MOTHERS AND FATHERS

EDINBURGH STUDIES IN SOCIOLOGY

General Editors: Frank Bechhofer, Patricia Jeffrey, Tom McGlew

The *Edinburgh Studies in Sociology* series publishes sociological works from the Department of Sociology at the University of Edinburgh. The majority of the books in the series will be founded on original research or on research and scholarship pursued over a period of time. There will also be collections of research papers on particular topics of social interest and textbooks deriving from courses taught in the Department.

Many of the books will appeal to a non-specialist audience as well as to the academic reader.

Titles already published

Kathryn C. Backett: MOTHERS AND FATHERS: A Study of the Development and Negotiation of Parental Behaviour

Frank Bechhofer and Brian Elliott (*editors*): THE PETITE BOURGEOISIE: Comparative Studies of the Uneasy Stratum

Tom Burns: THE BBC: Public Institution and Private World

Anthony P. M. Coxon and Charles L. Jones: THE IMAGES OF OCCUPATIONAL PRESTIGE: A Study in Social Cognition

Anthony P. M. Coxon and Charles L. Jones: CLASS AND HIER-ARCHY: The Social Meaning of Occupations

Anthony P. M. Coxon and Charles L. Jones: MEASUREMENT AND MEANINGS: Techniques and Methods of Studying Occupational Cognition

Harvie Ferguson: STUDIES IN EXPERIMENTAL PSY-CHOLOGY

John Orr: TRAGIC DRAMA AND MODERN SOCIETY

John Orr: TRAGIC REALISM AND MODERN SOCIETY: Studies in the Sociology of the Modern Novel

Forthcoming titles

Frank Bechhofer and Brian Elliott: THE SMALL SHOP-KEEPER IN THE CLASS STRUCTURE

Brian Elliott and David McCrone: PROPERTY AND POWER IN A CITY

MOTHERS AND FATHERS

A Study of the Development and Negotiation of Parental Behaviour

Kathryn C. Backett, Ph.D.

First published 1982 by
THE MACMILLAN PRESS LTD
London and Basingstoke
Companies and representatives
throughout the world

ISBN 0 333 28112 8

Typeset in Great Britain by
ART PHOTOSET LTD
Beaconsfield Bucks
and printed in Hong Kong

For Simon and Paul

Contents

Acknowledgements

The help and support which I have received from many people has been essential to the completion of this book.

In the early stages of the research project I received a two year postgraduate grant from the Social Science Research Council. Subsequently, my parents, Mr and Mrs Norman Hayes, and my husband, Dr Simon Backett, gave financial assistance which enabled me to complete my fieldwork and analysis without feeling pressured to find full-time employment.

Colleagues in the Sociology Department of Edinburgh University have given considerable intellectual support, not only in the shape of formal supervision but also in a willingness always to listen and comment on ideas as they were emerging. Special thanks must go to Professor Michael Anderson and Mr Tom McGlew who were closely involved with the research from its inception. Their contributions to the development and clarification of my arguments were, at all times, crucial. I am also grateful to Professor Gianfranco Poggi and Ms Lynn Jamieson for their useful comments on more recent drafts.

My warmest thanks go to those couples who took part in the various stages of the research. Not only did they give the continued cooperation which was so essential to a multi-interview study, but they did this with an interest and enthusiasm which made the fieldwork a stimulating and enjoyable experience.

I should also like to thank other friends and colleagues who have helped with the chores associated with producing a book and who have listened patiently through the years. My sister Mrs Alwyn Fox typed the manuscript accurately and efficiently.

Finally, my husband Simon has supported me in ways too numerous to mention. I am especially grateful for the unquestioning priority which he has attached to the completion of the book and for his sense of humour which, so often, has helped me to put the whole exercise in its proper perspective. Thanks also to Paul for being the kind of child who has allowed his parents to continue to pursue their own interests with relative ease, and for giving more pleasure than we could ever have thought possible.

Edinburgh, 1980   K.C.B.

1 The Objectives and Approach of the Study

I OBJECTIVES

This book is about the everyday experiences of parenthood and family life of a group of young middle-class couples living in Scotland. Although parenthood manuals abound, there are relatively few accounts from the parents themselves.[1] Most of us become parents, and everyone has opinions on how to bring up children, but although much of this valuable information circulates in conversation it is seldom recorded, let alone examined analytically. Hopefully this book will be of interest to the lay person who perhaps has his or her own theories about what actually goes on in families, as well as to the student of family behaviour who is interested in a systematic empirical analysis.

When I began this research I felt that there were some important gaps in our sociological knowledge of family life in Britain. Many of these still remain. Firstly, there was a dearth of information about the middle class, though a little more empirical work has now appeared (albeit concerned principally with conjugal rather than parental behaviour).[2] Many of the most stimulating insights in recent years have in fact come from the critics of the nuclear family, most notably the psychoanalytical writers, Marxists and feminists.[3] Although I agree with many of their arguments the work of these groups often lacks a satisfactory empirical base since it frequently comprises detailed theorising or draws its evidence from families with problems or alternative forms of communal living. My own interest lay rather in studying the dynamics of ordinary middle class family life and, in fact, I chose to study the stereotyped 'average' family of mother, father and two children.

Secondly, I was dissatisfied with the ways in which researchers had classically approached the study of the family in Britain. Much work for example had been based on the reports of only one family member, the wife or mother.[4] The Rapoports have rightly argued that the *couple* should be the basic unit of analysis.[5] I would add that, although the difficulties are enormous, the contribution to family dynamics of the other members of the nuclear group, the children, should also be considered. Thus, gaining a sense of how the 'whole family'[6] behaves should be the primary aim of the researcher, with subsequent decisions about empirical procedures being tailored to meet the particular research interest and the practical constraints involved in the project. Husbands and wives were equally involved in the present study, most of the children being too young to be interviewed. Studies of parenting of older children should, I feel, also incorporate detailed reports from the children themselves.

Thirdly, there appeared to be some important areas of substantive neglect in the sociology of parenthood. From the point of view of the present research two main issues were most pertinent. First whilst valuable work has been carried out on mothering and on socialisation practices in different classes and cultures, there has been a lack of direct research concerning fatherhood.[7] Not only have fathers themselves seldom been asked about their paternal behaviour but also their part in the complex nexus of childrearing has been left implicit in the analysis or conventionally partitioned off into the categories of 'breadwinner' or 'masculine role model'. Secondly there has also been a predominance of a one way interactional model for dealing with parent-child relationships. Thus the focus of most researchers has been on the effects on the *children* of aspects of their parents' behaviour. As Bell has pointed out, such a parent-effect model assumes a fixed and invariably applied repertoire of socialising behaviour. It finds difficulty in accounting for variations in, for instance, the behaviour of the same parent towards different same sex children in the family.[8] However, perhaps of greater significance to the sociology of the family, such a uni-directional model has diverted attention away from the effects of children on their *parents'* lives. Some useful work has been done on the initial impact of parenthood,[9] but the general neglect of a child-effect perspective has recently led the Rapoports to stress that 'Parents are People too'.[10] Hopefully the present study contributes towards a redressing of this imbalance, at least in the sphere of parenting; although much work has still to be done on the effects of children on all aspects of the lives of the adults who rear them.

II   AN INTERACTIONIST APPROACH

(a)   The legacy of structural-functionalism

Whilst my substantive areas of interest were determined in part by existing gaps in family sociology, an equally important influence on the study was a concern to apply interactionist concepts to the study of family processes. This concern stemmed in large part from a rejection of structural-functionalism and the central tenets of role-theory which have been so dominant in British family sociology. I hoped that the use of an interactionist approach would be profitable in two main ways. Firstly I believed that it would enable me to examine how the respondents themselves viewed the various family roles; these I felt should not be treated as 'given' but rather viewed as problematical and their construction seen as a topic for investigation in its own right. Secondly I hoped that it would facilitate an interpretation of family life as a 'unity of interacting personalities'; thus the definitional and interactional elements in the development of family behaviour as a whole might be studied.

Arguably structural-functionalism has influenced both the way family roles have been conceptualised and the range of empirical topics chosen for study.[11] The implicit assumption in most structural-functionalist work seems to have been that family members easily identify and follow clearly defined norms when they take up their roles. In fact, it has been found empirically that there are wide variations in how members perceive and interpret such norms.[12] It seems potentially profitable, therefore, to view norms rather as extremely broad constraints on action. Consequently actors' perceptions and interpretations of norms become problematical. Here I am in agreement with Lemert's argument that 'our society increasingly shows fluid and open structuring of situations' and that, in effect, 'norms become little more than a reference point for action'.[13]

Secondly, the structural-functionalist approach has influenced not only how family norms and roles have been conceptualised but also the choice of substantive areas to be studied. In particular it could be argued that the emphasis on an expressive-instru-mental axis in male-female family roles and the concern with child socialisation has led to the paucity of information on fathering and the neglect of effects of *children* on family life previously noted. By definition, interest has been focussed on the ways in which factors detached from the immediate familial interactions exert a signifi-cant influence over the form and content of that behaviour. For example, at one stage, inspired by the seminal contribution of Bott, this was evidenced in the work concerned with the relation-ship between social networks and conjugal roles.[14] More recently the emphasis has shifted to the influence of work patterns on family life.[15]

All of these developments have been valuable in adding to our understanding of the boundaries placed on family life by struc-tural constraints and normative pressures. But, by taking these features to be fixed and determinate, structural functionalists have necessarily ignored the interpretative processes by which members perceive and construct their family roles. Also, except perhaps in the form of a hint, the crucial importance of what could be termed 'the ongoing socialisation of one another by nuclear family members' has been largely bypassed in the work of those adhering to this perspective.[16] The alternative theories of interactionism would appear at present to offer greater scope for the study of the dynamics of family life.

(b)   Theoretical background to the study

The approach taken in this study was influenced primarily by concepts derived from symbolic interactionism and pheno-menological sociology. Until recently symbolic interactionist theories have been utilised much more in American rather than British family sociology.[17] For example, even in the 1920s Burgess was stressing the importance of members' own conceptions of family roles and of looking at how these were developed through interactions within the group itself.[18] Such early influences led later researchers to examine, for instance, the negotiation of meanings within the family,[19] communication patterns within the family group,[20] and interaction patterns in families with problems.[21] All of this work provides valuable information about family processes and the dynamics of living in family groups.

Whilst also stressing the importance of actors' subjective interpretation of meanings in the development of social action, phenomenological sociology has drawn attention to the highly problematical nature of these processes. It has its basis in the work of Schutz.[22] His concepts are referred to, where relevant, in the main body of the book. I shall, however, briefly mention his main influences on my approach at this point.

First of all, Schutz emphasised that man lives in an 'intersubjective world of culture', and that 'from the outset, the world of everyday life is a universe of significance to us, that is, a texture of meaning which we have to interpret in order to find our bearings within it and come to terms with it'. Schutz showed that 'even the socially most stereotyped ideas only exist in the minds of individuals who absorb them, interpret them on the basis of their own life situation, and give them a personal tinge'. Secondly, in order to go about his everyday life man is continuously engaged in constructing 'course of action' types. These are, however, taken-for-granted and seldom consciously examined. Thirdly, by contrast, the interpretative activities of social scientists can be seen as 'self-conscious' second order constructs. Following on from these points Phillipson paraphrased Schutz's main requirements for sociology as follows:

> Social action flows from and is sustained through meaning – that is, from the first order constructs through which the actor makes sense of his world. As the life-world comprises such meanings, sociology, if it is to provide organised Knowledge of Social reality must come to terms with the meanings from which Social action emerges.[23]

Berger and Kellner applied several of the above-mentioned concepts to the field of family sociology.[24] Their consideration of marriage and the construction of reality provides some stimulating theoretical points even though the potential empirical application of these was not clarified. I feel that much of their analysis of marriage can also be applied to parenthood. They are interested in the social processes which construct, maintain and modify 'a consistent reality that can be meaningfully experienced by individuals'. They suggest that one of the important areas in which such 'nomos building' occurs is marriage. The individual achieves his sense of the world essentially through validating experiences with significant others and, in marriage, this can be seen as an ongoing 'conversation'. These validating processes occur, however, not 'so much by explicit articulation, but precisely by taking the definitions silently for granted and conversing about all conceivable matters on this taken-for-granted basis'.

For Berger and Kellner then, the marital state is seen as providing a 'significant other' of major subjective importance. I would suggest that, for the couples in my group, the other spouse was also of such predominant significance in the everyday validation of *parental* behaviour. In the context of my respondents' perceptions of their particular situations parenthood only makes sense as *mutual* sets of behaviour.

Berger and Kellner note also that spouses do not have a shared past, even though their pasts may have similar structures. To me this implies that spouses cannot, therefore, take it for granted that they interpret their mutually held realities in the same way, and that, consequently, they must engage in continuous interpretative negotiations. Similarly, when they experience parenthood, with all its concomitant uncertainties, they must continually construct and reaffirm their views of this existence.

Berger and Kellner define the family in our society as more privatised than in the past when it was 'firmly embedded in a matrix of wider community relationships'. To them this historical change has increased the amount of effort which each couple has to put into constructing their family world. Societal prescriptions have become more ambiguous and therefore less easily and uniformly interpreted. Nowadays, they maintain, 'each family constitutes its own segregated subworld, with its own controls and its own closed conversation'. Whilst the couple might approach marriage (and parenthood) with taken-for-granted culturally derived preconceptions, 'these relatively empty projections now have to be actualised, lived through and filled with experiential content by the protagonists'. Accepting these views, this again supports the idea that the development of parental behaviour is most profitably studied as the result of interpretative activities negotiated within the nuclear group.

To summarise, drawing on the various approaches and concepts outlined in this section, my analysis of parenthood was guided by the following theoretical observations:

(1)   Parental role behaviour is relatively fluid. As Hess and

Handel have pointed out, family members –

> ... are engaged in evolving and mutually adjusting their images
> of one another. This mutual adjustment takes place in inter-
> action, and it is, in part, the aim of interaction. Since complete
> consensus is most improbable, life in a family – as elsewhere – is
> a process ongoing in a situation of actual or potential insta-
> bility. Pattern is reached, but it can never be complete, since
> action is always unfolding and the status of family members is
> undergoing change.[25]

Thus the development of parental roles is an ongoing and problematical process.

(2) Parental behaviour is meaningfully generated with
reference to other family members. Thus, in a two parent family,
one cannot analyse the behaviour, for example, of the father except with reference to that of the mother and child.

(3) The institutional constraints on family behaviour
emanating from the wider society are broad and lacking in
specificity. Given this, scope for variation is wide.

(4) Through their negotiating processes members continuously construct, sustain and reformulate working definitions
of behaviour perceived as appropriate to their mutually-held
family realities.

III.　METHODOLOGICAL ORIENTATIONS:
A QUALITATIVE APPROACH

Thus the framework for the study was derived from interactionist
and phenomenological theories. My interest in the meanings
which members attached to family life and their interpretative
activities led me to favour the development of a qualitative
methodology. This appeared, at this stage, to offer a means of
gathering grounded information about empirically valid concepts, and a way of re-examining some of the basic assumptions
implicit in much previous research.

Unfortunately, whilst sharpening up one's critical approach to
fieldwork, most advocates of qualitative methods still tend only to
offer suggestions of *possible* research strategies and tactics, and
these are often somewhat vague in their practical tenets.[26]

Garfinkel tried to reveal underlying assumptions by violating aspects of 'acceptable behaviour'.[27] Cicourel developed a complex procedure of 'controlled indefinite triangulation';[28] this involved feeding back to respondents' concepts which they themselves had generated earlier in the research. Glaser and Strauss felt that attention should focus on the *generation* rather than the *testing* of theory and that, in this way, 'grounded theories can emerge which, instead of forcing data into preconceived 'objective' reality, seek to mobilise as a research tool the categories which the participants themselves use to order their experience'.[29]

These suggestions influenced considerably the study design. I became convinced that structured questioning of respondents would not allow the wealth of meanings in this area of behaviour to be tapped. Also, the use of the 'one-off' standardised survey technique seemed inappropriate for obtaining valid data about the highly personalised and often sensitive domain of family life. My chief guiding concern was to discover the best ways of enabling respondents to tell me about their family lives in as free and frank a manner as possible. All of these reasons, combined with the limitations of time and resources involved in a one person project, led to my decision to carry out a multi-interview study of a small group of husbands and wives, using a minimally-structured interviewing technique.[30]

These then were the objectives and approach of the study. The fieldwork was stimulating and enjoyable and, during the analysis, I often experienced the excitement one derives from developing theories grounded in depth qualitative data. In the following chapter I begin my description of the couples' accounts of their family lives by examining a range of assumptions which underpinned much of their parental behaviour.

2 Underlying Assumptions about Family Life

I INTRODUCTION

In this chapter I shall describe some of the main assumptions underlying everyday family behaviour of the couples in my group. I focus especially on parental behaviour but treat this as necessarily to be seen within the wider context of family life generally. The development of this behaviour is treated as a particularistic process in which members are continuously creating and exchanging meanings special to each group. However, it is possible to extract from the accounts of these respondents certain broad precepts to which they all referred. These precepts seemed to form a taken-for-granted set of meanings to which each family group was oriented. It is these meanings which I call 'underlying assumptions'.

For the couples in my study, parental behaviour was developed in the context of many choices and uncertainties. One way in which they located themselves in this problematical world of parenthood was by establishing and sustaining belief in these underlying assumptions. Following Schutz the assumptions could be seen as providing a generalised set of objectified 'recipe knowledge'.[1] Such knowledge suggests the outline *forms* of behaviour, leaving the interpretation of its specific *content* up to the members of each particular family. The underlying assumptions had fluctuating relevances for each family member and the relevances varied through time. Also, in describing these assumptions I see the development of parental behaviour as derived from the individual's interpretations of both his/her social stock of knowledge *and* his/her biographical experience.

I describe the underlying assumptions by outlining their general forms and giving specific illustrations. An important point is that the forms are sufficiently generalised and flexible to allow considerable variation in their practical interpretation, both within and between families. This point is important because it suggests one way in which, despite their distinctive biographies, individuals within a family can sustain belief in its mutually constructed reality. Berger and Kellner said, specifically, about marriage and the construction of reality:

> Each partner's definitions of reality must be continually correlated with the definitions of the other.[2]

Accepting this theoretical point, I would suggest that the use of underlying assumptions provides an empirical illustration of how this 'correlating' process is actually carried out.

It is important to bear in mind that 'underlying assumptions' are analytical abstractions which I constructed as a means of describing the general beliefs about family life presented by respondents. This has two related implications. Firstly, the abstractions involve rather precise categorisations which do not actually exist in the everyday implementation of the beliefs. As David Silverman has pointed out:

> While the sociologist must *begin* from the first order constructs of the participants themselves, his work necessarily involves a distortion of their experience as he seeks to idealize and formalize, to talk about the typical where there is ultimately a number of unique cases.[3]

In many instances, therefore, when I have described a concept in, for example, the chapter entitled 'Underlying Assumptions', this same concept may also be utilised empirically as a 'legitimation' or a 'coping mechanism'. An example of this is the discussion of 'belief in fairness'.[4] Thus the categorisations are neither mutually exclusive nor exhaustive, but essentially a presentation device.

Secondly, the analytical abstractions are, in fact, considerably removed from the pragmatic use of these beliefs as recipe knowledge in everyday life. The assumptions were first objectified by respondents using them as legitimations in their accounts to me of family life. They were then further objectified by my process of selection and systematisation in order to present this account. Schutz commented that all everyday knowledge is incoherent, only partially clear and not at all free from contradictions.[5] The

two steps involved in creating the analytical abstractions have inevitably resulted in the false attribution of a certain clarity and
coherence to the beliefs, although many of the contradictions
remain.

II   FAMILY LIFE AS A LEARNING SITUATION ('TRIAL AND ERROR')

(a)   Marriage

'There's no-one who could tell you beforehand this is your first
step, this is your second step, you've got to learn it all yourself'
(I)[6] (Martin Chapman)

This was a very typical statement which reflected the belief held
by the couples that marriage and parenthood were learning situations. The major impression given was that modern middle class
family life lacked clear and precise behavioural and attitudinal
prescriptions. In some of my early questions, which aimed to gain
information indirectly about ideas behind conjugal behaviour, I
asked couples how they had viewed marriage *before* they were
married and what they would *now* tell other people to expect. The
overwhelming response was to state that they personally had had
few or no preconceptions, and often had not even thought about
what being married would entail, except in the most general
terms. They had seen it simply as a process of 'working things out
together'. Madeline Harris, for example, replied:

. . . very hard to put in general ways I suppose, because in the
end it's personalities that conflict at some point and are comple-
mentary at other points. You just work out your individual
marriage really I suppose within a social situation of certain
accepted norms which you either reject or accept as you become
aware of them. (I)

Many respondents felt that, in fact, it was *wrong* to do anything
other than enter marriage with a completely open mind. Even if
they *were* now able to articulate the problems and difficulties involved in family life, they usually felt that each individual should

learn about these through his/her own experience rather than be told about them beforehand. If a respondent *did* put forward some definite views, these were usually extremely generalised such as 'make sure you've got plenty of money', or were centred on the love relationship. Judy Davies said:

> . . . to begin with, you know, I felt that I really wanted to get to know my husband, know all his sort of feelings and what have you. This you'll experience yourself as you go on in married life, you'll find that you're thinking as one, sort of thing. (I)

To a certain extent this emphasis on learning through personal experience had as its correlate the view that each family was unique. The frequent rejection of my questions 'What would you now tell a young man/woman to expect from marriage?' was typically expressed by Andrew Jeffreys as follows: 'Depends on the conditions and the situation and the person, I just can't answer that.' (I) Alan Hemingway reacted even more forcefully when he said:

> Oh my goodness, you see, that's a generalised question. Em, you can't tell a young man that, because what HE would get out of marriage I would think would be vastly different to what I've got out of it. If you said to me what were the aspects of MY marriage that I considered the most important, or the ones that I'VE enjoyed most as it were, I could answer THAT. But I wouldn't necessarily say to a young chap that these were the things to expect from marriage because he's so different to me. (I)[7]

Several respondents also felt that each family situation was unique in its particular temporal context. This was usually expressed by the stated inability to take their parents' marriages as any kind of direct model (to accept or reject). They described, for example, the 'different' context of establishing a marriage during the war years, or spoke of their parents' attitudes as reflecting the kinds of values prevalent at that particular time. Louise Wilson illustrated this kind of qualification when she remarked:

> But every marriage must be different I would have thought. And I mean it must depend on the particular couple and the

time when they get married and this sort of thing. I mean marriage now of two career people in the 1970s is entirely different from even twenty years ago or even five years ago, and I think this is something that is peculiar to each marriage. (I)

This underlying assumption that each family had its own distinct subcultural reality was frequently used also as a legitimation or a coping mechanism. The assertion that 'it's different for everybody' apparently provided an extremely subjectively satisfactory means of sustaining belief in the particular reality being created.

Thus, although these couples now 'knew' about their own marriages, they usually felt that it was inappropriate or even irrelevant to pass on this knowledge, except in the most general terms. Such feelings would seem to sustain the kind of situation which Mayer described as 'pluralistic ignorance'.[8] He observed in his own work the preponderance of 'instances in which individuals have vague rather than erroneous conceptions of each other's family life'. If the views of my couples are typical they have considerable implications for both modern marriage *and* divorce. Despite arguments over detail and terminology, sociologists are agreed that, relative to previous centuries, the conjugal unit is both more isolated from the wider family and also a greater emphasis is now laid on the satisfaction of the personality, emotional and sexual needs of its members. It is also argued that one factor involved in the rising divorce rate is that individuals in fact value marriage *more* rather than *less* than in the past, and therefore choose not to continue with a relationship which is felt to be unsatisfactory. Arguably, the assumptions put forward by my respondents of the uniqueness of each marriage, and the inappropriateness of passing on knowledge about being married, can serve only to intensify both the privatisation and emotional challenges involved in marriages of the latter part of the twentieth century.

(b) Parenthood

Parenthood and childrearing were also seen as skills learned essentially through direct experience with one's own family. Here, however, the degree of uncertainty was perceived as being even greater since, as Margaret Barber pointed out: 'You choose your husband but you cannot choose your child.' (I) Just as respondents felt that there was no real preparation for marriage, as only by living with the person could one discover what it was really like, so they also felt that there could be no *realistic* prior preparation for parenthood.

One might expect the middle class to be likely to make extensive use of current facilities, now greater than ever, in the way of literature or classes about parenthood and childrearing. In fact, few of the respondents had done so with any seriousness. This applied especially to the husbands, and Andrew Jeffreys' remarks were typical; he said:

> As far as I'm concerned a lot of it's been intuitive rather than taking some nondescript person's advice out of a magazine. Because I think your reactions have got a great deal to do with the whole system rather than the imposition of an idea that you don't understand anyway. I think it's got to be a bit more from inside than from outside. I mean I haven't read anything about it. (F)

Shirley Jackson echoed this view from a slightly different angle, implying that preconceptions about childrearing were, in any case, often rendered irrelevant by factors of context or personality, she claimed:

> . . . well WE had strong principles, well *I* had, don't know about you (to husband), VERY strong principles of things that we WERE and we were NOT going to do when we had children. But children come along and they're PEOPLE and it just doesn't work, you know always. You know, you gradually see one principle being either swayed or going completely by the board and then another one because things that you THINK are going to work with children, they don't (F)

Moreover, even if an effort had been made to seek out prior knowledge through parenthood classes or childrearing literature, this was often seen as largely irrelevant once the baby actually arrived. Majorie Russell said:

> I think I read all the standard texts when I was expecting

Kathleen and then promptly forgot about them. Maybe some of it rubbed off but, er, I tend to go back to the old adage of bringing them up in the way that it feels natural to YOU to bring them up. You read the books but then don't go by the book, it's impossible! If you tried to go by every book you'd be a mental wreck, trying to decide what to do. I don't think you should DECIDE what to do; I think you should just DO something anyway. (I)

Interestingly, her husband, David, must have seen Marjorie's reading as so irrelevant that he had forgotten all about it. He said in a later joint interview:

Neither of us, er, neither Marjorie nor I have sort of studied child psychology, we don't read any books about the upbringing of the kids or anything like that. Whether we should or not I don't know. I think you've got enough to do to bring them up without studying HOW you do it you know. (laughs) (W/E)

Equally, even practical prior experience of dealing with children was often discounted on the basis that being a parent in one's own home situation was felt to be entirely different. Margaret Barber commented:

. . . the year I left school I went as an au pair girl to a French family who had five children, and I'd say that was an EX-CELLENT training for marriage. But again, O.K. I learned about children, but I couldn't appreciate it from a PARENT'S point of view. (I)

Shirley Jackson, an ex-teacher, remarked:

Mind you, it's awfully difficult, I mean I've seen a lot of knocks and quite a lot of bumps as far as children go, but it's difficult when it's your own child; you're emotionally involved with your own children. You know, I can stay VERY calm in somebody else's emergency but I'm not so calm in my own emergency. (W/E)

For all of the parents therefore, the emphasis was always on 'trial and error', and on trying to work out the appropriate situation for each particular family. In many ways these couples could be seen as operating in a situation where uncertainty prevailed for perhaps two reasons. Learning about appropriate behaviour through some sort of unquestioning process in the family of origin was increasingly irrelevant to them. Equally respondents did not seem to accord any particular efficacy to alternative methods of teaching oneself by making use of formal educational facilities.

It was, however, recognised that this emphasis on learning through experience could have many drawbacks. The majority of couples felt that they had, through inexperience, made various kinds of mistakes with their first baby which had resulted in problems either for the child or for themselves. Also, many mentioned that the sheer tension of learning as one went along was passed on to the baby and might well have been the reason for some of the difficulties. Martin Chapman said:

> Oh when Anne was a baby she wasn't as contented as what Judy is, nothing like it, and I think that is really our own, to a certain extent our own fault because we were inexperienced at the time and em, I think looking back on it, I would say that HALF the trouble with Anne was that, er, when she wanted to be fed we were frightened to feed her, whereas *now we've got the knowledge of how to bring up a baby and what the baby's crying for etc., but we induced a lot of the stresses on ourselves through Anne by our own inexperience.* (I) [my emphasis]

Alan Hemingway, another husband, who has having sleep problems with his two daughters, said about childrearing:

> But em, I DO worry about mistakes that we're making unconsciously; em, I don't KNOW that we're making mistakes. And a remark that I've made to Dianne, you know, more than once, that for all we've been breeding the human race for goodness knows how long, the problems that we face now are, em, have been experienced thousands of millions of times, but there is no way that I can benefit directly from that experience. (I)

Thus, albeit retrospectively, my respondents tended to devalue any set ideas or objective preparation for the parental role. Preparation was, by and large, seen as at best irrelevant and occasionally as a distinct hindrance. Maureen Rankin gave a good illustration of this kind of view when she was explaining to me why she was so critical of Dr Spock. She said of his advice:

> Well, I wouldn't say it doesn't work, em, it probably works with 80% of kiddies but it doesn't work with ours. It DOESN'T work, because we certainly gave it a try and instead of little problems improving they definitely got worse. *So we adopted other means.* (I) [my emphasis]

Flexibility and learning were thus seen as the keys to success!

Before the first baby arrived many of the wives went through the procedures provided by the medical profession to 'prepare' people for parenthood. They attended the ante natal classes and read the relevant leaflets. Most husbands were also 'involved' where appropriate. After the baby arrived, however, many of these parents described how they still *felt* unprepared for the plethora of everyday decisions about what the child wanted. It was the actual practical experience either of making decisions which they defined as 'correct', or else the retrospective 'under-standing' of wrong decisions, which made them *feel* prepared for the second child.

(c)   Images of Children

Already one of the most important themes of this study has been implicit in much of the preliminary discussion. Learning about marriage and parenthood involved ongoing definitions of what was perceived as real and relevant to each particular family. In addition, as I shall discuss in detail later, these respondents ad-hered to a basic belief that parents should try to *understand* their children.[9] Thus, in my analysis, I treat parenthood as an especially problematical situation in which couples faced a con-tinuous challenge of 'making sense' of their child and its world. I would suggest that the problematical nature of the development of parental behaviour derived in part from the fact that explanations of the child were frequently untestable, since too many uncon-trollable and unknown factors were involved. The main practical way in which parents therefore 'made sense' of their children was by developing typified images. These constituted subjectively satisfactory bases for action. This was a dynamic negotiated process in the course of which parental behaviour was being developed.

There were two main analytical levels on which respondents constructed images of their child. These I have called 'abstract' and 'grounded'.[10] Simplistically, abstract images can be seen as interpretations primarily of the social stock of knowledge, whereas grounded images were developed out of the ongoing biographical experience. Again, however, this analytical distinction does not operate in everyday life, since those abstract images which the individual *perceived* as relevant fluctuated according to his/her current definition of his/her biographical situation. In this way, for example, images of the differences between children and adults, and of the place of the child in the family group, typically alter as mutual biographical situations change. My presentation of respondents' images of children must therefore be seen in the context of their perceptions of their *current* family lives.[11]

Images of children provided crucial meanings around which parental behaviour was developed. They were constantly referred to in respondents' accounts. It seemed, therefore, that they were frequently used as legitimations in the everyday negotiating processes of spouses. A vital aspect of this was the subtle position of influence held by the mother over the father's image formation.[12] This stemmed in part from the underlying assumptions about parenthood as learning. Direct experience and grounded knowledge were thus accorded considerable importance. Empirically this was often illustrated when a husband qualified a statement about his child by attributing it directly to his wife. Also, the husband frequently maintained that his statements about a child would be far less detailed than were his wife's since *she* saw much more of the child and its world. Analytically this can be seen as one of the many implicit acknowledgements by respondents of the importance of context and situation in the formation of subjectively satisfactory images. All of these important points will be expanded in later chapters.

I shall briefly summarise the main images of children at this stage as these are also referred to in the following two chapters. The discussion of abstract images deals with respondents' generalised beliefs and ideas about their child. The vagueness of the concepts meant that there was considerable variation in each parent's practical interpretations of them in everyday life. Three main areas of abstract images were referred to most frequently.

Firstly, couples put forward ideas about children and childhood. They differentiated between children and adults in various ways which had considerable implications for the development of parental behaviour. They also held images which differentiated their own child from children in general. Such images isolated some of the special features of being a *parent*.

Secondly, they referred to ideas about children's needs and wants. These I have termed 'images of the child's psychology, personality and physiology'. Here respondents drew considerably on their social stocks of knowledge. Their practical interpretations of these images, and the choice of *relevant* image, were, however, continuously affected by their perceptions of the particular child concerned. Although he was taking for granted the definitional processes involved, D. R. Peterson illuminated one aspect of this complex interaction between belief and practice when he stated:

> It is often just as reasonable to assume that personality tendencies on the part of children appearing very early on in life and possibly of constitutional origin, have engendered modification of parental attitudes. The parents of a stable, predictable child can afford to be democratic. . . . the parents of an erratic, difficult, peculiar child may become apparently inconsistent out of sheer desperation.[13]

Thirdly, the parents developed current and projected images about the place of the child in their individual and mutual lives. Simplistically, the current images could be seen as affecting everyday decisions about the importance of different demands of family members. The projected images comprised ideas about the future character of the child, the parents' future relationship with the child, and the child as a future member of society independently of his/her parents. All of these projections had implications for *current* parental behaviour.

The discussion of grounded images illustrates the ways in which respondents used their personal experience of family life, and their interpretations of particular contexts and situations to make sense of the child. Again, they tended to refer to similar areas of experience, similar *forms*, whilst specific adaptations and *contents* varied. Grounded images have been separated into comparative and contextual images.

The section entitled 'comparative images of children' deals

with the meanings attached to the structural fact that each couple in the sample had two children. Here there are many practical implications of the underlying assumption that parenthood was a learning situation. The couples were very aware of the ways in which having *two* children affected their dealings with each individual child. They also formed many explicit images concerning the relationship between the two children themselves. Analytically, respondents' accounts showed that such images were often very self-consciously used as bases for action or as legitimations. Each parent also 'made sense' of his/her child by developing contextual images. The process of 'understanding' their child involved locating him/her and his/her behaviour in various social, temporal and genealogical contexts. This was perhaps the most dynamic area of image formation.

III FAMILY BEHAVIOUR AS LIFE CYCLICALLY-ORIENTED ('IT'S JUST A STAGE')

(a) General

Underlying assumptions about the family life cycle were another important reference point for respondents. In their accounts they constantly interpreted and legitimated current and intended behaviour by reference to time, temporal changes, and their meanings. In this section I discuss first the kinds of assumptions which were largely implicit in the accounts. I then present respondents' perceptions of their *current* position in the family life cycle. These can be seen as the *explicit* meanings which they attached to the objective characteristics of their current family set-up. Thus I shall be dealing with some of the interests to which Hess and Handel attached importance when they said:

> The relationships which develop among the various members of a family do not follow the intrinsic lines of age and sex. They are shaped as well by underlying family themes and *images which impart meanings to sex, age and other personal characteristics.*[14] [my emphasis]

In addition to the images mentioned by Hess and Handel another important component of assumptions about family life as cyclical was the social definition of time. The importance of considering meanings attached to time and temporal change was particularly well shown in respondents' accounts of parenthood. Their qualitative distinction between 'spending' and 'passing' time with children was one example. Another was the way in which the *amount* of time which each spouse spent with the child was perceived as affecting the kind of parental behaviour each developed. These specific points are discussed and expanded in Chapters 7 and 8. The general point about the importance of the meanings attached to time, however, is fundamental to this section.

There were various levels on which assumptions about the family life cycle were implicit in respondents' accounts. On an abstract level this was reflected in their construction of beliefs about permanence and temporariness in relation to people and circumstances. On a more grounded level respondents continuously attributed social and psychological meanings to the life cycles of individual family members. This was shown particularly in their images of age changes in children. Such grounded images of the ages at which, for example, children could 'understand' were crucial in the development of parental discipline. The best illustrations, however, of this area of underlying assumptions were the frequent use of the concepts of stage and phase.

As with the other underlying assumptions, the important characteristics of the life cycle beliefs were their vagueness and flexibility. This allowed considerable scope for specific personal accommodations. One illustration was the way respondents 'made sense' of their child's behaviour by locating it in one of the stages of child development, as they perceived it. Their accounts of such stages or phases showed considerable variation both in the age of child being discussed and the kind of 'stage-related' behaviour being described. This also provided a good example of the way in which interpretative acts drew on both the perceived social stock of knowledge (here the popular infiltration of psychology) and the individual biography (here, experiences with one's own child).

(b)   Perceptions of the family life-cycle

(i)   Permanence and temporariness

Implicit in respondents' accounts was the assumption that, whereas the spouses would probably live with each other for life, the child's full time presence was relatively temporary. Couples varied in their attitudes towards the permanence *per se* of marriage. At the time of the fieldwork, however, it seemed that all were assuming that, unless things went wrong, they would be spending the rest of their lives together. Many respondents claimed that such an assumption had affected their attitudes towards their married life. Specific examples of this varied. For some it had meant that they had tolerated temporary hardships because, as a couple, they would progress towards a 'better' situation in the future. Many spoke, for example, about giving up good clothes, good cars or good holidays when they married, in order to save for a house and furniture. For others it had meant that they had *had* to find some way of coming to terms with personal differences. One husband, for example, felt that he was gradually succeeding in accepting his wife's lackadaisical attitude towards time. Four wives spoke of their different adaptations to their husbands' time consuming hobbies of rugby, gardening and D.I.Y., respectively. An excellent summary of the general perception that belief in the permanence of the relationship affected behavioural adaptations came from Madeleine Harris. She said:

> . . . somehow the permanence of the situation is an influence in committing yourself to each other. I mean, there are many points where we could easily have come apart if we hadn't felt it was permanent and we were just going to work it out. And without this feeling of, 'well, we MEAN this to be permanent', we probably wouldn't have bothered to work it out. It was too hard, it was too painful and meant too much soulsearching and too much change for yourself. (I)

In contrast to this assumption of spousal permanence was the image of the child as a transient being, a full time visitor to the spousal relationship for probably only about twenty or so years of its total existence. This image had implications for the spousal relationship in that couples talked about the dangers of becoming over-involved with the children to the neglect of each other and their own personal development. It also had considerable implications for the parent-child relationship in that, even at this early stage, these parents were very aware of potential future difficulties associated with giving the child 'freedom' and 'letting go'. The Rankins illustrated *their* awareness of the parent-child relationship as follows. They saw the whole process of the child growing up and becoming independent as involving the parents in continually having to gauge how much trust and freedom they could safely give the child. Talking about their elder child, Lynne, Maureen Rankin said:

> *Maureen:* It's always a worry just how much more freedom I should give her at this age, you know, am I giving her enough? I don't feel that she's got too much because she's proved to be trustworthy in as much freedom as I've given her, she's never let me down YET, but that's not to say that she never will. [laughs]
>
> *Derek:* And you can't keep too stiff a control otherwise at the age of fourteen or fifteen they're going to rebel aren't they? But it IS difficult. (F)

A further illustration of this point came from the Coulsons in their final interview:

> *Barry:* I reckon em — you know, I will allow the boys a certain amount of freedom over the years, progressively increase it, and just HOPE that the way we've brought them up will keep them on the straight and narrow. Also the understanding ultimately they're gonna go their own way earlier than WE did most probably, em, that regardless of what trouble they get into or what their problem is, they can always come back here.
>
> *Jean:* Yes, I was going to say that I think if you have the right sort of relationship with your children right from the start, that they're always gonna WANT to come back to you. (F)

Further implications of the image of the child as only a temporary full time visitor to the parents' lives will be discussed in a later chapter.[15] Here it is interesting briefly to reflect on the fact that these couples were operating with different underlying assumptions concerning the place of the spousal and parental relationship in their total life span. Demographic changes over the past hundred years mean that the periods of reproduction and childrearing are now compressed into the early years of marriage, which itself is occurring at a younger age. These facts, together with a considerably greater life expectancy result in the situation that couples can now anticipate a lengthy period of anything up to forty or fifty years together, once their children have left home. The couples in my group seemed to have made a realistic appraisal of the relatively short time that they would be involved in active parenting. Hopefully, this might equip them for a happier adjustment in the future to the 'empty nest' phase than is suggested by the somewhat depressing conclusions reached by those who have studied the later years of marriage of previous generations.

(ii)   Stage or phase

The concept of stage or phase was used by respondents in three main ways: as a benchmark for their present existence, as a legitimation of many items of family behaviour, and as a coping mechanism for tensions and dilemmas. In this section I shall be dealing with the first usage. At the level of an underlying assumption, the concept of family life as a series of stages had two related aspects. Firstly, it implied an acknowledgment of family life as a dynamic entity. Secondly, it helped the individual meaningfully to locate him/herself and others. The abstract notions of permanence and temporariness can also be seen as part of this process.

Implicit assumptions seemed to be held about the 'right/wrong' age or the 'right/wrong' time for a certain stage. The most frequent examples were associated with individuals being defined as at the 'right' or 'wrong' time in their lives to cope with perceived changes involved first in marriage and then parenthood. Maureen Rankin, who felt that she and Derek had married at the 'right' age, said of him:

. . . well, there again he was 26, and that meant he was old enough and he was prepared in that sense. He was old enough and he felt ready to settle down. He'd been reasonably well off until that age; he'd had a good life up to that point; he'd had good holidays, he'd er, he was stable you know, and quite ready to settle down in that sense. (I)

Sometimes an assumption about the 'right' age to embark on a particular stage was expressed indirectly. Some respondents spoke, for example, about being slightly too young or too old when they married or had children. Often these notions about age were implemented on the level of a legitimation. Marjorie Jeffreys, for example, wondered if her problems in controlling the behaviour of her two young sons were connected with her being 'older' when she had them. Mary Clark associated the arguments and dissatisfactions of her early married life with her being 'too young'.

All such statements about being the 'right age', 'too old' or 'too young' involved the attribution of social and psychological meaning to age and stage in the family life cycle. An important way in which respondents evaluated their current stage in the family life cycle was to relate it to their perceived biographical experience. Anna Robson said:

There are times, it's just that, you know, a child's yelling its head off, it's teething and you haven't slept much and your husband and you are bickering and I thought 'well it couldn't always be as bad as this.' But, see if I was twenty-one, I would have wanted out, I'd have felt I was missing something, but the six years before I was married I knew I wasn't missing anything because I'd seen most of it all. I was lucky again, I mean, I'd done all the things I wanted to do apart from going to America and Canada. (I)

Concepts which related to life cycle were also expressed on a more general level in terms of stage as part of the life span of the individual. Andrew Jeffreys, talking about his wife's feelings of frustration at being at home with small children explained:

Marjorie feels she's got less time to do what she likes; we both KNOW that it's a comparatively temporary thing. If you're going to have children, even if they are frustrating at times, em, you've gotta put up with them for that length of time, their, well, here's another good cliché, their formative years. [laughs] You know, you've got to sort of bear with it for that length of

time until you've become sort of more free again; then you can
decide what you would like to do. The thing is, it may be a sort
of fifteen year chunk, may sound an awful long time but, you
know, after that period of time things gradually get back to
where you would like to be. (I)

Obviously, the stages usually discussed were those so far experienced by the couples, that is, early marriage before children
and then married life with small children. Throughout, however,
there was also an awareness both that there were several more
phases involved in this stage of being parents with children at
home, and also that this stage would, at some point, inevitably
end. Some aspects of present behaviour were seen as in part desirable in view of anticipated future stages. They felt, for example,
that both individual identity and the basic husband/wife relationship should not be overwhelmed by the children. This was rooted
partly in feelings about what each of them wanted out of their
current existence but, for the majority, it was also anticipatory of
future stages. Frequently, for example, a cautionary tale was told
about people whose lives had been so centred around their
children that they had little meaning in life when the children left
home. Many respondents, especially the wives at home with small
children, felt, therefore, that it was imperative for them at least to
try to have some interests independently of the home and
children, despite the organisational difficulties this might involve.
They also stressed the importance of having time away from the
children to enjoy things together. Barbara Johnson, for example,
felt that:

Barbara: We don't do enough on our own and I feel that you
can grow apart if you don't. Perhaps this is something else
to advise a young man or woman. Even when the children
come along DO reserve some time to yourselves because you
can grow apart and it might be too late before you realise.

K.B: Do you mean doing things with each other or doing
things separately?

Barbara: No, doing things with each other. Also doing things
separately, but doing things with each other, doing things
that you did before you had the children because you find,
you CAN find, I reckon there's the danger that you find that
you've developed like this [made a gesture indicating 'at a

tangent'] and you've lost the bridges that you HAD across to each other. (I)

These examples illustrate some of the ways in which family life cycle assumptions provided implicit reference points for these couples. They were one way of locating oneself in and attaching meaning to current family existence. Respondents' accounts were characterised, moreover, by the attribution of very broad temporal dimensions to the various phases and stages. They operated with essentially flexible interpretations of the specific ages at which individuals would 'be ready' for certain stages. This was applied to their own lives and to their 'understandings' of their children. In this way quite considerable variation could be legitimated.[16]

(iii)   The current 'stage'

In this section I shall describe how the couples perceived the most recent change in their family life cycle, that is, the addition of children to the marriage. The importance of considering respondents' definitions of the situation was stressed by McHugh as follows:

> To fully describe an institution as a locus of group rules, for example, requires some description of how the institution looks to those engaging in the action, because they will be acting according to how it looks to them, and in so doing the institution will be maintained and changed.[17]

Respondents' perceptions of the effects of children are presented to illustrate aspects of the material, physical and social psychological contexts within which they *all* saw themselves as operating. The discussion will, however, indicate that images of children played an important part in explaining variations in *individual* respondents' practical responses to these typically perceived contexts.

All of the couples stated that, whether or not they had wished it to happen, the children had considerably affected their personal and married lives. Margaret Barber, for example, felt that this was absolutely inevitable and said:

> Maybe we aren't particularly good at coping but when people tell me that they won't allow children to change their lives, I either think they must be very poor parents in that they must pretty well IGNORE their children and very self-indulgent people, or that they must be stinking rich and pay other people to do what they should be doing, or that they have a horde of Edinburgh grandparents who are all doing it with love. (Jt)

The most obvious immediate change was that all of the women had given up full-time employment in order to have the baby and, even if this was viewed as a temporary necessity, it was seen also as having had far-reaching effects on many aspects of the conjugal relationship. Only two of the wives in the sample, Kathy Hislop and Jean Coulson, had not continued in full-time employment immediately after marriage, and this had been with the explicit intention of becoming pregnant as soon as possible. Ian Johnson expressed a commonly-mentioned view as follows:

> I think it's all tied up with the children, really, the amount to which she'd be tied up by the marriage; if you don't have children then you keep on leading the sort of life that you did before you were married. But once you've had children I think it makes much more difference to a woman than it does to a man. (I)

Although specific issues varied, there were three main areas of effects which were usually mentioned. These could be categorised as material, physical and social psychological. No doubt there are endless possible additions to any list of effects, but here I will describe those aspects which the couples in my group saw as especially relevant to their own lives. The examples given cover all of the effects mentioned by respondents and are intended to provide a background of how they saw their lives after having children. Obviously the fact that, at the time of study, all of the children involved were under six years of age, was a relevant variable to be borne in mind when considering the effects which these particular parents saw fit to mention.

(iii)(a)   Material effects

The immediate effects of the man becoming the sole earner and the obvious cut in income was, interestingly, talked about more in terms of its social psychological implications, with the purely financial aspects being much less stressed. There could be many explanations for this but two would seem to be especially pertinent. Firstly, all of the men were earning salaries sufficient to give a fairly comfortable standard of living; all but one, for example, were in the process of buying their own house, and all but one ran a car. Secondly, a minimum of three years had now passed since the birth of the first child. During this time it seemed that the couples had either adapted financially, or a few of the wives had gone back to part-time work. Whatever interpretations might be made, the fact remained that there were few memories of financial impoverishment or material difficulties which were vivid enough to merit being stressed.

The comments actually made were connected more with changes in attitudes towards money and its earning. A few of the wives, for example, talked about not feeling that the money was their own since they had not personally earned it. Most of the wives said that, if they had any spare money, they would now tend to spent it on things for the children, especially clothes, rather than on themselves. About three quarters of the wives, however, talked about giving up their own jobs in terms of this being a temporary personal sacrifice, and made practically no mention of any changes involved materially. Most of the men saw the implications of their becoming the sole earner in terms of its heightening their personal responsibilities, since two and then three other individuals became totally financially dependent on them. Only Ian Johnson really contradicted this overall impression when he talked about feeling he was different from other middle class fathers. He said that he did not feel burdened down with responsibilities, had continued to spend money on what might be considered by others to be frivolous items such as leisure equipment and holidays, and had continued to live in rented accommodation. (The Johnsons in fact bought a house towards the end of the study.) A more typical statement was made by Derek Rankin when, during the joint interview, he reflected on the differences after having children. He commented:

And if I lose my job and have to take less salary well that affects everybody, whereas if we were both working, well, you could afford to do these sort of things. (Jt) *(iii)(b)   Physical effects*

Children were perceived as imposing considerable physical effects in two main ways. Firstly, the sheer activity of looking after the children was seen as extremely tiring, both physically and mentally, especially if they were also waking through the night. Several of the wives said, for example, that being at home and looking after children was far harder physically than it had been to work full-time before the children were born. About two thirds of the couples had either had in the past, or were currently experiencing, sleep problems of various kinds with the children. They talked about how exhausting this could be, and of the various schemes they had instituted in order that each of them had as much sleep as could be arranged.

Secondly, children were seen as restricting in various ways the physical mobility of the spouses, both individually and jointly. The most obvious effect, mentioned by everyone, was that the couple could not now go out together in the evening or at weekends without making arrangements for someone else to take over responsibility for the children. Although a third of the couples had relatives living in the Edinburgh area, none were near enough to be regarded as 'instantly available'. They all talked about how the physical restrictions of not leaving the children alone had resulted in changes in their activities outside the home.

The use of babysitters in order to be able jointly to leave the children was, in fact, the least regularly implemented response to the mobility limitations. The most regular response was for one spouse to stay in and babysit to allow the other to pursue activities independently, whether these were connected with leisure, or work and household responsibilities.[18] John Clark, for example, said:

> But there's no doubt we have to go our separate ways more than ever we did because there's no doubt we were a couple who did things together a lot, we weren't interested in going our separate ways. (I)

Alternatively, three of the couples simply became more housebound, seldom went out individually or jointly, and carried on the majority of their leisure and other activities outside the home as a family unit. If these findings are at all typical they would suggest that the segregated dimension of the leisure activities of middle class couples has been considerably under-estimated. Most of the men and women in my group chose to have activities separate from one another not only because having children made it difficult to do things jointly, but also, quite simply, because they *liked* to have independent pursuits.

The degree to which respondents felt *physically* limited by the children varied considerably, with ideas about children's needs and wants playing a large part in this process. For example, couples put forward very different views of how much they were restricted, based on the one hand on the image of children *needing* to stick to their own little routines and, on the other, that children should learn to be adaptable (i.e. to their parents' lives). Even so, many of the most mundane activities requiring physical mobility, such as shopping outings, were seen as considerably restricted by having to organise and transport around two small children. As Dianne Hemingway said:

> . . . it's affected our married lives in that you have to cater for four and not just two and because they're small they can't just be carried everywhere with us and, which some people DO. *It depends on the children, if they're placid and don't mind being humped around, but I'm afraid ours, ours protest rather loudly and we tend to really NOT do things because of them.* (I) [my emphasis]

Even Barbara Johnson, who was one of the respondents perhaps most keen not to let having children alter her life said:

> It's 100% giving yourself up, you have GOT to put the child first although you may not want to, in fact earlier I said that if it was a question of me or them, the sods came second and *I* came first. But in fact that isn't true, that is just how I would like to be, but if you've planned to go out for the day and the child is ill, you can't do anything about it, you stay at home. (I)

(iii)(c)   *Social psychological*

In this area, the most frequently mentioned effect of children could be described broadly as a restriction on the spontaneity of the couple's behaviour. On a practical level this was expressed in terms of the much greater need to organise all aspects of life, since they felt the responsibility of ensuring that the children's requirements were catered for adequately. The chief examples voiced by almost everyone was that they were now unable to simply decide to do a whole range of things, such as spontaneous trips to see a film or out for a drink, or to visit friends. Also, all of these parents, to varying degrees, felt restrictions on their ability to say whatever they felt like saying in front of the children. There were obviously a variety of implicit meanings behind this as well as the reasons which were actually articulated by the respondents. Some illustration of this wealth of beliefs and ideas is given by the following quotations, which are representative of the range of statements generally made. Philip Barber, in reply to my question 'What things are the same or different now from when you were first married?', explained:

'You're very much more housebound, er, you have very little time even to speak to each other, very much LESS time to speak to each other`and this CAN become a problem sometimes, it really CAN. Because as soon as the kids wake up, which is from 7 o'clock in the morning, if not earlier, there are certain subjects that you just can't speak to each other about', and he later went on 'you find that this sort of thing goes on in a child's mind and you begin to be very much more careful about ALL your conversations in front of her.' (I)

Sylvia Chapman remarked in their joint interview:

Sylvia: This is where I feel we don't have so much time you know, I sometimes feel we haven't had any time at all to say hello to each other, I feel sometimes we haven't had time to, you know, communicate in ANY way, em, [*Martin:* Oh aye, aye, well], so that in that way it's different, em, you know, it's er

Martin: [laughs] Although we've been in the house all day, mmmhmm. (Jt)

Sheila Pringle said:

Ben and I don't seem to talk as much, as we don't have time. It's not that we don't talk, we just don't have the time for the past two years. And especially for the children, you go to have a conversation and they want something and you break it off and then you forget about it. (I)

These three quotations say a very great deal about the attitudes towards children of these middle class couples. Each quotation suggests that the immediate needs of children were felt to be predominant in the everyday familial interactions (whether or not the spouses felt this to be a desirable state of affairs). Communication between the spouses was either deliberately censored or seemingly inevitably curtailed when children were present. However, it is important to note that, no matter how inevitable this behaviour might have seemed to the participants, it was in fact a social construction, and very dependent on their images of children. How different their behaviour might have been had they felt that it was legitimate to ignore a child's emotional development, to expect a child only to 'speak when spoken to', or that a child's needs and desires did not require speedy parental attention!

Moreover, having children was described as altering the spousal relationship even when the children were not physically present. Such feelings of restrictions on mutual and self expression were described by many of the couples. A few people mentioned restrictions on the spontaneity of their sex lives, but the majority talked about differences in their personal relationship in more general terms. Madeleine Harris, for example, said that the presence of children had meant 'a removal of the kind of sort of face en face, just the two of us relationship, which is a kind of maturing, I think.' (I)

This change from the claimed intensity of the dyadic situation was often illustrated when couples talked about differences in their patterns of moods and disagreements. About two thirds of the respondents made statements similar to that of Margaret Barber in her joint interview when she observed:

I think one of the things it's probably done for us is that, er, any arguments we have now don't last for more than five minutes. (Jt)

Helen Moffat expanded on this kind of change as follows:

I think your relationship's, well I mean obviously it can't be

100% right, but I think right at the roots it's got to be right because *I think children will smell it a mile off.* [my emphasis] So that I think we do take things or any differences of opinion that we have more seriously and not leave things hanging over. I mean if we DO have a disagreement we try and sort it out, we wouldn't have a sort of muttered squabble going on for about a fortnight or something like that, which you can afford to do when you've got no children. (I)

Madeleine Harris elaborated on her earlier statement when she explained:

. . . and so, when there are other parties, even though they be just children forcing you to take a more objective or, you know, just to cool off a bit, or just to cope anyway and keep going you know. That I think is very healthy, you know, and good thing because it gives you a perspective, a wider scope somehow so that you don't look into small things and explode them, you know. (I)

Most people remarked that having children around had had similar effects on their marital relationship, whether it had meant that the form of their disagreements had altered, or that the scope for conflict had widened. A few claimed, for example, that most of their current arguments were, in fact, about the children. Barbara Johnson made an interesting point about her own experience:

Well I think of necessity it forced us to understand each other better because things arose which needed discussion. And you might find areas of vigorous disagreement which wouldn't have cropped up unless you'd had children; because I think, even if you've never thought much about kids before you eventually HAVE them, there's some kind of residual attitude towards child-rearing. (I)

IV   FAMILY LIFE AS A SHARED REALITY ('GIVE AND TAKE')

This final area of underlying assumptions deals with the couples' accounts of family life as a mutually created shared reality. The following theoretical statement from Schutz provides an excellent summary of the complex interactive nature of the development of family behaviour. Schutz stated:

> My constructing the Other as a partial self, as the performer of typical roles or functions has a corollary in the process of self typification which takes place if I enter into interaction with him. I am not involved in such a relationship with my total personality but merely with certain layers of it. In defining the role of the Other I am assuming a role myself. In typifying the Other's behaviour I am typifying my own, which is interrelated with his, transforming myself into a passenger, consumer, taxpayer, reader, bystander, etc.[19] [and here, a spouse or parent]

Throughout their accounts respondents continually expressed an awareness that their behaviour was being developed in the context of the other family members. This aspect of family life has been addressed by sociological theorists with very different evaluations of its benefit to the individual. For Berger and Kellner such an awareness of the other family members, most notably the other spouse, has a 'nomic instrumentality' – the world is more real and solid for the individual because of this central core of mutually created meaning.[20] For Cooper such mutuality is constraining and damaging to each individual, stultifying and warping his/her very perception of the world and its possibilities.[21]

Three main underlying assumptions characterised my group's descriptions of family life. Firstly they frequently referred to an awareness of being part of a 'family unit'. By this they were, at these points, referring to their family of procreation. According to respondents, there was practically no aspect of family life where one could be 'unaware' of the other group members. Secondly, although reactions to this 'unit feeling' varied, they all maintained that the needs and wants of the other members had to be seen to be 'fairly' accommodated. This underlying assumption of mutually negotiated 'fairness' was typically expressed in terms of 'give and take' and 'coming and going'. Thirdly, all of the points discussed so far indicate another frequently stressed assumption – that family life should involve 'open communication'.

(a) Unit feeling

The relevance of feeling part of a family unit was mentioned in various ways. It was seen as having both positive beneficial effects as well as detrimental ones. On the positive side, some people described a feeling of security or of having become less self-centred: Edward Jackson said, for example:

> I mean I've got friends who are still bachelors the same age as I am and these blokes are miserable. They're always having to seek friendship whereas, well I'll tell you maybe what the answer is, if I can put it this way. OK, we've got Shirley and I, the two kids and the two dogs, now that gives me a one in five chance of getting a friendly welcome when I come home at night. It means you're coming home in fact to an actual environment where, OK, you're bound to get a welcome, and because of this, it stabilises you. (I)

Other people saw themselves as having become less self-centred. Anna Robson, for example, claimed:

> I'm a much nicer person now, I like to think so. I don't think about myself and I think this is the big thing for anyone thinking about marriage, don't think about ME anymore, think about US.' (and later) 'Your whole life changes, Kathryn, I mean, I've got three people who need me now. It's a nice feeling, you know, I mean, before it was just ME, me, me, me. (I)

Similar feelings were expressed in terms of being unable to indulge in introspection, simply because the time was not available. Louise Wilson felt that:

> . . . you don't spent as much time worrying about what you should be doing or what you ARE doing or in fact what you would like to be doing. (I)

David Russell felt, though, that this was just one aspect of children having narrowed his perspectives, 'because you're so much concerned with thinking about THEIR [children's] future, YOUR future with THEM'. (I)

Equally, others in the group sometimes found 'unit feeling' to be oppressive in that it tended to detract from individuality, privacy and freedom. Both husbands and wives mentioned this but perhaps the women stressed it more because at this point in their lives they were more *directly* involved with the 'unit' than were the men. Both Barbara Johnson and Marjorie Russell said that they felt, at times, that they were completely oppressed by a lack of personal freedom. Barbara said of the mother that:

> . . . when there are children around, she isn't ever on her own. This is something that I've actually had to fight for a bit, you know, just a bit of time on my own. I think it's just that men don't realise you need it, at least *I* do. (I)

Marjorie Russell added the further point that, when there were children around it was so much more difficult,

> . . . to give vent privately to your emotions, you can't let them, not that it happens very often, but when there's one of the local bugs going round and you're feeling low as low and nothing's going right, all you want to do is hide in a corner and bawl or something. (I)

The general impression was perhaps summed up by Madeleine Harris when she said:

> One has to find some way of not depriving them but also of keeping yourself, you know. (I)

Respondents frequently described how they tried to cope with the needs and wants of the individual in the context of this 'unit feeling'. Marjorie Russell again explained:

> I think probably we are still adjusting to the fact that we are now a unit of four, not a unit of two nor two individuals. I think it's difficult to make it a good unit and also retain some area where you are personal and private together, and separately. (I)

Alan Hemingway put forward the image that children were potentially overpowering, and reasserted the importance of the needs of the *parents* in the face of, as he saw it, the current emphasis on the *child*. He argued:

> I think that WE have to work hard at giving ourselves as adults
> a place in this household if you like, because if we DON'T work
> hard at it, they just take over in terms of attention and they
> come first. Well I think they come first in MOST families but I
> don't think that they should to the extent that they appear to
> everywhere else, and the whole sort of society is geared down to
> the great sort of god, the child. Well, at this particular stage in
> life, I think we're in a position to enjoy ourselves most and we've
> jolly well got to make sure we do. (I)

In this way respondents could be seen to define their own needs,
wants and satisfactions within the unit by reference to its other
members. Basically, whilst expressing 'unit feeling' as some sort of
taken-for-granted benchmark, they always balanced this with
notions that individuals should neither be allowed to dictate nor
have their individuality swamped by the group.

(b)   Fairness

A second important assumption was that individuals should be
treated 'fairly' within the group. Each spouse should feel that he/
she was making a 'fair' contribution to the unit's functioning and
was also getting a 'fair' share of the rewards. This was frequently
expressed in terms of marriage being a 'partnership of equals'
which should be run on the basis of 'give and take'. Such assumptions were also extended to their views about children. The
assumption that children were entitled to 'fair' treatment within
the unit was a frequent legitimation of the kind of treatment, and
the amount of time and attention, which they were given. Again,
'fairness' was negotiated in terms of each particular unit and, as
will be described in Chapter 5, various coping mechanisms were
developed to sustain belief in its reality.

When talking about this assumption respondents frequently
apologised for speaking in clichés, but insisted that these really
did apply. In fact, the avoidance of any *specific* statements was an
integral part of sustaining beliefs in fairness. This meant that a
feeling of flexibility could be retained whereby their system *could*
be altered if either of the spouses challenged it and maintained

that he/she was *not* getting a fair deal. Once again the picture was one of respondents holding similar generalised assumptions in common, the actual practical implementations of which were seen as idiosyncratic. Martin Chapman said, by way of advice to a young man getting married:

> I wouldn't try to be too specific because, because you're dealing with individuals and you could be misguiding them. I would try to generalise and always tell them to put something into it as well as to get something out of it. And try to remember also that they won't always get their own way, there will be frustrations. They've got to consider each other and each other's feelings as well as their family [children] when they come along. (I)

Such generalised assumptions had important implications on the practical everyday level. The range of behaviour which could be subsumed under the heading of 'fairness' and sharing was vast as can be illustrated by the following two quotations. Contrast Patrick Hislop who said to Kathy:

> I saw it [marriage and parenthood] as a partnership of specialists. I'm the specialist at bringing in the goods if you're the specialist at making use of them. (Jt)

with the very different framework of 'fairness' put forward by Philip Barber. He said:

> We both feel that these things should be shared, er, that everything about family life should be shared as much as possible. A reasonable division of labour in that I, well I don't regard housework, rearing the children and so forth as Margaret's, as the WIFE's duties, and that mine are to go out and earn the bread. We see this very much as a question of these chores have to be done, and we sort out an arrangement that suits both of us. (I)

The maintenance of belief in this underlying assumption of fairness was an important factor in the negotiation of family behaviour. As will be shown throughout the book, various gestures and coping mechanisms were used to maintain this *belief*, in the face of practical contradictions.

(c) Open communication

All of these assumptions about give and take, marriage as a partnership, and learning things together, implied another important underlying assumption – open communication. Everyone stressed that this was important, even if they did this in the context of complaining that their own communication processes were inadequate or impaired. Communication was seen as a process of exchanging both factual information and information about ideas, beliefs and feelings. Respondents saw this as important not simply to organise everyday existence but also to retain the closeness of the personal relationship. Margaret Barber said, for example:

> If you can't talk over your problems I think you're sunk from the beginning, or at least it would have to be a very superficial kind of marriage. (I)

A few people in the group said that the ability to openly communicate ideas and feelings was so vital to the marital state that if I was *not* actually studying that angle then I really *ought* to be! Ben Pringle argued:

> I think this, if you are able to communicate, particularly with your wife, and I don't mean just talking about the latest TV programme or talking about things that people usually talk about, er, this isn't communication to me, it's getting an opinion across to somebody and yet being able to accept one back and then knocking it about a bit and arriving at a mutual decision. Not an easy thing to do and I don't quite honestly think that we WERE good at it when we got married, better than most I feel sure, but we're better at it now. (I)

From the perspective adopted in this analysis, that marriage is a process of negotiation of a mutually held reality, communication can be seen as a vital means of reaffirming the belief system. If modern middle class marriage does involve members orienting themselves to sets of ill-defined generalised assumptions, with the means of attaining these being varied and uncertain, then communication between the spouses is an essential factor in creating the belief that both are working along lines similar enough to ensure the continued viability of the unit. Empirically, some of the couples saw proof of a successful process of communication in terms of 'thinking as one'. Judy Davies, who felt this very strongly, explained:

> Well, you often, you know, I often say to him, or I'll be about to say something to him, in the course of conversation and I'll find he'll say 'oh I was just going to say that', so obviously there is, you know, this understanding, and obviously our love has deepened, well this is how *I* feel, since we got married, otherwise we wouldn't be going along the same sort of line, would we? (I)

Obviously the extent to which couples claimed to think alike varied, as did the areas on which they claimed accordance. All, however, made some statement about being increasingly able to anticipate each other's reactions over the years, and that differences of opinion had at least become more tolerated, if not actually lessened. Ian Johnson said:

> There are lots of other things where I'm sure we originally differed and now we don't. And a lot of the things we just don't need to talk about because over the years, em, we haven't said very much, at any one time, but we've said enough over the years to exactly to know the other person's point of view. (I)

Throughout the book many of the taken-for-granted aspects of the communication processes of these couples will be illustrated. A major point will be, for example, the importance of the mother's position as an agent of information to the father concerning the child. However, much of this later consideration of communication points to the conclusion that, for a variety of reasons, it was usually at best only partially 'open', and even deliberately so. Nevertheless, this does not detract from the strength with which respondents themselves adhered to the importance of openness. This was in many ways the lynch pin of their social construction of family reality.

V SUMMARY

Analysis of respondents' accounts showed that they held similar underlying assumptions about family life, although these might be expressed in different kinds of behaviour. With reference to parental behaviour in particular, such assumptions provided sets of benchmarks amidst a plethora of uncertainties.

Three main areas of assumptions were outlined. Firstly, couples emphasised that marriage and parenthood were situations of 'learning'. They felt that there was no realistic prior preparation for parenthood; essentially one learned about being a parent through direct experience including 'trial and error'. Secondly, behaviour was related to the family life cycle. Couples described their family lives as constantly changing, and interpreted their own and their child's behaviour in terms of its appropriateness to the family life-cycle stages as they perceived them. Finally, respondents emphasised that family life was a shared reality. They defined themselves as being part of a family unit, and saw this as having a direct effect on many items of behaviour. Communication and fairness were vital elements in these processes and respondents stressed that 'give and take' was a crucial feature of family life.

Thus family life was viewed by this group of couples as a learned, shared and life-cyclically oriented reality. Such beliefs, however, provided only a broad framework for the development of their parental behaviour. In everyday life considerable variation in the practical implementation of these beliefs was possible. Respondents were therefore engaged in ongoing interpretative activity. Their beliefs had to be constantly re-created, re-affirmed and sustained. This took place in the processes of negotiation of the mutually-held realities with other family members. It is to these negotiating processes that I turn in the following chapter.

3 Negotiation: the Development of Parental Behaviour

I NEGOTIATION

Being a parent involves continuously making choices and decisions about how to deal with one's children. For many parents, however, this process is not a lone activity but is carried out intimately with another adult, one's spouse. In this chapter I shall discuss some of the interactional and definitional factors involved in this mutual development of parental behaviour.

The underlying assumptions discussed in the previous chapter provided spouses with a generalised sense of their mutually-held reality of parenthood. The problematical nature of the process arose out of the fact that varieties of behaviour could be claimed as 'legitimate' in terms of these very broad assumptions. As Walsh has stated:

> . . . the social world is also a world of multiple realities, in the sense that members may focus on social situations in different ways and thereby read (account) what are the same situations differently.[1]

This applies as much to marriage and parenthood as to any other sphere of the 'social world'. In order, therefore, to achieve some sense of acting in the same reality, each couple was engaged in a continuous process of *negotiation*. In Berger and Kellner's terms they were continually correlating their individual definitions of reality.[2]

The main focus of the present study was to look at how spouses defined their social worlds and negotiated these definitions with other family members in order to achieve a subjectively satisfactory construction of 'being a parent'. This process of negotiating parental behaviour was characterised by the use of legitimations and legitimating tactics. These involved explaining behaviour to oneself and others so that it could be seen to be compatible with the mutually-held reality being created. As Schutz pointed out, negotiation is a process of reassurance that the 'right' prescriptions are being applied.[3]

The negotiation and legitimation of parental behaviour involved extremely complex exchanges of meanings at many different levels. For example, it is important to remember that the *subjective* meaning attached to a particular activity by a family member might bear little relationship to its actual *practical* contribution to the administration of family life, as assessed by the researcher. Throughout my fieldwork I was constantly reminded of this very important point. Occasionally respondents *themselves* defined certain actions as making minimal *practical* contribution, or as being 'an indulgence', but at the same time stressed their importance. During the analysis I realised that one aspect of the subjective importance of such actions was that they sustained belief in the various underlying assumptions which were crucial to the mutual reality being created. I shall give two examples to illustrate this point. Both deal with the reaffirmation of meanings: the first through the practical division of labour, the second through verbal communication.

Firstly, great importance was attached by respondents to the regular *voluntary* execution of various domestic tasks by the husband.[4] Many of these could be seen, objectively, to be simply 'gestures' whose importance was to sustain a belief in the fairness of the mutually shared domestic responsibilities.[5] The kinds of 'gestures' varied between families, as did the actual number and range of domestic tasks which the husband carried out. All couples, however, cited certain of the husband's domestic activities which, although often making a *minimal* practical contribution, could be analysed as of great importance in sustaining the belief in fairness. The most frequent examples were that the husband made tea or coffee, or washed the dishes, in the evening. Other more complex examples were that he bathed the children in the evening, or looked after them totally for a short period. As will be discussed later, the exchange of meanings behind these various activities could be seen as of greater significance than the practical contribution of the task itself.[6]

Secondly, most of these husbands and wives said that they tended to talk a considerable amount about the children with one another. This, they maintained, was not at any particularly self-conscious level of 'let's discuss the children', but rather it was a taken-for-granted exchange. Respondents themselves often said that this could be viewed as a sort of smug self-indulgence about their children's pleasant qualities. On another level they legitimated such discussions as helping them to be consistent with the children, and to maintain a 'united front'. Analytically, however, it can be suggested that this interchange between parents was a vital means both of coping with the uncertainties of their parental situation, and of mutually-legitimating and reinforcing each other's beliefs in the appropriateness of their actions. Talking about the children was much more than an indulgent exchange or even a discussion about how to deal with them. It was inextricably linked with underlying assumptions that children should be understood and that, for consistent parental behaviour, spouses should sustain the belief that the understandings were subjectively satisfactory to them both.[7] Such communication was not only an integral element in the construction of parental behaviour but it was also a means of sustaining belief in the viability of the unit in the face of all the contradictions and dissatisfactions.

II LEGITIMATIONS

Legitimations were an integral part of the negotiation of parental behaviour. Respondents used them to justify both previous and intended actions. Many legitimations involved the stating of underlying assumptions previously described. These were the broadest possible common denominations of taken-for-granted meanings. The dynamic of the negotiating processes stemmed at least in part from the vagueness and generality of the assumptions. In addition the assumptions were frequently incompatible. All of this meant that the practical implementation of these meanings provided great scope for variations in interpretation and strength of adherence. Legitimating behaviour was therefore a continuous element in the everyday decision-making involved in being a parent. This everyday decision-making was, in itself, a means of re-affirming underlying assumptions since, in the process of surveying possible courses of action, individuals and couples often legitimated their intended actions in terms of these generalised meanings. In this way belief in a mutually-created reality was being constantly sustained.

In this section I shall first illustrate how legitimations were used in the development of parental behaviour. I shall then discuss the special importance of assumptions about children (images) being used as legitimations. Finally the *ways* in which these images of children were used as legitimations will be described. This is treated as an evaluative, selective and interactive process.

(a) Examples of legitimating behaviour

All of the couples had made the decision that the woman should stay at home to look after the children, at least in their early years. During their accounts respondents legitimated this decision about parental behaviour both to myself and to one another. This involved referring to various underlying assumptions, and either defining them as being upheld or else rationalising their perceived current infringement. The Robsons, for example, discussed this as follows:

Anna: I feel at the moment that all my married life seems to have been taken up with small children, although I've only got two. I mean, I've been married what, seven years.
Jim: Yes, but you've got to remember, em, you'll be possibly married if you're lucky for fifty years, so seven years out of fifty is not a big amount to be mixed up with small children, Anna, when you think about it.
Anna: Oh I know this, but try telling me this. I mean, I'm here at the moment because the children are small enough to need me here at the moment. (W/E)

Most couples, like the Robsons, legitimated this decision in two main ways. They put forward abstract images of children's needs and wants, often, as in this case, stability and security.[8] These were usually supported by assumptions about family life as cyclical. Respondents maintained that, in the context of modern day western society, such a home-bound period was inevitable but temporary. A similar legitimation came from Philip Barber when he said of the 'toddler stage':

Your life's very much centred on the children, and I think that whoever is looking after the children has got to make this kind of sacrifice, that they have to accept, for the period in which the children are up and about, able to move around and yet not sufficiently well able to be, well, not old enough to be off to school for a day to give them a free period, they have to commit themselves. This is the mother's role, the mother has to commit herself to this kind of life. (I)

Another area of parental behaviour which illustrates the use of legitimations was the degree to which children were expected to fit in with the parents' lives or vice versa. Unlike the first example, this was an area on which respondents held almost polar views. Here the potential incompatibility of various underlying assumptions was clearly shown. Images of children's needs and wants could easily conflict with assumptions about family life as a shared reality in which individuals should neither dictate nor be swamped. The following quotations are typical and illustrate the different parental decisions made by James Gilchrist and Jim Robson compared with Jean Coulson and Ian Johnson, and the ways in which they legitimated this behaviour. James Gilchrist said:

When we go visiting, we're back for 7 o'clock because that's the time the kids are washed and in their beds and have their supper. We sort of made that rule up between the two of us and that's it . . . we don't, em, we don't spoil their sleep or their health in any way or their routine by enjoying ourselves and letting them suffer.

Jim Robson said:

I see children that are lumped about every place their parents go. I think this is wrong, they're brought home at all the odd times of night, I think this is wrong.

When asked why he thought this was wrong, he replied:

Because I feel that a child needs its own environment when it's time to go to sleep. I find that my children don't settle any place except their own home or a home they know very well, such as

their grandparents or something like that. I wouldn't for instance dream of taking my children along to a party and lobbing
them into a bedroom and then lobbing them out at 1 o'clock in
the morning. I personally don't think this is a good idea, *I don't
think it gives a child a sense of security.* (I) [my emphasis]

Jean Coulson put forward a different view, she explained:

> . . . although we consider our children first obviously, em, at the
> same time, you know, THEY'VE got to fit into OUR existence
> rather than you know, US adjust to THEM. [and later] I think
> a lot of families, you know, once they've got children they say,
> 'oh we can't go away now, it's impossible', but if we want to go
> you know, we pack up the car and off we go you know, we don't
> want THEM to make a difference from that point of view. I
> don't think it's good for the child, you know, basically, I mean
> when Matthew was small you know, we travelled around
> abroad and took him with us. We'd rather he came with us, em,
> than leave him behind with somebody else to look after him. (I)

Ian Johnson said:

> When we lived in London we travelled about quite a lot because
> a lot of our friends lived out of London. And we'd go away for
> the weekend or overnight and the kids would just sleep in the
> back of the car or they'd sleep in a bed at the other end and we
> could transfer them from one bed to another and they wouldn't
> wake up, or, if they did, they'd go back to sleep in five minutes
> . . . and they've just accepted this. And I think probably a lot of
> kids wouldn't do this, em, you know, you hear of parents saying
> to tiptoe out and be very quiet. Well they don't care where they
> sleep, they'll sleep anywhere. (I)

These quotations are interesting in many ways. They show how
these parents used images of children to legitimate their behaviour. James and Jim defined children as needing their own
home environment and fixed routines in order to foster good
health and a sense of security. Jean and Ian defined children as
being much more adaptable than this, and saw their having a
break from home and routine as valuable (i) because it kept the
family together (unit feeling), or (ii) because it encouraged

children to learn to be flexible (family life as a learning situation). At the same time, however, they also legitimated their behaviour in terms of the needs of *all* the members of the group rather than just those of the children.

The underlying assumptions were essentially very flexible. This was shown by the wide ranges of behaviour which respondents claimed reflected these beliefs. Assumptions were also used selectively, and were assigned varying priorities when they were used as legitimations. Many parents, for example, felt that the children's needs and wants restricted their own freedom. This could be seen to violate assumptions about fairness. In this situation they tended, therefore, to implement the assumption that family life was cyclical. They emphasised that they had enjoyed considerable freedom of action *before* children and would be able to do so again in the future.

Parents also legitimated their behaviour to the children themselves. Analytically this can be seen as a practical interpretation of their assumptions about family life as a shared and learning situation. It is also connected with their images of the child as a future friend.[9] Descriptions were given of how decisions had been made, or actions had been taken which favoured one child at the expense of the other. Typically this occurred when the elder child was asked to give way to the perceived special needs or demands of the younger. It was apparent from respondents' accounts that they felt such behaviour on their part had to be legitimated to the elder child, or else alternatives created which sustained belief in fairness. In such circumstances the notion of phase or stage was frequently used as a legitimation. An example came from the Chapmans who, at that time, maintained that they thought they were treating their elder daughter somewhat unfairly. Martin said:

And I, I find myself, er, getting on to her a lot more, I think probably just with the lack of sleep I'm a bit more irritable just now. Just general circumstances that em, I think we're being a bit unfair to the child really, in that respect, we're pulling her up for things that normally we wouldn't have said anything . . . We've even tried to explain to Anne that, em, we aren't getting our sleep, with Judy teething and even Anne herself occasionally says: 'Did I disturb you last night, daddy?' (F)

(b)   Images of children as legitimations

The legitimation to one another of past and intended childrearing
activities was an important element in the spouses' negotiation of
being parents. Here, images of children were constantly ex-
changed and discussed. Several couples maintained that they
were in agreement about how to bring up the children. However,
even those who claimed this overall agreement discussed and
debated the management of everyday issues in much the same
way as did couples who made no claim to such concordance of
views. Discussions took the general form of each spouse legitimating alternative methods of defining and dealing with a situation,
often by appealing to different underlying assumptions. Sometimes disagreements on methods were perceived as irreconcilable.
Even then, however, these were frequently tolerated, and were incorporated into the mutual repertoire of parental behaviour if
each spouse was able to put forward a legitimation which proved
subjectively satisfactory to the other. The uncertainties of practical parental behaviour were so great that a mother or father was
seldom totally confident that his/her methods were in line with
their intended meanings. The following quotation, for example,
was part of a discussion where one spouse legitimated his appeal
for firmer control of the child by putting forward the image that
children need well-defined limits of behaviour. His wife challenged this, arguing for a more lax approach based on the assumption that a child's individuality had to be allowed to develop. In
reply to Eric's statement that their son had a 'mild discipline
problem', Carol Burns argued:

> *Carol:*   I think it's simply because he's at school and he's grow-
> ing and learning and you know, managing himself a bit more,
> you know, he comes home from school now.
> *Eric:*   It's just as he gets older.
> *Carol:*   It's just growing up, and he's bound to be exerting his
> personality more and more as he learns more and see others
> em, he'll just try it on a bit more you know, just to get his own
> personality going.
> *Eric:*   Obviously the older he gets, the worse it would get
> unless it's stamped on, I mean it must do.
> *Carol:*   Yes, but you know, *how* do you stamp on it without
> crippling it, you know, without stunting his personality?

Eric: Well you see, this is where the problem arises. (F)

This extract was, therefore, part of an exchange where spouses legitimated different approaches to a defined problem. This was part of the process of negotiating parental strategies, and illustrated several assumptions which were often implicit in such discussions. Both spouses were operating with the image of the child as a learning, dynamic entity. They tried to understand his behaviour by placing it in the context of different physical and social environments. They also used projected images of how their own behaviour might affect the child's future personality. Here already then are three fundamental images of children which were common to all respondents, and which will be elaborated upon in later chapters.

Thus, legitimations of the *child's* behaviour as well as their own were further elements involved in negotiating parental behaviour. Here respondents were implementing the most crucial underlying assumption – that being a parent involved understanding the child. Assumptions about phases and stages, were perhaps the most frequently used legitimations in this area. This was often well illustrated when the child behaved in ways which the parents defined as 'incomprehensible'. One way of legitimating such behaviour, and their response to it, was to explain it as a phase. Many couples, for example, told me about their children being cheeky to them and calling them all sorts of silly names. Hannah Gilchrist gave a typical legitimating response as follows:

I think they all go through the same sort of stages, children, you know, the cheeky mischievous stage is about three years old. (I)

The use of the notion of stage as a perceived aid to understanding a child's behaviour was nicely illustrated by Madeleine Harris when she was talking about a student who had recently 'au-paired' for them, she said:

Frances is at an age where she's not a little baby anymore and I think she felt the girl was a bit condescending to her, I don't think the girl knew how to cope with *that age* you know, because *they're not babies and yet they're children*, and *it's some balance between a bit of grown-upness and still a bit of being very little*. (W/E) [my emphasis]

(c) Legitimating parental behaviour: an evaluative, selective and interactive process

The negotiation of parental behaviour was characterised therefore by the constant use of images of children to legitimate actions. Evaluation of these images was a crucial element in developing courses of action. For example, one way in which these parents constructed understandings of their child was by the definition of various personality traits.[10] At its simplest, they then had to decide whether a defined trait was good or bad in order to make their response. Patrick Hislop, for instance, said of his younger daughter:

> Anna, on the other hand seems to be much more aggressive (than Julie), has no fear of people, em, is perhaps too aggressive for her own good – which has to be occasionally trod on. (I)

A further illustration of the potential importance for behaviour of the parent's perception and *evaluation* of various traits came from Carol Burns. She spoke as follows about her reaction against a medical questionnaire which she had been required to answer concerning her son, John. She said:

> You know, you could have just put 'yes' to everything and you could have just put 'no' to everything because, em, well it said 'is he obedient?', well of COURSE he's disobedient, 'is he argumentative?', YES, thank goodness. And yet I'm sure if I'd answered 'yes' to this lot I'd have had a very aggressive child on paper. (I)

The use of images of children as legitimations was also a *selective* process. In everyday life images were usually drawn upon in an essentially spontaneous and unreflective manner. Legitimations were essentially context bound. In the present context parents were being encouraged to verbalise their ideas about their children for the benefit of a piece of research. Several of them remarked that they would usually reflect in such a self-conscious way only when a problem arose. My impression was that individuals and couples had repertoires of images which were drawn upon for different purposes in different situations, and which were frequently internally inconsistent. When respondents actually described and elaborated upon specific domestic events, their accounts were characterised by an essentially pragmatic and *ad hoc* use of images. Margaret Barber's comment seemed to reflect this and would probably have been echoed by most of the respondents. She said:

> . . . one tends to act as one genuinely feels at the time with children, you don't generally have time to reflect what's the right thing to do. (I)

The selection and evaluation of images of children was also an *interactive* process between spouses. This was a crucial way in which belief was sustained in their mutually-held reality of being parents. The vagueness and generality of many of the images of children put these spousal interactions at a premium. They talked to one another about the child in an attempt to develop understandings which would, ideally, be subjectively satisfactory to them both. These mutually-held understandings could then be a taken-for-granted base for the parental behaviour of both spouses. In practice, it would seem from respondents' accounts, that it was often disagreements and misunderstandings during such interactions which undermined their claimed ideal of inter-parental consistency.[11] The wide range of possible legitimations, both of the child's behaviour and the parent's response, meant that respondents frequently vacillated and disagreed about which interpretation could be used as a credible view of reality at any particular time. During the course of the interviews spouses often revealed and debated with one another their different images of children. Madeleine Harris, for example, showed how her reaction to certain aspects of the children's behaviour would be different from that of Jeff, simply because she interpreted them differently. She reflected:

> I'm trying to think if we DO have any conscious rules about their behaviour, what we want them to be like – to be honest and not tell lies. I think you're (to Jeff) more CONSCIOUS of that than I am because I don't think children lie, half the time they just make up imaginary tales. (F)

Here Madeleine defined herself as reacting less strictly to situations where both she and Jeff felt that their children had been dishonest. She put forward an alternative abstract image of children to legitimate her response. In this particular instance the Harris's simply accepted one another's different reactions. Often, however, arguments took place when one spouse tried to persuade the other to change his/her parental behaviour by claiming the greater validity (evaluative), or relevance (selective), of a particular image.

III   SOME CHARACTERISTICS OF LEGITIMATIONS

Legitimating parental behaviour involved continuous choices about the kinds of knowledge which made subjective sense to each respondent. As Schutz said:

> Not only *what* an individual knows differs from what his neighbour knows, but also *how* both know the 'same' facts. Knowledge has manifold degrees of clarity, distinctness, precision and familiarity.[12]

(a)   This was shown on a *general* level when, for example, respondents contrasted knowledge perceived as 'common-sense', with that of science.

(b)   It was also illustrated when they legitimated a *particular* piece of behaviour of their child. In this instance, the most frequent choice was between using a taken-for-granted image of the child, such as a perceived personality trait; or gaining further 'understanding' by reconstructing the *context* in which the child was defined as acting.[13]

(a)   Some of the general choices of kinds of knowledge which were perceived as subjectively satisfactory were discussed in the previous chapter.[14] Most couples stressed the irrelevance, in practice, of knowledge or experience *prior* to being a parent; and emphasised the importance of learning through *direct* experience of the situation. One way of explaining the preference for this kind of knowledge was the image that all children are different. Ben Pringle, a father who *had* read various things about parenthood remarked:

It's not a knowledgeable subject, you know, I don't think a great deal of knowledge *helps* you. If there is a science of parenthood, er, I don't think there is, children are so different. (I)

The high degree of subjective satisfaction accorded to knowledge derived from one's 'own experience' was also shown by legitimations defined as 'common sense'. In their accounts respondents constantly indicated that, whilst they were aware that whole ranges of 'scientific' analyses could be applied to being a parent, they preferred to rely on the intuitive experimental brand of knowledge called 'common sense'. Barry Coulson illustrated this when he talked about their dealings with their children as being different from those of some friends. He explained:

But we have some friends that, you know, it makes us feel rather, well, as I say, sort of simple, you know, the way they sort of treat their children. It sort of bothered me, and we said 'oh crikey, are we doing the right thing?' They treat it all sort of 'oh, how will it affect the child sort of thing?' I mean, we DON'T, we just do what is normal, em what WE feel is normal and natural. (I)

Respondents were aware that parents had different ideas about which knowledge 'made sense' to them. For example, some recounted, with delight, instances where they or their friends had followed 'scientific' advice about childrearing, with no successful outcome (i.e. the suggested methods had not achieved the desired results). The Rankins, for instance, said that they had only managed to deal with their son's refusal to eat when they *stopped* taking Dr Spock's advice and used their own 'common sense' instead.

Parental behaviour which was legitimated by 'common sense' knowledge was also felt to be subjectively satisfactory partly because being too 'scientific' was equated with not being 'yourself'. Several parents further maintained that *children* were especially sensitive to such 'falseness'. The first part of this quotation from Barbara Johnson was typical. She said:

I think you can worry too much about whether you're doing the right thing or the wrong thing. I feel that perhaps you just ought to follow your instinct and hope for the best. I think, actually, you can't dissemble anyway, children realise if you're not being true to yourself. And, em, as soon as you try and make out that you are different from what you really are, I reckon you're creating more anxiety than ever, so I hope they just know me as a bad-tempered old bitch (laughs) and they'll just have to like it or lump it. (I)

Interestingly, however, certain kinds of 'scientific' legitimations of children's behaviour, such as those provided by doctors, were perceived as being extremely satisfactory.[15] Most of these parents did not challenge the perhaps more esoteric field of medical science. They felt, however, that their everyday knowledge (common sense) was more pertinent to their own family lives than were the social sciences of psychology or sociology. I would suggest that, in part, this is because medical legitimations usually come with a prescribed and easily administered 'solution'.

(b)   The choice between different levels of knowledge was also affected by the particular *context* in which behaviour was seen to take place. Parents' accounts were characterised by continuous decisions about the most subjectively satisfactory legitimations of the child's behaviour. It seems likely that they had ranges of legitimations which were explored either systematically or randomly in making decisions about everyday parental behaviour. Physical, personality or contextual images were, for example, the bases of three possible kinds of legitimations.[16] Sometimes a great deal of parental behaviour was legitimated in terms of one particular image of a child, which had achieved temporary predominance. This occurred when, for example, a child was defined as 'going through a phase' to which distinct characteristics had been attributed. A frequent illustration occurred when mothers legitimated all decisions about going to places with or without their children in terms of his/her 'going through a clinging phase'.

The subjective satisfaction of a legitimation also varied through time. The overall uncertainty, and the number and complexity of variables involved in making sense of the child, meant that respondents' accounts were simply those sets of legitimations which were satisfactory to them *at any one point in time*. Occasionally this process was laid bare when respondents 'realised' that they had in fact 'misunderstood' the child and had developed 'wrong' legitimations of his/her behaviour.

Examples of this were given by the Moffats and the Hislops who related similar experiences of forming 'wrong' understandings of their elder daughter's behaviour. In each case, they had perceived the child as behaving abnormally by becoming tearful and easily upset and claiming physical symptoms. The parents had defined all this as stemming from social psychological factors. The Moffats thought Pamela was worried about school; the Hislops thought Julie was being upset by her very dominant small sister. When doctors eventually diagnosed a tonsil infection for Pamela Moffat and a urinary tract infection for Julie Hislop, both sets of parents subsequently accepted a physical account of the behaviour, and said that they now felt somewhat embarrassed and abashed by their previously inaccurate understandings. The change in understanding their children's behaviour resulted in different parental acts. Basically both sets of parents stopped either 'humouring' their children or encouraging them to face up to their 'problems', and allowed the children to stay off school for a while to 'get better'. These were just two instances of many situations described by respondents where they defined themselves as having 'misunderstood' their child at a certain point in time. Subsequently, they had changed to a different 'understanding' and different behaviour to which they *then* attributed a greater legitimacy.

In these ways legitimations were characterised by the selection of different kinds of knowledge, and by the varying satisfaction of the underlying assumptions at different points in time. In addition, the process of legitimating behaviour was pragmatic and tactical in another sense. In creating their mutually-held reality spouses also developed constellations of meanings which I shall call 'explanatory incidents'. These were frequently referred to during their accounts and involved a respondent describing an incident in the *past* which was now used as a legitimation of *present* behaviour. The use of 'explanatory incidents' as legitimating tactics links in with the following point made by Berger and Kellner. They wrote:

> The couple thus constructs not only present reality but reconstructs past reality as well, fabricating a common memory that integrates the recollections of the two individual pasts.[17]

Obviously each incident was being described specifically for the information of an outsider, the researcher, but it was, nevertheless, a tacit reference point for the couples concerned, and had been incorporated into their mutual stock of knowledge. Marjorie Jeffreys, for example, legitimated as follows her continued decision to stay at home with the children rather than go back to work as she would have liked. She said:

> I think the child would eventually get the idea that you were more interested in what happened outside than what happened at home. (I)

She went on to refer to an incident which occurred when she was listening to a series about professional women going back to work, explaining:

> And one day I switched this on and I was doing some job about the house and Brian was pottering about, he switched it off, and I asked him why he switched it off, 'because I don't want you to go back to work, Mummy.' And he thought I was listening to that programme because he thought I wanted to go out to work and he didn't want me to go out to work. (I)

Barry Coulson, who never did any cooking, legitimated this as follows:

> But I don't enjoy it em, even if Jean is away I will never cook for myself. Only the bare essentials, you know, I just have no patience with it. I used to cook when I HAD to, if Jean was in bed when we first got married and she'd had a miscarriage, I cooked for six bloody weeks [everyone laughing] . . . it drove me insane. W/E

An 'explanatory incident' could also be used to support a belief in the feasibility of an item of *intended* behaviour. An extreme illustration of this was given by Kathy Hislop when she speculated that her husband would help in the house if, in the future, she went out to work. As she had virtually never gone out to work at all since she was married, and as her husband currently made no contribution to the household chores, she legitimated her belief as follows:

There was three weeks when I did work when we were in the flat (first married) and Patrick was always home before I was at night. And towards the end of the second week he was starting to get the tea ready before I came in, and I think it only gradually dawned on him that these things had to be done. (I)

An 'explanatory incident' was often used as a sort of negative form of legitimation. This frequently occurred when couples were legitimating a strong and fairly inflexible preference for *always* allocating an activity to one spouse in particular, or for always behaving in a certain way. They reinforced their confidence that this was the *'best'* course of action by using an 'explanatory incident' to illustrate that the alternatives would be unsuccessful. The most common example was the reference to the 'nappy disasters' which had occurred when the father had attempted that particular chore. Another frequent example was the overspending or purchasing of a wrong item when the husband had done the shopping. Although these examples did not apply to all of the respondents, most of them, at some point, used the tactic of an 'explanatory incident' to legitimate, in their particular situation, one spouse's monopoly of a certain activity.

On a wider level an 'explanatory incident' was sometimes used to reinforce a decision *not* to take a particular course of action. A somewhat extreme example came from the Robsons, who only very rarely left the children with someone and went out on their own. Anna Robson explained:

I'm NOT very lucky with babysitters, well I have neighbours who offer you know, but anytime we DO have a babysitter one of them wakes up yelling. It's just one of those things you know. As I say, when we DO go out it's usually a family treat. (I)

To support this, both she and her husband related independently the incident of one New Year's Eve when they had gone next door to their neighbour's house for a few minutes, only to find on returning, their distraught child screaming in the hall.

This brief consideration of the use of the 'explanatory incident' has some interesting wider implications. In many cases it would seem that *one* experience or incident had been sufficient to concretise a set of beliefs about appropriate behaviour. It was again evident that, in the area of family behaviour, formalised learning techniques, or rational scanning of possible modes of behaviour, were usually regarded as irrelevant, and that personal experience was the prime way of deciding on a course of action. In addition to this, decisions about family behaviour and organisation were made not only on the basis of acceptability, but also of habit. In the area of the division of labour, for example, the person who carried out an activity the most frequently was often eventually regarded as the 'best' for the job, from the point of view both of standard of work, and of economy of time and effort. Routines were quickly developed on the basis of 'explanatory incidents', and the belief that the potential inconvenience of trying alternative methods was not worth the bother because the present method had been *experienced* as, at the very least, acceptable.

That a particular personal experience may have provided objectively inaccurate or inadequate knowledge was irrelevant; the important factor was that the respondent *believed* in that knowledge. This was particularly evident in the area of childrearing where much behaviour was evolved on the basis of 'explanatory incidents' and recollected experience. As I shall discuss later, experiences with and recollections of the first child were very much referred to as an aid to dealing with the second child.[18] Parents tended to use a sort of working model of what had happened with the first child to legitimate their actions with the second. The progress of the second child was, for example, seen very much in the context of that of the first. This was a constant reference point for the parents, even though several of them also mentioned that it was difficult to remember exact details of the first child's progress. Spouses, for example, frequently disagreed with each other during the course of an interview about what had actually happened at certain times. Thus, putting the situation somewhat baldly and provocatively, a fair amount of the child-rearing behaviour of the couples was constructed by reference to often admittedly hazy and badly recollected experiences, especially those with the first child. These are some examples of respondents telling of this situation. Margaret Barber said:

> It's quite interesting, er, you saying 'how would you describe them?' because you see, if I didn't have medical charts, I would say that Karen was a small, unhappy, delicate looking little baby when she was Mary's age; Mary is round and rosy and contented. And yet, having been to the clinic and having them

weighed, I discover that not only has Mary gained less, in spite of being a heavier baby than when she was born, she is now half a pound less than Karen was at this age. And if I didn't have the proof RIGHT in front of me, I would never ever believe anyone, I would say Mary is pounds heavier. (I)

Shirley Jackson disagreed strongly with her husband when he maintained that their second child was now more advanced than the first had been at the same age, she argued:

Well, *I* don't think so, I think YOU can't remember what Simon was like at fifteen months because *I* certainly really can't remember, so neither can you. Well *I* remember thinking at one point, 'gosh, Elaine's doing that much quicker than Simon ever did it' and I kept a record, a MUCH more informative record about Simon than I've ever kept about Elaine [laughs]. And *I* looked up the record, now *I* was SURE that Simon had done this particular thing at a much later stage, and I looked up my book and he HADN'T, now that just shows in that very short space of time how you forget. I mean I can remember when he walked, you know, which is quite a MAJOR thing in a child's life, but, you know little things about how he was sort of fitting pegs into holes n' things, well now I was SURE Elaine was doing it quicker than Simon and, you know, she wasn't. I think this is a mistake that people make. (W/E)

IV SUMMARY

In this chapter aspects of the negotiation of the mutually-held reality of parenthood have been discussed. In part this process involved the interpretation in everyday life of the underlying assumptions discussed in Chapter 3. The very vagueness and generality of these assumptions meant that their practical interpretation could vary considerably. The legitimation of behaviour was therefore a constant feature of the decision making involved in being a parent.

I treated the development of parental behaviour as emerging from the negotiating processes within the family group. There was continual discussion between spouses on how best to manage all

a parent, they preferred to rely on the intuitive experiential
kinds of everyday issues in childrearing. A central feature of this
parental conversation was the use of images of children to legitimate a spouse's preferred course of action.

Legitimating parental behaviour was an evaluative, selective
and interactive process. It also involved spouses in making
choices about the kinds of knowledge which made subjective sense
to them. For example, 'common-sense' knowledge, or knowledge
legitimacy than 'scientific' knowledge. Finally, these legitimating
processes were also pragmatic and tactical. This was exemplified
in the use of 'explanatory incidents', where a single experience or
incident was often regarded as constituting sufficient evidence on
which to base a whole set of beliefs about appropriate behaviour.

In my concern to describe these negotiating processes I may,
however, have conveyed the sense that they proceeded un-
problematically in everyday life. This was far from the case. One
family member's legitimations were regularly challenged by the
other participants. Also, considerable effort was necessary to
sustain even the basic assumption that family members actually
comprehended one another's actions in a similar fashion. I now
turn, therefore, to a discussion of how these couples perceived and
attempted to deal with the problematical features of their everyday family lives.

4 Coping Mechanisms

I INTRODUCTION

Conflict and misunderstanding were continuous possibilities in the negotiation of parental behaviour. Schutz indicated that this was a feature of any process of constructing reality. Speaking of the 'recipe knowledge' which provides the meanings at hand in everyday life he said:

> It embraces the most heterogeneous kinds of knowledge in a very incoherent and confused state. Clear and distinct experiences are intermingled with vague conjectures; suppositions and prejudices cross well-proven evidence; motives, means and ends, as well as causes and effects, are strung together without clear understanding of their real connections.[1]

In this chapter I shall consider how, at the level of everyday behaviour, respondents developed 'coping mechanisms' to deal with contradictions, dilemmas and problematical elements involved in their mutual development of parental behaviour.

The preceding chapters must be seen as essential background to the following discussion. I described various underlying assumptions which provided a framework of meanings around which a wide variety of behaviour could be developed. Legitimations then came into operation as that part of the process of negotiating parental behaviour whereby respondents explained and justified their actual or intended conduct. This was often done by referring to the generalised framework of assumptions. The maintenance of their belief system was seldom, however, as straightforward as this theoretical presentation would seem to suggest. Scheff saw negotiation as implying the resolution of *conflicting* interpretations of meanings. It was intrinsic to the concept of negotiation that members involved in defining a phenomenon might disagree over its 'true' meaning.[2] Although

the underlying assumptions provided a basic outline for agreement, their generality meant that practical interpretation was
very much open to negotiation. Also, situations were often too
problematical, too changeable, or too much the subject of basic
disagreement to accommodate behaviour which could be defined
as 'adequately' legitimated. It was here that the coping
mechanisms tended to be used to provide a more pragmatic
support.

There were two main levels on which coping mechanisms were
developed:

(1)   In the first part of the chapter I shall describe how they
      were used to deal with situations involving tensions and
      dilemmas which couples perceived as flexible, and open
      to compromise or change.
(2)   Then I shall outline how they were used to deal with
      differences of opinion which were perceived as too
      fundamental to be reconciled. Equally, they were
      applied in situations involving aspects of behaviour
      which were regarded as unacceptable or incompre-
      hensible, but basically unavoidable or immutable.

The purpose of this chapter is twofold. On a descriptive level I
shall illustrate some of the problematical elements in this area of
family behaviour, as presented by the parents in my group. Many
of these tensions can be seen as stemming in part from the underlying assumptions themselves. On an analytical level the chapter
deals with the various ways in which spouses coped with these
problematical elements, thus continually recreating and sustaining the reality of their family lives. Berger and Kellner's comment
about marital conversation is widened here to apply to the whole
range of verbal and non-verbal spousal interactions. They
maintained:

> In the marital conversation a world is not only built but it is also
> kept in a state of repair and ongoingly refurnished.[3]

II COPING MECHANISMS TO DEAL WITH SITUATIONS AND DIFFERENCES PERCEIVED AS FLEXIBLE

In this section six overlapping kinds of coping mechanism will be described. These are: articulation of the problem, practical compensation, phase or stage, myth, the avoidance of disruptive topics, and the use of tactful deception. They are illustrated principally by reference to problematical elements involved in: (a) the current situation of the woman, (b) mutual involvement with the children, (c) the overall division of labour, and (d) communication.

(a) The current situation of the woman

Difficulties facing the woman at her present stage of parenting were frequently mentioned during the interviews. Essentially the couples felt that in practice assumptions about 'fairness' in family life were contradicted by the fact that, after the arrival of children, the woman's everyday freedoms of choice and action were more restricted than were those of the man. The main coping mechanisms which were brought into effect were (i) *verbal articulation of the problem*, and (ii) *practical compensations*. These can be seen as pragmatic attempts to alleviate any disruption or dissatisfaction which arose out of the contradictions of the assumptions of fairness.

Basically the problem centred on the fact that, at least for a few years, all of the wives in the group had given up full-time paid employment in order to stay at home and look after the children. Only two of the wives *preferred* being at home, and saw great freedom in the fact that they felt that they were in control of their own work situation. The majority, however, wanted to return to some form of paid employment as soon as possible, and felt that their lives had been more drastically altered by marrying and having children than had their husbands'.

Such views provided a fundamental challenge to the validity of the assumption that marriage and parenthood should be a 'fair' partnership. Here are two quotations which illustrate a frequently expressed opinion. Helen Moffat said:

But I really feel men aren't just as much married as women, I don't think it honestly changes their lives completely at all. (I) [and later to her husband] I mean, you've still got your work and if you change your work it's not because you're married. (Jt)

Barbara Johnson, who at that point had just started a new professional career, argued:

I would say that, to my mind, in a general view, the husband has more rights than the wife, I think the wife is in an inferior position, but it could just be ME being em [Ian: Emm, bolshi] defensive. I don't think that's the situation in OUR marriage, but I think that is general. (Jt)

Usually these kinds of views were expressed in connection with changes following the birth of children rather than marriage itself. They were always qualified by the belief put forward by all of the couples that one parent should be at home to look after the children, at least in their early years, and that, in the context of present day society, this was most conveniently the mother. Here then was a conflict of beliefs which, at their current stage of the family life cycle, they did not believe could be resolved by *changing* the situation. It was acknowledged, however, that it *would* change in the future. Jeff Harris stated neatly the view which was common to all of the couples when he said about his wife's adaptations to parenthood:

Well I think the best way to put it is not so much more adaptations but, perhaps has had to em, has been much more constrained in terms of, you know, what choices she can actually undertake. I mean, given the fact that we're committed to the children and want to em, bring them up basically ourselves, you know, there isn't much choice, one of us has got to be home with them. (I)

Here was a situation, then, where respondents' stated beliefs about fairness were being somewhat contradicted by the exigencies of parenthood. Alternatively, from a theoretical perspective, this could be seen as an incompatibility in practice between those assumptions dealing with children's needs and wants, and those about fairness. No matter how the situation is analysed, the relevant point is that the majority of the couples felt that, in this respect, the woman was getting the worst of the family bargain. A major aspect of this perceived inequality of the conjugal situation was that the man could not only *physically* leave the problems of home and family each working day, he could also do this *mentally.* The woman was not only primarily responsible for the physical organisation of home and family, she was also, at this point, much more mentally preoccupied with the home. Helen Moffat, for example, explained:

> A lot of women, and when the children are difficult, you feel quite self-critical, you know, are we bringing them up the right way? Everybody's the same, I think there's a feeling of guilt, though not all the time. (W/E)

Her husband, George, later commented that he only very occasionally felt like that and said:

> I mean, a man out working all day, em if he sat and reflected all day, he'd soon have the sack. (W/E)

Many of the respondents suggested in various ways, that, despite the claimed jointness of the whole family enterprise, the fact that the man went out to work each day led to his having a different attitude to home and family problems. The following conversation occurred in the Gilchrists' joint interview:

> *Hannah:* I expect YOU to listen to my problems [*James:* Oh aye] but YOU don't consider them as important as yours [pause] do you?
>
> *James:* Your house problems?
>
> *Hannah:* Well anything [*James:* Anything?] Anything that's cropped up during the day.
>
> *James:* Well no, em, I don't consider them important in comparison to MY problems. [*Hannah:* No] They're not AS important, they're they very well may be important to US as a family if we were only involved AS a family, but because I'm involved in my work, em, I relate the problems of the, the HOUSE in relation to my problems at work and they're [*Hannah:* They're secondary to your work really.] well,

they're not the same sort of problems. [pause] It's a bigger problem at my work if I can't solve it. (Jt)

(i) Various coping mechanisms were implemented to alleviate any disruption which might arise out of the situation described above. The most frequently utilised mechanism was simply verbally to acknowledge the perceived inequalities. It seemed that respondents felt that as long as both spouses, and especially the husband, reiterated an *awareness* of the woman's problems, then the situation was not so potentially disruptive. These are some illustrations of the ways in which spouses articulated this awareness, both to myself and to each other. Barry Coulson said:

> I think she's lost some of her freedom, freedom of action. She's more tied em to the house and then with children, em, you ARE tied and damned hard, I don't think *I* would like it if the roles were reversed em, I don't think I'd take it. I don't think, you know, I'm suited to it. (I)

Jim Robson argued:

> All my wife does in the house is, I think, more of a job, is a harder and more arduous job than she probably had at the office before she was married . . . to do the same chores day in day out, and this is an intelligent woman by the way, er, with a reasonably high IQ, I think for her to do all those things and say very little about it, to me I think is great because I couldn't do it Kathryn, I'd be bored to tears doing that sort of thing. (I)

Ray Mitchell talked about his wife's adaptations to marriage as follows:

> I suppose I would say it's committed her to a line which has got far less freedom of action within it than a man. (I) [and he later said to his wife in their joint interview] But the big difference comes when children arrive, when YOU had to stop working em, and then responsibilities sort of multiply, [Alice agreed] and the big difference was to YOU, not to me, because *I* kept my job. (Jt)

Similar kinds of statements to these occurred sufficiently frequently during the course of the study for them to be viewed as standard responses to problematical situations, such as when the woman was particularly dissatisfied at the end of another busy day of childminding and housework. (Also when an outsider – researcher – asked about the position of the woman in marriage!) In addition, the women themselves, in their individual interviews, often pointed out that their husbands acknowledged that they would not like to change places with their wives. The husbands were reported to sympathise with their wives' loss of freedom, and to have said that they would find it boring to be at home permanently. A further way in which the problem was articulated was to put forward images of children as being oppressive to the woman because their demands were so constant.

(ii)   Although such verbal acknowledgement of the situation was the most constant form of coping mechanism, there were also some more practical measures. In many ways, the actions I shall outline accentuate even further the fact that spouses perceived a contradiction in their assumptions of fairness and equality within their current family organisation. Many activities were geared towards making the woman *feel* that she had equal freedom and that the man was both aware of, and making compensations for, any unfairness in their family bargain.[4]

The majority of the wives, for example, felt that their previous occupations had been much more intellectually stimulating than was the routine of house and children. Apparently as some form of compensatory coping mechanism, therefore, the husbands tended to stress the importance of their wives' present activities and to make a point of conversing about them to their wives, even if these conversations appeared mundane. In addition, they felt a responsibility, by their attitudes and actions, to alleviate what many wives saw as intellectually undemanding routine. Barry Coulson, for example, saw his wife's activities as much less stimulating than his own, but felt the need to compensate in some way for this inequality by making the effort to show interest in her routine. He explained:

Being a husband is being responsible, em, you've gotta take a responsible view of marriage I think, em, it's not a game. I feel very strongly this equal partnership although you're fulfilling different roles, one is the housekeeper and one is the breadwinner. But, you know, you've gotta listen to the wife, em, understand that, you know, her life centres around the home which is perhaps NOT as exciting as the office or whatever your particular job is. And that's important to her, and I think you've gotta listen and participate, just as SHE likes to know what your work involves. (I)

From the interviews it seemed also to be important that the husbands did not appear to devalue their wives because they were perceived as currently involved in mundane activities. Louise Wilson stressed the importance of the husband's attitude as follows:

I would like to think of a husband, of MY husband anyway as, as considering my ideas. I would hate, I'm not working at the moment, and I would hate to think that because I'm stuck in the house, that he regards me as someone who just buys the cabbages and this sort of thing. (I)

The subtlety of the coping mechanisms which were necessary to create a feeling of fairness and equality, can perhaps best be illustrated by quotations from one marriage where the exercise was felt to be successful, and another where it was judged a failure. (Here I introduce a concept which becomes central in later chapters: that of the husbands' voluntarism.) Firstly Madeleine Harris reflected:

How's he different from other husbands? I think he's much more willing to just be part of the whole, children, life, em you know. That I feel very often our partnership is very much more a partnership, you know, we're much more, living with each other you know, as two people who are equal, you know and not one somehow, you know, has the ascendancy over the other, you know. (I)

Secondly, the Wilsons described to me the situation of another couple, whom they knew, where they considered that the husband was *not* compensating for his wife's lack of freedom of action. The consequences, they felt, were manifested in the wife's cycle of depression, stemming from her restriction, and in the children's behaviour problems. Louise Wilson explained:

But I think that the BASIC reason for this, although we think the husband DOESN'T control them [the children] much, is that *I* think the husband isn't giving her [his wife] the kind of husbandly support that she needs. I mean, if, if the husband would come home just to let her [his wife] out for a few hours, she would get away, she would forget about it and she would come back with an entirely different attitude. (I)

On a practical level, husbands sometimes took over responsibility for house and children, perhaps for an afternoon or evening.[5] This also could be seen as a coping mechanism which aimed to create a *feeling* of fairness and equality. In the context of the limited human resources of the nuclear family, the husband in the situation of the families in my group, had become the focal person whose co-operation was vital for many of the free time and entertainment opportunities of the wife. Martin Chapman talked about his wife's frustrations and his attempts to help, as follows:

I mean it's fine for me, I can get away to my work and, I mean I've got the communication with people at my work, and to a certain degree I sympathise with Sylvia, but I can't do anything about it. It's just one of those things, you know, I try to give Sylvia as much time in town as I can. (W/E)

From the point of view of a wife who felt that she was getting quite a fair deal out of her marriage, Maureen Rankin said:

The main thing is that he's quite prepared to take charge and give me the freedom if I want to go, if there's anywhere special that I want to go I know he doesn't mind me going. (I)

Obviously, within the group there was a variation in attitudes towards this particular issue, and a few of the wives were extremely independent of their husbands in their organisation both of personal and family entertainment. There was, however, at the level of compensatory coping mechanisms, a general point which applied to all of the couples. The husbands all had an awareness, expressed in various ways, that they should somehow compensate at a *practical* level for their wife's greater restriction of freedom of action. They put this awareness into practice, in varying degrees, by such things as relieving her of familial duties from time to time, or making sure that some joint outings were organised, or simply encouraging her and co-operating in her arrangements to take up interests outside the home.

In these ways couples developed coping mechanisms to sustain belief in the fairness of their marriages in the face of perceived contradictions. For all of them, becoming parents had meant that the woman was removed from the outside world of work to the confines of home and family. (Throughout, the implicit legitimation of this situation was in terms of the assumption that family committments were life cyclical and that this was simply characteristic of the present stage.) In this process, however, crucial aspects of the spouses' lives were altered. By and large respondents gave a picture of the man retaining a much more consistent life pattern and having a greater realm of choice and freedom of action since, at this stage, practical responsibility for home and children lay primarily with the woman.[6] Articulation of the problem and practical compensatory actions were two ways in which couples alleviated these perceived unfairnesses of the current situation of the woman.

(b)   Mutual involvement with the children

Another area where assumptions about fairness could be challenged was that of childrearing. The issue of sharing 'fairly' the mutual reality of being parents was here further complicated by assumptions about children's needs and wants, and the appropriate relationships between parents and children. In this section I shall describe some of the ways in which spouses sustained belief in mutual involvement with the children. This discussion of coping mechanisms introduces some of the important factors which will be considered in detail in Chapters 8 and 9.

All of the couples had opted for the mother to devote her energies full time to childrearing, at least for a few years. They therefore took for granted *her* active involvement in the early stages of the child's life. The dilemma which then faced these parents was how to establish and sustain belief in the active involvement of the *father*, in the face of the much more limited amount of time which *he* had available for the child. Current medical policies associated with pregnancy and birth enabled respondents to establish belief in the father's involvement with the actual *arrival* of the child. Fathers are, for example, encouraged to participate in some of the ante natal instruction and also, increasingly, to be present at the birth of the child. Several couples made a point of telling me that the husband had been present at their children's births, thus overtly laying claim to involvement from the very beginning. Subsequently, however, the father had less time available for the child than did the mother. This created problems for the couples in defining the father as taking an objectively 'fair' share in child-related activities.

The importance of mutual involvement with the children was stressed by almost all of the couples. (Only one wife actually felt that it was unimportant. She maintained that, unlike women, men were not interested in children. Her husband, interestingly, felt that she tried to keep a whole range of domestic matters from him, and *he* professed a considerable interest in the children. He was, however, only minimally involved in *practical* childrearing.) The reasonings behind the stress on father involvement were complex, and varied between respondents. Assumptions about parenthood as a learning situation were relevant here. Respondents put forward beliefs that the father *had* to be involved with the children in order to form understandings, and so *learn*, through his own experience, how to deal with them and what they were like. This was perceived as a basic feature of the father's forming an adequate future relationship with his growing child. Maureen Rankin, for example, said:

> I think fathers should be very involved with the children and I think the time for them to be involved is right from the word 'go'. I think if they're going to get on well with their children when their children are older, they've got to start right from the beginning and develop a, the relationship at the same time as the mother develops a relationship. (I)

A feeling of mutual involvement with the children was also seen as important for the husband's relationship with his wife. This was illustrated in different ways by the following quotations. Margaret Barber argued:

> I feel, rightly or wrongly, that the husband has to make the move as soon as the children are there, to be right alongside his wife [Philip agrees] because otherwise, I think in SOME

women, the maternal instinct is SO strong that if the husband
moves away in the early stages, the wife won't move away from
the children to join him. She'll stay right there beside the
children and this could become habitual. (Jt)

Dianne Hemingway felt that:

> If there are children I think it's very important that he shows
> them lots of love and plays with them, takes an interest in all
> their doings. It's important for the children, it's also important
> for the wife if she knows that he's taking an equal part in their
> upbringing, not just providing the money. (I)

These then were the kinds of views expressed by the majority of
parents in my group. As will be outlined in Chapter 9, however,
there were many levels on which father involvement could be
claimed. These ranged from an administrative interest in the child
to a regular practical involvement in everyday childrearing activities. At each level, however, respondents' accounts showed that
they saw frequent disparities between their *beliefs* in a fair and
mutual involvement, and what actually happened. One way in
which they sustained belief was simply to *articulate the problem* and
to reassure one another that they *were*, in fact, adopting the
'fairest' solution in the prevailing circumstances. The joint interviews when I was not present, were particularly characterised by
the use of this kind of coping mechanism. Barry Coulson's
comment to Jean was typical. He said:

> It's a joint effort to bring up children [Jean agrees]. And
> although you carry out most of the tasks, I reckon really, you
> know, I see MY part. (Jt)

The verbal reassurance often took the form of stressing the
jointness of emotional, intellectual and decision making responsibilities for the children. For example, Margaret Barber said to
Philip in their joint interview:

> You're not out of sympathy with my day time activities with the
> children and I'm not out of sympathy with your day time activi-
> ties with work, but that we just both just have to jolly well get on
> with what we have so that, I suppose you might say that the

responsibility of the children in FACT is more with me, but emotionally I would say it's very evenly divided. [Philip agrees] (Jt)

Madeleine Harris felt that Jeff was very much involved and said to him:

Yes I think that we in general share the whole notion of teaching them, you know, playing with them. I mean, just taking care of both emotional and intellectual and cultural development [Jeff agrees], and everything else. That it's nobody's function to do any one thing in particular (Jt)

Different coping mechanisms came into effect to sustain belief in a mutual involvement on the level of *direct* childrearing activities. Although some of the fathers *did* carry out a considerable number of practical tasks and activities with their children, the simple fact that, for most of them, their return home in the evening usually coincided with the end of the children's short day, meant that their overall *direct* involvement in this area could in no way be considered equal. Beliefs were sustained by maintaining a generalised practical involvement, by developing specific 'father times', and by using notions of phase or stage.

Couples claimed that the father took an active interest in the children during the time when he could actually be with them. The predominant way in which this generalised practical involvement was expressed was by playing with the children, or otherwise keeping them occupied. Several respondents felt, however, that the *potential* involvement of the man in *all* aspects of looking after the children, *even if this was only to a limited extent and sporadic*, added to the feeling that it was a shared enterprise. This was also perceived as creating a good relationship with the children. Barbara Johnson, for example, said:

If you've got *no* relationship with the child as it is developing, I don't think you're ever going to understand it. So I feel that men ought to be prepared to muck in with the babies, in ALL the sordid details. I mean there's nobody better at changing nappies than Ian. But em, I think it creates a relationship which is valuable. (I)

Andrew Davies felt that the extent of *his* involvement could be shown by the reaction of his eldest boy Robert, he explained:

> He knows that either one or the other can do any of the jobs both in running the home, in doing the meals, or attending to Robert, and he's quite happy that either one of us do it, and I think this is how it should be. [He added later:] I always make a point of telling him when I'm off on a Saturday, to remind him that tomorrow Daddy will be home all day. This seems to mean a lot to him, and I think this is how I would want it to be always. I think a direct involvement with your children you know, none of this shunning responsibilities and shouldering it on your wife, on the mother, I think it's, it's unfair. (I)

Couples also treated the perceived current problematical elements of father involvement as *a phase or stage*. This coping mechanism involved stating that the father's involvement with the children, compared with that of the mother, would become more overtly fair as the children got older. This was (i) because the children would see less of the mother as they progressed into other social milieux, therefore the overall differences between parents would narrow, and (ii) because it was claimed the father would be better able to become independently involved in doing things *with* the children when they were older. This latter rationalisation was put forward by most of the respondents and was an excellent coping mechanism since it obviously dealt with anticipated future developments which could not be disproved at this point in time.[7] It was usually expressed by maintaining that men were not very much interested in 'babyish' activities, but that the husband had every intention of taking a greater share later on by, for example, taking the children swimming. In this way the totally fair and equal involvement of the father was perceived as, to a certain extent, impossible during the current stage. Belief in the reality of the underlying assumption was, however, sustained by maintaining that he was equally *interested* in the children, and did as much as could be expected for them *at the moment*. Additionally, and most importantly, degrees of objective parental involvement would even out in the future.

(c)   The division of labour

Whilst this study is primarily concerned with the development of parental behaviour, this must, in part, be seen within the context of the overall division of labour. This is because meanings in one area have implications for behaviour in the other. It appeared, for example, that respondents preferred that the man should spend any limited time actually with the children, rather than becoming involved in specifically *household* chores. A range of images of children was put forward to support this negotiated activity 'preference'. In this section I shall focus on the *use of myth as a coping mechanism* to support belief in a fair division of labour. Examples are drawn from the areas of child-related and general household tasks.

For all of the families the majority of activities connected with looking after the house and children devolved on to the wife during the stage when she was not employed outside the home. This is, therefore, an admittedly limited discussion of the division of labour, since I am not considering the other ranges of 'domestic' tasks such as gardening, car maintenance, or decorating the house. In this I am reflecting the content of respondents' accounts since they were more concerned with *husbands'* participation with house and children. These then were the tasks involved in the basic routine aspects of everyday living, such as shopping, cooking, cleaning, washing and ironing, and dealing with all aspects of childcare. Even among those couples who claimed that the husband took a considerable share of these activities, the wife was still viewed as having the overall responsibility. All respondents expressed ideas about fairness and sharing. Nevertheless, most of them also saw the woman as, at this stage, taking a much greater share of what they defined as the more mundane and generally less rewarding aspects of the total family work load. Obviously, to a certain extent, couples felt that circumstances made much of this inevitable, and it was legitimated in terms of stage or phase. Coping mechanisms on an everyday level, however, came into operation where the *man* was seen as available to participate equally, but as not actually doing this. The degree and nature of the husband's *actual* participation in household activities varied within the couples in the group. Also, the perception and definition of what constituted a 'fair share' were obviously subjective variables. There seemed, nevertheless, to be a repertoire of coping mechanisms on which spouses tended to draw as a tactic for alleviating tensions which arose in their own particular circumstances.

Paradoxically, one set of such coping mechanisms (i) relied on a belief in the husband's competence whilst another (iii) maintained that he was in certain respects, incompetent. There was also an intermediate set of coping mechanisms (ii) which implied that competence existed, but that it was constantly undermined by a lack of awareness. I refer to all of these as *myths* since they required either minimal practical proof, or even no substantive proof at all.

(i) Firstly, beliefs that the household division of labour was fairly shared were sustained by reference to the following claims: that husbands had demonstrated ability by carrying out various activities in the past; that they were in fact *willing* to do things; and that they would be able to cope if the necessity arose. Although all respondents did not necessarily draw on this entire repertoire of coping mechanisms, everybody used at least one of them at various times. These are some illustrations of the ways that these notions were implemented. Firstly, there was *the use of the claim that the husband had done things in the past*. Andrew Jeffreys said:

> We can share things, even if it's an unequal share we still do the same sort of things. So the proportion may be different but the activities are similar. I mean, I don't think she would say much different, because *most of the things that SHE does, I have done*. (I) [my emphasis]

Maureen Rankin claimed:

> He's helped a fair bit in the house, he's not afraid to lift a hand and help with the dishes, this sort of thing, it's not beneath him, he helps out, and at weekends he'll often fry the breakfast and this sort of thing. When the children were babies he helped out with them. *He could do things that I don't suppose he ever imagined he would do* [laughs]: he's helped out, I mean he HAS changed a nappy, em, not regularly, but I mean he HAS done when the children were babies. (I) [my emphasis]

Secondly, *the belief that the husband would be willing to do things* was obviously an important coping mechanism. Helen Moffat said to George:

> ... but I mean, you WOULD, if I asked him he WOULD go and make me a coffee [*George:* Yes], you WOULD [*George:* Yes, yes]. (W/E)

Kathy Hislop said, talking about what she thought marriage would be like:

> The main thing that we did sort of discuss and agree on was, I felt that I would be in the house all day and would have everything done, and *he agreed that if he ever had to, if I ever worked then he would help.* (I) [my emphasis]

Thirdly, *the idea that the husband would be able to do things if the necessity arose* was a twofold coping mechanism. This notion not only supported beliefs in a fair division of labour but it could also be seen as a kind of theoretical safety net for the lack of human resources of the nuclear family. Such feelings were evident in the next two statements. Margaret Barber explained:

> As far as I'm concerned, any time that there has been a REAL crisis or a real need, Philip has always, even if there's been something on, found time to cope. (I)

Madeleine Harris described their situation as follows:

> We don't in fact feel now that anybody has to do any sorts of things that the other person should never do. What happens, because of just the way the day falls out mostly, that I do most probably most of the house things and Jeff will certainly do them or help do them if he has time, or if I'm just fed up with them he would do them. He's certainly not averse to cooking a meal or anything else; he can certainly cope em, I can and have gone to an Open University conference for a weekend, he can cope quite easily. I don't have to find someone else to come in and do the jobs that I would normally do. (I)

(ii) Secondly, there was an intermediate set of coping mechanisms which still presupposed the husband's willingness and

competence but simply asserted that he was somehow not aware
of things to be done; this in itself being a basic contradiction of the
assumption that family life was a learning situation. Patrick
Hislop presented a rather extreme illustration of this kind of
attitude when he said:

> I very seldom do anything to help on the domestic scene. I have
> dried dishes on about three occasions since we got married, em,
> if I'm asked I'll stand on my head but by and large *I don't recog-
> nise the things which have to be done*. [my emphasis]

This attitude was accepted by both of the particular spouses involved but would undoubtedly have been too extreme to have
been completely accepted by the rest of the couples in the group.
Nevertheless, to a lesser degree, the notion that the husband did
not recognise certain things which had to be done was put forward
by almost all of the respondents, both male and female. Sylvia
Chapman argued:

> I think he was quite domesticated but, I don't think they're ever
> as domesticated as a woman. I think they've got to adapt more,
> em, to runnning their own home than a girl has. Although it's
> quite a big step for a girl, I think it's even bigger for a man you
> know. Like Martin he'll wash the dishes but he'll not wash and
> dry them, things like this, you know. You can't always be ASK-
> ING him to do things, but *he just doesn't see them to be done*. (I) [my
> emphasis]

Carol Burns gave another illustration; she explained:

> I'm beginning to learn as I go along that he just doesn't SEE.
> This is what makes him as he is, em, *he just doesn't SEE trivia*. But
> if I point something in his direction he'll attend to it. (I) [my
> emphasis]

(iii)   Finally, there were numerous examples where a spouse
claimed a lack of knowledge or skill in a certain activity. This was
used to account for situations where one of the spouses seldom or
never undertook a particular activity. The most recurrent examples were as follows: it was claimed that the majority of
husbands in the sample never changed nappies because they were

no good at it; it was claimed that many of the husbands did not dress the children because they were either too slow, or did not know where the clothes were, or which ones should be used; at least three-quarters of the husbands seldom cooked, because, it was claimed, they simply did not know how. Equally, there were various activities, such as digging the garden or mending the car, where it was generally claimed that the wife had inferior knowledge or skill. It did seem, however, that, given that the study focussed primarily on the negotiation of everyday internal domestic affairs, the husband tended to approach the situation from the viewpoint of 'opting *in*' whereas at this stage the wife's area of choice was from the viewpoint of 'opting *out*'.

Occasionally a respondent 'stood back' from this process of maintaining that the division of labour was fairly shared. Arguments usually occurred during interviews if one spouse 'blew' the coping mechanisms which were being used to sustain belief in the underlying assumptions of fairness. Anna Robson did this during their fourth interview. Previously she had constantly stressed her husband's willingness to be involved in their ongoing domestic responsibilities. Now, on a miserable and cold December evening, she proceeded to argue that men had 'an easy life' as regards the household division of labour. Jim protested:

> No, just a minute, it's a joint effort, *I* set the table [to which Anna replied:]
> But you'll find, you'll find a joint effort, Kathryn. Your husband puts out the cutlery while you put out the tablecloth, the condiments, the jam, the goodies. You make the fish fingers, you make the chips, you make the toast [laughs]. But THEY put out the cutlery so it's a joint effort. (W/E)

Later she could be seen to acknowledge that the husband's participation was more to sustain a *belief* in fairness, rather than an objectively fair share, when she said:

> He stands at the other side of the hatch and I pass him through the things to put on the table. That's a joint effort, Kathryn, *you don't feel you're* being left on a limb to do it all by yourself. (W/E)

This is an early illustration of the precariousness of coping mechanisms. Myths were only sustained by the collaboration of all members of the family. These, along with other coping mechanisms were often open to challenge and were frequently 'blown' during the course of the interviews. This 'blowing' of coping mechanisms is further discussed at the end of the present chapter. When this occurred the *social* construction of reality was highlighted.

(d) Communication

As I argued in Chapter 2, an underlying assumption of all of the respondents was that there should be open communication and debate between the spouses. This was viewed as the correct state of affairs even if the couples felt, at that point, that their own patterns of communication were inadequate. Many of the parents also said that they were aiming for a similar kind of relationship with their children, and hoped that, in the future, the children would always feel that they could approach them with any ideas or problems. In practice, however, the underlying assumption of open communication tended to be modified by problems involved in its implementation. In simple terms, the outcome seemed to be, that in order to cope with the practicalities of everyday life, the accomplishment of routine tasks and the maintenance of harmony were usually given priority over open communication. Most of the couples, for example, said that, at this stage of their family life, communication between spouses tended to be altered or disrupted by the presence of children. Shirley Jackson explained:

> When you start to talk about something if the children are there you'll be interrupted [*Edward:* That's right, yes.] Quite often you find you don't finish a conversation that you've started, in fact, you do nearly all your discussing n' that when your children go to bed. (Jt)

Philip Barber said:

> That's the major problem at the moment, that communication with each other even on important issues tends to be neglected, because the sheer practical problems of running a family just make it like that. (I)

Various other factors were perceived as altering both the extent and nature of communication. Spouses maintained, for example, that the amount of active communication was altered because one had learned about the ideas and beliefs of the other spouse, and vice versa. The logical extension of this, which was expressed by most respondents, was the lack of necessity to discuss a wide area of matters because the outcome was predictable. Many people said things similar to this statement by Louise Wilson. She remarked:

> I think that the longer one spends with one person and the more one gets to know them er, the less you really have to say and the more they, you you can anticipate their reactions to almost everything, and you just sort of get settled in I suppose. (I)

Not only had much been learned about the other spouse but also many activities had been experienced jointly, and this might decrease the need for communication and discussion. Alan Hemingway said:

> We don't really em, we don't TALK about things because everything we do is together and therefore, therefore we're there when everything's done, and therefore there's not much to discuss that we do together, apart from my job or something. (I)

Although there were obviously variations in the degree to which couples felt that such factors altered the amount of communication, the fact that a mutual feeling of the taken-for-grantedness of a common stock of knowledge had diminished the need for articulation of, and communication about, many issues, became very apparent during the course of the interviews.

The assumed openness of communication was further complicated in practice by the fact that learned information about the other spouse led as much to the *avoidance* of issues and situations as to their free expression. A very relevant mechanism for coping with the stresses involved in the intimacies of family life was the *avoidance of topics known to be controversial or potentially disruptive.* Illustration of this point was given by Martin Chapman who claimed:

> Well, I think we have come to the, I think mutual understand-

ing, that we just, we don't discuss topics or anything like that, because ultimately it ends up in a blazing argument because we can never, she always says that I want to get the last word in and I always think I'm right, and *I* think the same about her. [laughs] (I)

Most of the respondents outlined how the claimed atmosphere of somewhat intense communication in the dyadic situation of early marriage became more muted, and in some ways calculating, as information was amassed through the years. Colin Duncan explained:

When you're first married, you know, well it would lead to a big fight then but em, you're just finding out then, whereas now you KNOW what's gonna cause friction or what's gonna really please her you know. (I)

The possession of knowledge about the other spouse could also lead to alternative objectives being given priority over the open communication of views. Mary Clark said, for example:

It's very difficult, although we SHARE a lot, it's often very difficult to know exactly about how I think he feels about something. I'm quite sure he says anything to sort of either pacify me or to make me feel better about the situation. (I)

For the couples in my group, therefore, the assumption of open communication can be seen as contradicted in practice by two main factors. After children arrived there were increased practical demands, and also their mere presence was often seen as restrictive. A further contradiction stemmed directly from the assumption of family life as a learning situation. Learning about other family members meant getting to know a great deal about what *not* to say. Not only were various areas avoided, but open communication was also modified by *the coping mechanism of 'tactful deception'*. Some examples of this occurred in the initial individual interviews. Occasionally a respondent gave me a piece of information, or an opinion, about his/her spouse with the proviso that I should never mention this to the person concerned. Equally, during their joint interviews, respondents frequently glossed over some of the more critical views expressed in the *individual* sessions. Barbara

Johnson, however, felt that problems could arise from all of these modifications of open communication. In reply to my question 'What things are the same or different from when you were first married?', she said:

> One of the differences maybe is that, we don't NEED the great long sort of heart to hearts because we know each other's thoughts on that particular matter. Although there comes a time when you've misunderstood the other's thoughts and there can be a lot of difficulties, a lot of minor irritations, before you actually throw the whole problem open. (I)

The notion of disrupted or impaired communication patterns obviously has considerable implications if one is viewing parental behaviour as achieved by a process of negotiation between family members. From the accounts given by my couples, family behaviour seemed to be evolved on the basis of communication systems which aimed to uphold the assumption of openness but which, in practice, were, for various reasons, considerably restricted. In some ways these restrictions were, as in all areas of social activity, the inevitable practical outcome of attempts to organise and rationalise behaviour. In other respects, however, they simply served to illustrate how 'tactful deception', and the avoidance of potentially disruptive areas of communication, was at a premium in the complex emotional interdependencies of family life. I would suggest, therefore, at the same time as respondents stressed the importance of open communication, their actual behaviour generally proceeded on the basis of often disrupted flows of information, inferred cues from other family members, and stocks of knowledge which were felt to be common and were usually taken for granted until problems arose.

III COPING MECHANISMS TO DEAL WITH PROBLEMATICAL ISSUES PERCEIVED AS INFLEXIBLE

To a certain extent the problematical issues discussed so far involved tensions and dilemmas, the impact of which was at least partially forestalled by an implicit belief that sufficient flexibility existed to cope with them. Frequently, however, respondents gave accounts of situations or characteristics which were felt to be irreconcileable, incomprehensible, and unchangeable. At the time of the study, couples were continuing to live with these perceived problematical issues. It is relevant, therefore, to consider some of the coping mechanisms which they evolved to try to lessen the associated tensions and dilemmas.

Four coping mechanisms will be described in this section. They are: phase or stage, attribution of permanency, the notion of balance, and disapproved expedients. It was difficult to select general examples in this area partly because the issues perceived as *inflexibly* problematical were even more family specific. (a) The first two coping mechanisms will, however, be illustrated with reference to characteristics and behaviour of children and parents, which were perceived by respondents as incomprehensible and/or unchangeable. Each family had its own particular range of these. (b) Examples of the second two coping mechanisms are taken from childrearing dilemmas, specifically disciplining and child management.

(a)　Behavioural and personality dilemmas

When certain aspects of the behaviour of family members were seen as irrational or incomprehensible, one way of coping with any resulting tension was to regard it as a transient situation, that is, as a *phase or stage*. Between the adult members of the group such difficulties might be articulated, discussed and rationalised. Alternatively, sometimes the issues were ignored, or regarded as too sensitive for this process to take place (in which case 'tactful deception' might be used). Even so, a generally comforting conclusion might still be in terms of phase or stage.

The most frequent examples given by respondents were of the use of this coping mechanism with regard to children's behaviour. Crucial to this study is the notion that the task of interpreting and understanding children's behaviour was a fundamental part of the process of developing parental behaviour. The notion of phase could also be used as a sort of generalised coping mechanism, always there to be fallen back on when the need arose. As will be discussed in the next chapter, children were viewed as constantly changing. Although parents tried to comprehend these processes and constructed beliefs that they 'knew' what was happening, there were, inevitably, times when the child's behaviour was felt to be incomprehensible or impossible to tolerate or deal with.

Here are some illustrations of how the notion of phase or stage was used as a coping mechanism when these parents encountered situations and behaviour which they felt they could not understand. Carol Burns, for example, said about Alison's 'clinging phase':

> We'll just see how she goes, you know, two doors down, my friend's little girl had this a couple of months ago, you know, she wouldn't go to parties where before she went everywhere by herself quite gaily. But em, she's had about a month or so of not moving from the doorstep and she's fine. This is it with children, you wait till you've got yours, you see, one phase passes and you breathe a sigh and another one comes [laughs]. It's always a phase, and everybody will say 'never mind, dear, it will pass.' (W/E) [and she said in the final interview,] Nothing really bothers me [laughs]. I just accept every next trauma as a phase [laughs], and we'll be out of it and into the next one next month you know. But nothing really bothers me particularly, even this cheekiness I know will go. (F)

Parents also implemented the notion of phase to cope with any qualms they might be experiencing about the best way of dealing with their child. This was done both in terms of seeing the defined problematical behaviour (i) as a transient episode in the life of that particular child or (ii) as a transient episode which was common to most children. Interestingly, examples of these two approaches were given independently of one another by the Barbers. Talking about their eldest daughter, Karen, Philip Barber said:

> You tend to think you've spoiled your kids in some way, maybe we HAVE with Karen, I think she may be a bit more dependent on us than some of her friends, that's certainly true. Er, one hopes that she'll grow out of it, I think she probably will grow out of it. (I)

Margaret Barber commented:

> Her emotional ups and downs, her waking in the night, etc., I think it is, I think it's common to a lot of her age group, I don't

look upon it as a problem that's peculiar to her, or as a problem that's peculiar to us as a family anyway. (I)

Respondents' accounts indicated that the subjective satisfaction of the notion of phase or stage as a coping mechanism increased as their personal experience of children increased. This was especially well shown when parents identified current behaviour of the *second* child as being the same 'phase' which they had already experienced with the first. Madeleine Harris explained:

I mean we remember Frances who is, I think LESS persistent than, than Ian by nature, and at two years old, we went through a few, well, incredible times that were just beyond anyone's understanding. Why any child would fling themselves on the ground when offered an ice cream, you know what I mean? [laughs]. I mean, it HAS to be some frustrating thing they're going through in their own little emotional lives you know, because it doesn't seem to have any RATIONAL explanation in experience, so you sort of live with it and see them through with it, and they DO come out of it at the other end, so we do just keep that hope alive [laughs]. Ian, he's louder though so it's harder to live with [laughs]. (F)

This kind of statement was typical and also showed how narrow is the line between grounded images of the child and abstract images. Here the initial grounded image of 'my child behaved irrationally at two years' is moving towards an abstract image that 'it is common for children to behave irrationally at two years.'

No matter how incomprehensible an item of the child's behaviour appeared to be parents had still to evolve some kind of response, even if this was inaction. For example, speaking of the 'cheeky phase' of his three year old son, Michael, Andrew Jeffreys said:

He is in the peak of his cheeky stage, and when you are called very sort of odious things you have to sort of let it brush over. I don't mind being CALLED things at all because I know that sooner or later, if you don't react to it, they'll forget. This is the stage where we're getting called all sorts of horrible things and Marjorie and I seem to agree that it's best to try and ignore this.

Er, it DOES change. (I)

The uncertainties involved in developing parental behaviour were heightened in such situations where is was felt to be impossible to reach subjectively satisfactory understandings of the child. The assumption of family life as a learning situation was thwarted by encountering the 'incomprehensible'. The notion of phase or stage provided one coping mechanism for alleviating any associated feelings of responsibility or worry.

Respondents also told of tensions stemming from problematical behaviour and characteristics of the adults in the group. Some examples have been given in the earlier section on communication. Such tensions obviously involved issues much broader than the negotiation of parental behaviour. They are relevant to the present discussion, however, since they will illustrate further meanings involved in the negotiation processes. The couples themselves maintained that some such tensions had in fact been frequently aggravated or brought to the surface by the exigencies of parenthood.

The ultimate coping mechanism to deal with certain personal or interactive dilemmas took the form of regarding them as stemming from fundamental and immutable characteristics or habits. This I have called the *attribution of permanancy*. The exact nature of these dilemmas was obviously family specific and all of the spouses talked about their own various past or present tensions. The coping mechanism of labelling these dilemmas as permanent and unadaptable was implemented both as an aid to avoiding potentially disruptive consequences, and as a means of sustaining beliefs in underlying assumptions and the viability of their family set-up, despite practical contradictions. Although issues were mentioned, often jokingly, by all respondents, Ian and Barbara Johnson were amongst those respondents most able and willing openly to state such dilemmas. Ian said of Barbara:

She's got this uncanny knack of making you feel that whatever she says or does or thinks is by definition right and you're WRONG, and you're silly for thinking anything else. It's very difficult to live with really. Still, I'm sure I've got traits which are just as bad. (I)

Barbara said to Ian that she saw as a difficulty:

. . . the fact that your personality's so totally different from
MINE, you find yourself threatened by MY type of personality
and I find myself frustrated by YOUR type of personality [and
she concluded:] Well it's just a conflict of personality, I think. I
can't see how you can change your whole personality to suit
another person, even though it IS your spouse. [Ian agrees] I
mean there ARE adaptations that one makes but to make a
FUNDAMENTAL change is asking [*Ian:*   too much] too
much of anybody. So I mean that is one problem we've had to
cope with, and I think we'll never resolve it, we'll just have to
compromise, find the least painful way out. (Jt)

Although many of the difficulties which were coped with in this
way were similarly idiosyncratic, the general point can be further
illustrated by two other issues which came up quite frequently.
About a third of the couples, for example, told of difficulties
associated with differences between themselves in sleeping and
waking patterns. Even if, initially, attempts had been made, in
their terms, to try to change each other or adapt themselves, such
habits and characteristics were eventually labelled as fundamental and unalterable, and routines were developed around
them. Another recurrent issue was the amount of patience which
each was defined as having with the children. Everyone talked
about wanting to have *more* patience with their children but each
couple seemed to have developed working definitions of each
other's relative tolerance and patience levels, and negotiations of
parental behaviour progressed in the light of these perceived
'givens'. Barry Coulson said, for example:

I haven't patience, well not only am I intolerant, I haven't
patience with them to em, give enough time to them for playing
and talking and constructive things and em, just generally you
know, sort of developing them and I'm AWARE of it. (F)

Also, in this situation, some respondents felt that their own lack of
patience was 'balanced' out by their spouse's activities. A frequent claim was that husbands had more patience at the end of
the day, because they arrived home 'new' to the situation.
    The effectiveness of this coping mechanism of attribution of
permanency depended on its being acknowledged by *both* spouses.
In fact, this was one of the prime areas which was challenged

when dissatisfactions were being voiced. A simple avowal of disbelief that a particular trait could *not* be altered was sufficient to negate this particular coping mechanism. It was interesting to note that while, during *some* interviews, spouses talked about each other's characteristics and habits either jokingly or as a matter of fact, at *other* times the coping mechanisms lapsed and the same items were put forward as definite sources of tension and resentment.

(b) Childrearing dilemmas

One of the mechanisms employed to cope with situations where respondents saw their behaviour or attitude as irreconcilably different from those of their spouses was the *notion of balance*. This sometimes came into operation when respondents felt a situation to be sufficiently disturbing to define it as problematical but, at the same time, wanted to find some positive way of coping with it. Obviously, again, the situations so defined were very much family specific. There was, however, sufficient indication that the area of childrearing activities might throw up these kinds of differences to warrant taking it as a generalised example.

This was especially so in the area of discipline. Although a few of the couples maintained that they were in agreement about methods, the majority gave several instances where one spouse felt unhappy about, or even interfered with, the other's activities. Most of the time such differences were unreflectively presented as a fact of life which caused friction but had to be accepted. When, however, parents *did* reflect on the differences, some notion of balance tended to be employed. Carol Burns gave a very good example when she talked about the fairly extreme differences in childrearing methods which she perceived between herself and her husband. She explained:

> In fact, I only said the other day, em, we had guests in and we were talking about children, and I said how I thought Eric was too harsh with them and didn't show them enough love. Because I think it's just his family, to show open love, you hardly see it, it's there, but you rarely see it you know. And this boy was saying, 'well you're probably the other way, you show TOO much love and it's a good counterbalance you know to

have, you'll probably get a good mid line there. If you're both sloppy you know you end up spoiling the kids.' (I)

On a less extreme level, Ben Pringle felt that he should balance out his wife's rather soft-hearted and generous attitude towards their daughters. He said:

I'm sure she thinks, and she may well be right, that I'm too strict with them, and I AM on occasions, possibly to try and compensate for Sheila's trying to do everything for them. I try and instil a sense of proportion into them that they can't have everything. Either because they're exhausting their mother, or because I just instinctively feel that they shouldn't be given everything. (I)

Finally, the Moffats felt that their disciplinary methods were completely opposed. George saw Helen as far too 'soft' and Helen was appalled by George's strictness and his use of physical punishment. George, however, had no qualms about his methods and maintained that, overall, their parental discipline balanced out.

The notion of balance thus came into effect as a coping mechanism when one spouse was in opposition to the other's childrearing behaviour, but was unable to change the situation. Respondents also expressed an awareness that, in their *own* behaviour, they frequently contradicted, in practice, what they considered to be the *correct* course of action. Their accounts showed that one way of coping with such qualms was to adopt a pragmatic attitude, and to label such items of behaviour as *disapproved expedients*.

Disciplining children was one area where the use of disapproved expedients was often described. Parents related incidents which they prefaced by an expression of guilt or embarrassment. Frequently, such incidents were described as occurring in a certain context which necessitated speedy action. In retrospect the ensuing behaviour was defined as theoretically incorrect but defensible, given the prevailing circumstances.

There were two kinds of situations which were coped with in this way. Firstly, everyday occurrences were described where it was felt that the immediate pressures and demands had been so overwhelming that there was no opportunity, at the time, to reflect on appropriate courses of action. Secondly, respondents talked about various items of their parental behaviour of which they basically disapproved, but had adopted as a consequence of giving precedence to other priorities. Labelling these items of behaviour as 'disapproved expedients' was a coping mechanism which was perhaps the most frequently implemented, but at the same time was perceived as the least acceptable, both by the user and by other family members. A lengthy but useful description which brought out very well points mentioned by most of the other parents in the group, was given by Barbara Johnson. We were talking about her feelings that Ian had a better understanding than she of their younger child, and she had just remarked that she often referred problems about Thomas to him when she felt unable to cope. The conversation continued as follows:

K.B. (to Ian):   And does it generally work that you CAN cope with him?

Ian: Don't know, suppose so.

Barbara: The whole situation seems to dissolve doesn't it? [*Ian:*   Mmm] [pause]. Cos usually we're in such a rush that the em, situation is sort of overwhelmed by the next situation you know, like the fact that he hasn't finished all his breakfast. Oh, the scene over breakfast, he took a second helping of cereal and we knew, we BOTH knew, that he wouldn't eat it because he never eats ONE helping, so you MADE him, you tipped most of it back, didn't you? [*Ian:* Yeah] you got very cross with him [*Ian:*   Oh I didn't]. Yes you did, you upset him and made him cry, and I booted him up the stairs, I couldn't STAND the crying at that time in the morning. . . . The whole situation didn't, sort of wasn't logically pursued, and it wasn't sort of fully developed, because by that time I, it was nine o'clock and we had to get out of the house, so he was hauled down again, put into his anorak, and bundled off into the car. (F)

Examples of the second kind of situation often came from those parents who were having sleeping problems with their children. About a third of the couples described such problems and their attempts at remedies, many of which they basically disapproved of. None of them claimed that they felt it was the 'right' course of action either for a parent to take a turn in sleeping with the child, or to have the child in the parent's room beyond a certain age. A few, however, had resorted to such actions as a consequence of giving priority to the child's sense of security, or, more simply, a better night's sleep. Other examples came from some parents who felt that they had sacrificed certain of their basic beliefs in order to create a more harmonious atmosphere. Shirley Jackson said:

> Mind you, I do something that I thought I would NEVER do, that I think I should say as well. If I'm going into the super-market I take my children to the sweets counter first and I buy them you know, small things, [*Edward:* But that gives you peace and quiet to do your shopping] so that I can shop in peace going round the supermarket. (F)

Kathy Hislop illustrated how situations could overwhelm a parent's desire to be fair with the children. She explained:

> I find it difficult to be fair to Julie when Anna's there, because she doesn't assert herself and I feel she should be getting more attention being the older one. She tends to give in too easily which makes it, well, fair enough, *I* do as well and feel this isn't fair to her. I haven't found a way round this without actually causing ructions with Anna because of it. And I feel if Julie's prepared to give in, it keeps the peace, although I don't feel it's always the best way. But then at breakfast time, where's the point in causing rows? (F)

This latter quotation points to the main reason why respondents felt the need to define certain kinds of behaviour as 'temporary expedients'. Usually they expressed guilt or embarrassment because they felt that a family member had *deliberately* been treated unfairly. Also, underlying assumptions about understanding children, and being consistent, were violated by the demands of prevailing circumstances. This area of coping mechanisms was particularly tenuous and open to challenges from other family members. One spouse might, at a certain point, accept the contextual rationalisations and go along with the process of labelling the act as a 'disapproved expedient'. At another time, for example during an argument, the label might be challenged. In such a situation the same act might be redefined and then be used to illustrate that the 'offending' spouse was an inconsistent, unfair, or impatient parent.

IV THE 'BLOWING' OF COPING MECHANISMS

This example leads on to a final point concerning the maintenance of belief systems. It was a continuous process of reaffirmation and reassurance. It was also open to the possibility of challenges from any family member. Coping mechanisms were used to stem those tensions which might result in such challenges. Occasionally, during the fieldwork, the importance of such coping mechanisms was laid bare when respondents violated them. During their joint interview John Clark gave a frank account to Mary of her faults and irritating habits. His refusal to engage in 'tactful deception' led to a considerable argument. Mary eventually said, jokingly, that, after all that, she wondered how they had managed to stay together.

Kathy Hislop, in her first interview, had initially used a coping mechanism as an explanation for her husband simply not *seeing* things which had to be done about the house. She later admitted, however, that when house and children became oppressive, she felt another interpretation to be true. She argued:

> I think he's the same as a lot of other husbands cos the husband on the other side of us was completely undomestic and he wouldn't think to do anything in the house unless he was asked to do it. Which annoys me because I think he should SEE things that need to be done. And it's not until things really get on top of me that I sort of blow up about them. And then he says 'well if you had asked me I would have done it.' [N.B. husband here invokes *another* coping mechanism.] It's something that's always happened, but it's something that I just won't accept, that, if I ask him, to do something he'll do it, but if I don't ask him, he's too lazy to do it. (I)

In everyday life the coping mechanisms were frequently challenged and 'blown'. This was evident from respondents' accounts, and revealed the precariousness of the reality being created. Berger and Luckmann would relate this analytically to marriage and parenthood being situations of secondary socialisation. They pointed out that:

The more 'artificial' character of secondary socialisation makes
the subjective reality of its internalisations even more vulnerable to challenging definitions of reality; not because they are
not taken for granted or are apprehended as less than real in
everyday life, but because their reality is less deeply rooted in
consciousness and thus more susceptible to displacement.[8]

Respondents' accounts suggested that, what in my analytical
terms could be seen as a temporary refusal to acknowledge family
life as a shared reality, was a frequent practical result of such challenges. Refusals to communicate or to co-operate were outward
signs of this temporary denial. Minor examples of the results of a
lapse in coping mechanisms also occurred during the interviews
themselves. Occasionally a hurt or angry spouse withdrew from
the conversation for a while, or showed distress by a change in
demeanour. Sometimes a respondent used the protective atmosphere created by an outsider's presence to issue threats of future
non-co-operation or refusal to carry out certain tasks.

V SUMMARY

This consideration of coping mechanisms completes the preliminary analytical discussion of how respondents negotiated and
sustained their mutually-held parental reality. The negotiation of
parenthood involved continuous possibilities for conflict and misunderstanding. Often situations developed which were felt by
spouses to be too problematical, too changeable or too much the
subject of basic disagreement to accommodate behaviour which
could be defined as adequately legitimated. Therefore, a more
pragmatic set of supportive mechanisms also operated and it is
these that I have called 'coping mechanisms'.

In this chapter two main levels of coping mechanisms were
described and these were illustrated by a selection of the most recurrent problematical issues presented in the interviews. The first
set of coping mechanisms related to those tensions and dilemmas
in family life which the couples in my group felt were amenable to
compromise or change. The second set of coping mechanisms per-
tained to problematical issues about which respondents felt they
could do little. These were used, in effect, simply to make the
issues *feel* bearable.

Having considered some important aspects of *how* spouses negotiated meanings behind parental behaviour, I shall now focus further on the meanings themselves. In the next two chapters I shall describe the images of children which played a crucial part in the development of parental behaviour. This will be followed by a consideration of issues involved in being a mother and being a father, as described by couples during the interviews.

5   Making Sense of the Child: Abstract Images of Children

I   INTRODUCTION

Parents are faced every day with constant stimuli from their children which, apparently automatically, they decipher and evaluate as part of the process of childrearing. Ordinarily the underlying meanings involved in such interpretative activity remain largely implicit unless, for example, a problem arises which results in their articulation. A main aim of the present study was, however, to uncover some of these underlying meanings. As these couples talked about their family lives it became increasingly apparent that one such set of meanings was their ideas about, and interpretations of, children. Such 'images of children' played a crucial part in how they acted and reacted as parents.

In this chapter and the next I shall show how negotiating parental behaviour involved spouses in developing, exchanging and sustaining images of the child and its world which could be used as subjectively satisfactory bases for action. Parents derived images of children both from their social stocks of knowledge and their ongoing biographical experiences. There was continuous interplay between these two spheres of knowledge. For purposes of presentation, however, I have separated my discussion of images into two sections. In the present chapter I consider 'abstract images', and in the next the more dynamic 'grounded images' will be discussed.

The process of image formation appeared to most respondents to be essentially spontaneous and unreflective. Such taken-for-grantedness of everyday life was described by Schutz as follows:

. . . in everyday life, as I share experiences with my fellow-men and pursue the ordinary pragmatic motives in acting upon them, I find the constructs ready made and I take it for granted that I can grasp the motives of my fellow-men and understand their actions adequately for all practical purposes. I am highly unlikely to turn my attention to the various strata of meaning upon which my comprehension of their conduct is based.[1]

Indeed, the taken-for-grantedness of image formation was illustrated by some of the parents who denied that they had formed any clear cut notions about their child; maintaining, for example, that he/she was too young and still developing. This kind of reaction seemed unrelated to any objectively measurable criterion, such as age. One respondent, for instance, felt that there was little to say about a thirteen month old baby, whereas another launched into a detailed description of the personality of one who was one month old! In part parents were reluctant to define and articulate characteristics which they *disliked*, as being permanent personality traits. Anna Robson, for instance, saw her two and a half year old daughter as bad mannered and boisterous but told me there was very little to say about her because 'her personality's not formed yet.' Helen Moffat perhaps gave some indication of one of the reasons behind this occasional reaction against consciously formulating and articulating images of children. She said:

Helen: I think perhaps if you think about your children an awful lot you're in trouble. You know you start thinking and asking what's different about them, I don't think it's a terribly good idea really.

K.B: Yes, why not?

Helen: Because you DO start totting up their, the pros and cons of their personality. I don't think it's a good idea to do. (I)

All of the parents, however, even those who for some reason claimed that they were reluctant or unable to speak definitively about their child's character or personality, always then proceeded to put forward some images which, albeit in a qualified fashion, were, nevertheless, being used as a working model. The data show quite clearly that, no matter how simplistically this was being done, images were continually formed of even the smallest baby. Shirley Jackson gave a good example of this kind of qualified image formation when she talked about Elaine who, at that point, was eight months old:

> *Shirley:* Edward and I were just talking about this the other day. We THINK that, we don't KNOW of course because she isn't old enough, but Simon we can talk around, you know, we can sort of REASON with Simon and sort of get him round to our way of thinking. We don't think we'll be able to do the same with Elaine, we don't KNOW, but we think that she's going to be very much em, Simon HAS a mind of his own but you can always you know, make him see your point of view. And if it's the one that you think is right for him, you can always sort of bring him round to that without very much of a scene.
>
> *K.B.:* Why do you think Elaine is going to be different?
>
> *Shirley:* Well, we find NOW with her that, em, she's VERY contented and she's a very placid wee girl until there's something, you know, just not quite right, you know, something which she feels or, and she has a right wee temper, you know. (I)

Equally, in their joint interview, the Jacksons provided an example of parental negotiation of images about a baby.

> *Shirley:* And Elaine, well she's an average ten month old baby. Her character's developing, hasn't as yet em.
>
> *Edward:* But definitely she seems to be very very strong willed.
>
> *Shirley:* Yes, but she's also a very amenable wee girl, always been very good. [*Edward:* Oh yes] The only time we ever have any bother with her is when she's cutting teeth and it's never drastic. (Jt)

Here the Jacksons had already developed a tentative image of their daughter as being of strong-willed character. They were also aware, though, that she was only ten months old and, as such, still 'developing'. They were therefore reluctant to make very positive statements about her and related some of her determined reactions to the trials of babyhood, such as cutting teeth. This then provides an early example of making sense of the child by vacillating between a personality and a physiological image.[2] Subsequent parental behaviour could be very different depending on which image attained predominance at any one point in time.

This example from the Jacksons is reminiscent of the classic dilemma, which must have faced every parent, of whether to pick up or leave alone a crying and demanding infant. Interpretations of the child's behaviour are usually reduced to a choice between 'there's something the matter with the child' (physically or emotionally) or 'the child is "trying it on"' (asserting its own personality and will).

Only one respondent actually consciously reflected on the process of forming personality images of children, and her spontaneous comments were very interesting. Margaret Barber explained: 'The other anxiety one could have is whether we have defined them either wrongly or too early and will maintain our definition.' (F) She went on to talk about how she felt that her parents had made this kind of mistake with her sister and herself, perhaps with disadvantageous effect. Later she returned to this point and said:

> *Margaret:* . . . and I could see that we might make the same kind of mistake: that you say 'Karen's the sensitive one and Mary's the resilient one.' How much this is that Karen communicates her anxieties and things and Mary may very well NOT be the kind of child and em I've written down here you know, I worry sometimes in case Mary isn't making her needs more plain [*Philip:* Yes] because we tend to RESPOND possibly less to them.
>
> *K.B.:* Do you see this definition of the children as being an important factor?
>
> *Margaret:* I think it's an important thing in that it affects your attitude and very often your action towards them, yes. And therefore possibly one should be more careful NOT to define them, you know, to keep on the lookout the whole time possibly. (F)

II GENERAL IMAGES OF CHILDREN AND CHILDHOOD

(a) Children should be 'understood'

Making sense of the child was, for these parents, a complex interpretative activity. The major image which seemed to dominate their parental behaviour was of the child as a being to be 'understood' by its parents. They put forward this image both in the sense of comprehending and of empathising. 'Understanding' the child was perceived as an ongoing challenge and, as such, reflected the underlying assumptions about family life as a learning situation. This crucial image was important for several reasons. In one sense it defined for respondents the broad outline of being a parent. It also designated for them the main difference between their own and other children. Some examples should help clarify these important points.

'Understanding' the child was perceived as fundamentally a parental responsibility. At this stage couples felt that their own 'understandings' would have the greatest validity, since they had the broadest experience of the child.[3] They also felt that other people did not have the same reason to make the effort adequately to understand the child, since he/she was not their 'responsibility'. (Another basic image.) An example of this was that all couples generally went to great lengths to resolve and administer any problematical elements associated with their nuclear group before outside help, either practical or theoretical, was sought. By outside help I mean essentially medical or other professional help. Informal exchanges with friends or relatives were seen by respondents as qualitatively different. Such exchanges seemed to be perceived more as gathering wider personal experiences on which to base decisions.

Most of the parents described instances when they had tried out various tactics to deal, for example, with children's sleep or behaviour problems. This had often gone on for a long time before outside help was sought. Margaret Barber had not confided Karen's sleep problems to the playgroup leader for many months. The Mitchells persevered with Rachel's hysterical clinginess for over a year before they sought professional advice. Against his wife's wishes, and only when Alan Hemingway felt his work was suffering because of lack of sleep, did he go to the Doctor about Laura's wakefulness. About a third of the respondents actually indicated that to resort to outside advice was somehow an admission of failure to cope with something that they should have been able to manage themselves. Thus, albeit on a more mundane level, the couples in this study tried to contain their difficulties within the group in much the same way as did the other family members in Jackson's study of alcoholics.[4]

In this way the image of the child as a being to be 'understood' was an important meaning behind parental behaviour. Interestingly, at some points, children proved *so* problematical that, even though parents did not feel that they had reached a subjectively satisfactory account, they nevertheless gained some consolation from the fact that they had at least gone through all the processes of understanding, i.e. considered all angles and attempted a variety of solutions. The Barbers, for example, said in their final interview:

> *Philip:* Well obviously we've had Karen now for over four years so we've had more problems with her [than Mary], er, I think we tended to try and look for a positive solution to it.
>
> *Margaret:* Rather than just live on with it.
>
> *Philip:* You know, rather than just live on with it, you know, like the bedtime problems, the sleeping problems.
>
> *Margaret:* Although I'm not sure that the end result wouldn't be the same, *but at least we feel that we're doing something.* (F) (my emphasis)

A further implication of this image was related to the different meanings attached to one's own and to other children. Couples obviously varied in the degree of interest expressed in children other than their own. Nevertheless, their accounts indicated that a rather different overall attitude existed. Other children were taken very much more at 'face-value' and less effort was made continuously to interpret their behaviour, that is 'understand' it. The parental bond was perceived not just as a blood tie but also as a continuous responsibility to make sense of that particular child. I would suggest that this interpretation of being a parent is one explanation of why a few respondents, who said that they did not particularly like children in general, had, nevertheless, a great interest in their own. Derek Rankin, for example, said:

> Well I enjoy having children whereas before when I was single I used to hate them. Now, friends of mine who were married and had them, as far as I was concerned, they just got in the way, if anything I was embarrassed to come near them, or if they came near ME what do you say to a kiddie?

Ian Johnson, who expressed similar sentiments, expanded as
follows on his comment that he and Barbara never talked to other
adults about their children because it was boring:

> WE don't think our children are boring. We think, well we
> KNOW that other people find the topic of children boring. [...]
> we are mutually interested in our own children. (F)

Thus the image of one's own child as a being to be 'understood'
was an important factor differentiating perceptions of that child
from those others outside the nuclear family group. This group of
parents tended *not* to take their own child's behaviour at its 'face-
value'. In addition, they were usually reluctant to make any defi-
nitive statements about their child which might be construed as
harshly critical. Rather, they preferred either to furnish explanations for any problematical elements, or to regard them as a phase
or stage. Occasionally a respondent *did* make a critical statement
about a child. Almost every time this occurred either the *other*
spouse quickly qualified the remark, or the respondent him/her-
self followed it up with a softer comment or an itemisation of the
particular child's *good* points. The fact that such exchanges
occurred frequently during the joint interviews, when I was not
present, suggests that this was not simply an 'interviewer effect',
but was also characteristic of the negotiation processes
themselves.

This observation of the special meanings behind *parental*
behaviour had some further implications. Through 'understanding' the child the parents developed the belief that *they* could make
the most valid final judgments on the child. Here again we see the
great legitimacy attached to personal experience in the family
situation. Many interpretations were possible of a child and his/
her behaviour, but the nuclear group was the primary definitional
unit. This was especially highlighted by three separate situations
where respondents knew other families in the group, defined their
children as problematical and presented alternative images to me.
Given that these 'interested outsiders' had presented their ver-
sions of these children's behaviour to me, it was fascinating to
listen concurrently to the parents themselves giving their own interpretations of the particular situations and their meanings. The
main point which emerged was that none of the actual parents
defined the particular children as having special problems and

they put forward whole ranges of legitimations and coping mechanisms to support their views. The Coulsons, for example, saw Karen Barber as a very neurotic child whose elaborate imaginative play was totally odd. Margaret Barber, however, felt that there was nothing to worry about and said:

> Her emotional ups and downs, her waking in the night, etc., I think it is, I think it's common to a lot of her age group, I don't look upon it as a problem that's peculiar to us as a family anyway. (I)

The Robsons saw Brian Jeffreys as a very odd child who was frequently very late for school and was completely defiant of his mother in public situations, such as the School Medical Examination. The Jeffreys felt strongly that, although they perceived their children to be frequently rather awkward, nevertheless, they should not be repressed or constrained, and that any difficult situations usually arose from their own inability as parents to understand and deal with them. They talked as follows about Brian in their joint interview:

> *Marjorie:* I think Grandad's the only one with any real influence when it comes to it. [*Andrew:* Yes] It's a pity they're so far away. [and later]
> *Andrew:* There's perhaps some way of reasoning that escapes us, perhaps we're too direct.
> *Marjorie:* I think perhaps we expect too too much from him, I don't know. [*Andrew:* Oh] And one thing *I'M* sure, my Dad's got more patience with him than *you* have.
> *Andrew:* Oh, inevitably, yes. (Jt)

The Wilsons were critical of the general family set up of the Mitchells, seeing Ray as principally to blame for being insufficiently involved. They saw both of the children as inadequately disciplined and spoiled, and said that Rachel Mitchell behaved so badly that she was being excluded from gatherings in the neighbourhood. Alice Mitchell talked about difficulties in getting Rachel to leave her and go to nursery school, but she basically felt that she was a bright extroverted little girl who was just going through a phase. Thus, given that the parents always had the ultimate decision as to which interpretation of the child was to be implemented, the study indicated a strong tendency for parents to avoid harsh judgments, and to try to keep any potential problems within the family's sphere of influence by seeking out further 'understandings'.

(b)   Children are different from adults

Respondents' accounts also revealed the basic image that a child was different from an adult. Consequently, interactions and patterns of behaviour different from those of the adult world had to be developed. Many illustrations were given both directly and implicitly. The Barbers, for example, had the following conversation in their joint interview:

> *Margaret:*   It's, I mean it's far more of an adjustment having children than getting married [*Philip:*   Oh entirely, yes] because with any luck, when you get married you know what you're marrying and you have been mentally adjusting to it for some time.
> *Philip:*   Also you're dealing with another adult [*Margaret:* Yes] who can come half way to meet you, but with kids they can't. (Jt)

Children were perceived as inexperienced humans. Implicit in these parents' accounts was the image of the child as continuously learning adult definitions and boundaries. Examples were constantly given of children behaving 'badly' because they had not yet absorbed these definitions. This assumption had considerable impact on parental behaviour. Many respondents, for example, had avoided eating in restaurants with the children, or taking them into certain kinds of shops, because they did not behave in an 'adult' fashion. Often illustrations were given indirectly when parents talked about difficulties having arisen because they perhaps expected too much of a child (i.e. where evaluating their child's behaviour in an adult context?). Sylvia Chapman said, for example, that when Judy was born, she began very much to use three year old Anne as a helper and, because the child apparently understood everything so well, she became very impatient with her if she did things wrongly. At a certain point, however, she realised that she was simply expecting too much of Anne who was 'just a child, herself, after all.'

Since they could not take it for granted that a child comprehended things to the same extent as an adult, parents were
engaged in the continual interpretative activity of assessing the
level of a child's 'understanding'. Their accounts showed considerable variation in the degree of 'adult' behaviour attributed
to, and expected of, a child. Sheila Pringle found great pleasure in
observing her daughter's 'nice' behaviour when she took them out
for coffee. To the Jeffreys, whose sons were of equivalent ages,
such an activity was unthinkable, since they did not expect their
children to respect such adult boundaries of behaviour. As has
been shown earlier, especially in the discussions of phase and
stage, these parents operated with broad and flexible notions of
child development. This was again illustrated in their everyday
interpretations of the extent to which children should absorb
'adult' definitions of appropriate behaviour.

Further distinctions between children and adults were made
indirectly in the preliminary interviews. These occurred when I
asked respondents first to describe their children and later to
describe their spouses. Whilst everyone was able to talk unself-
consciously and at great length about the children, only about half
a dozen people responded in a similar manner about their
spouses. Meanings behind the often embarrassed reaction to the
latter question were obviously infinitely complex. No doubt an
important factor was simply the research situation itself and
suspicion, at this stage, of how I might use such information.
Nevertheless, some brief speculative comments about this may
add substance to the main point about images of children.

About a third of the respondents who actually remarked that
the 'describe spouse' question was difficult, said this was because
nowadays they never really sat back and thought about their
spouse. Alternatively, they said that the spouse had become so
much part of their world that it was virtually impossible to put
such things into words. Inasmuch as they *had* been able to talk
about their children, very different definitional processes were
obviously at work. First of all, children were perceived as constantly changing and developing, whereas spousal characteristics
were usually felt to be relatively stable. Although, during the
course of the multi-interview study, rates of change and development were perceived as progressing spasmodically, that is, sometimes many things had happened and at other times very few,

nevertheless, the Jeffreys' comments about their children in their joint interview were fairly typical.

> *Marjorie:* They change, don't they, they change from one month to the next, don't they? [*Andrew:*   Yes] Since we've talked about them this last time I'm sure they've changed.
> *Andrew:* Yes, well, they've BOTH changed since then definitely. (Jt)

A second distinction was that children were seen as much more of an administrative responsibility than was the spouse. Another adult in the group was seen as, by and large, able to fend for him or herself, whereas children were defined as not able to do this, and therefore as having to be administered. The following two quotations illustrate that, no matter how the actual childrearing situation was viewed, the fact remained that the adult saw him or herself as exercising overall administrative responsibility for the child. Barbara Johnson said:

> I think we both agree that a lot of the upbringing of a child is conditioning anyway, em, so er 'jump to it' or else, clonk! (I)

Ben Pringle argued:

> I think being a PARENT involves providing an atmosphere in which children can grow up with security and stimulation and a complete lack of any inhibition at all, in fact, an atmosphere of freedom and yet, and yet within the confines of growing up in present society. (Jt)

Here, both of these parents, whilst advocating different approaches, took it for granted that children could not bring themselves up, and that adults were therefore in administrative control.

A corollary of this image was that parental definitions of the situation tended to be paramount. Whilst the child's innate drives and stated motives might be acknowledged, they were not usually accorded legitimacy in the same way as were those of an adult. Children were, after all, only inexperienced humans. This kind of overall parental power was illustrated in a discussion between Colin and Mary Duncan. Mary argued throughout that children should simply comply with their parents' wishes without question. Colin, on the other hand, had elaborate reasons for feeling that a child's motives *must* be considered. Even he, however, still saw this as ultimately within the parental sphere of control. Arguing that a child's reasons must be seen within their childlike context, he said:

Colin: But in HIS mind, in a five year old's mind, it's maybe quite logical and sensible [*Mary:* Mmmhm, sometimes] I mean why should you go about saying 'don't do this and do that and do this?'

Mary: There's usually a reason, you know, a REASON.

Colin: Aye, maybe for YOU. [*Mary:* Mmmhm] But why do you want him to do certain things, just em, YOU don't want him to do them. (F)

Colin's basic feeling, however, that the parent always retained the choice of definition had been established in a previous interview.

Mary: He has to be kept you know, DOWN, and this is where we disagree sometimes, you know.

K.B.: (to Colin): You don't think that keeping him down is the right way to deal with his temperament?

Colin: Well no, and neither, neither did the doctor at the place [Sick Children's Hospital to which they were referred after Alistair had behaved very temperamentally at a School Medical], he said that, he said, 'well don't try and win all the arguments, let him win some of them, but not them all. If you win, I mean, if it's something really *important*, well, you make sure you win it but, if not, well you've to let him.' He said that he was quite sort of intelligent and this was why he was so bad you know, this is going back to what I think, that if he gives reasons for things, you know, and he said that er, he said that it's very difficult to bring them up you know, because they won't just ACCEPT what you're saying. (W/E)

A third distinction between adults and children was implicit in respondents' descriptions of their dealings with their spouses and their children. By and large the children were dealt with in a much more *overtly* manipulative manner than were the spouses. Management of children was carried out by *open* dealings and negotiations between spouses, whereas any attempt to deal similarly with one another would generally have been regarded as unacceptable. This was partly because each spouse was regarded as another adult whose definitions and reasonings, unlike those of the children, were accorded legitimacy. Also, the *overt* application of rational management criteria to the spousal situation would have been regarded as a violation of the romantic love concept and as some form of selfish manipulation. Dealings between spouses were therefore much more covert and subtle and, consequently, more difficult for them to describe.

In this section various images of children and childhood have been described. By and large these were implicit in respondents' accounts. They can be seen as providing the taken-for-granted legitimations behind parental behaviour. In the next section I shall present further abstract images which were more explicitly articulated. Once parenthood *per se* was taken-for-granted the couples then developed notions about children's needs and wants. These were frequently used as legitimations in the negotiation processes.

III   CHILDREN'S NEEDS AND WANTS

Images of children's needs and wants constituted a major element in these couples' accounts of their everyday family lives. When actually talking to respondents it seemed that so many of these images were being generated that it would be impossible to present these in any kind of ordered fashion. Although, at that point, images of children were already starting to be considered as vitally important factors underlying parental behaviour, it was difficult to see them as anything other than diffuse and idiosyncratic sets of meanings. Considering the problem purely empirically this must still be taken to be the case, and, in fact, it might be suggested that this characterises all personal belief systems. Nevertheless, once removed from an intense direct involvement with the respondents, it gradually became apparent that, on a more abstract level, they were addressing themselves to similar *forms* of images, even if specific *content* differed. Again, parents were orienting themselves to broad assumptions about children, but the actual practical implementation of these had to be arrived at idiosyncratically by the members of each nuclear group.

In this section I shall first describe those psychological and physiological images of children's needs and wants which were mentioned most frequently during the interviews. Some of the implications of these images will be given at this stage. Further illustrations are incorporated in the later chapters.[5] Finally, I discuss instances where the parents were unable to develop an appropriate image of a need or want. Such instances, where aspects of a child's behaviour were defined as 'incomprehensible', highlighted, by indicating its problematical nature, the *social* construction of the reality of parenthood.

(a) Psychological images

(i)   I have termed 'psychological images' the complex of definitions relating to the perceived mental, emotional, and personality characteristics and requirements of the child. As was previously discussed, such images were being formed of the child from a very early age.[6] Here my distinction between abstract and grounded images also becomes particularly blurred. However, by way of a general framework for their parental actions, respondents usually put forward some broad images of the psychological make-up of children. They related their own behaviour either explicitly or implicitly to these.

These images frequently dealt with the way that children were defined as learning or developing. The range of these beliefs within the sample is illustrated by the following questions. All of these implicitly assume that the child is a 'learning' entity, but their differing images of exactly *how* he/she learns had considerable implications for parental behaviour. Martin Chapman argued:

> I think you can become too old too quick. It's a gradual, and I think it's wrong to accelerate the natural development of the child anyway. All you should do is guide it and let it develop itself, and just watch the direction it's taking and, em steer it the right way. I mean a child'll develop at its own pace and it'll get there eventually. (W/E)

Nick Wilson gave his views when explaining that he disapproved of modern teaching methods because he believed that there was no such thing as free expression in a child. He maintained that:

> Children imitate, they set their own standards by their parents
> or by their teachers, em, whichever is the most part of their life.
> (I)

The Pringles' general image of children was somewhat different
from this; Ben said:

> Well I think inhibition is a very bad thing anyway, to suppress
> anything in a CHILD which must be natural and to a large
> extent innocent MUST be a bad thing. Natural forthcoming
> things in children should NEVER be suppressed, because all
> they're doing is demonstrating their, well, their childishness,
> their innocence, their natural inquisitiveness, and their adven-
> turousness, or or, even their ANGER, er, suppressed ANGER
> is almost as bad as anything else. (F)

The somewhat opposed views about children of these last two
respondents were frequently expressed during their interviews to
legitimate decisions about child management. Ben Pringle took
great pleasure in the openness of his daughters, and encouraged
them in 'free expression' which he tolerated with good humour.
He commented:

> We're both naturally CLOSE to our children in that you can
> see for yourself, neither of them are inhibited. In fact, they don't
> even do you the goodness to wait till you've finished a sentence
> till they're blabbing you know, which I think is a good thing, to
> have inhibited children is a bad thing. [*Sheila:*   Oh it IS yes]
> And I'm pleased to say my children aren't. (F)

Nick Wilson, on the other hand, expressed anger when the
children failed to 'imitate' adult behaviour to his satisfaction. He
said he was very intolerant when the children spoiled his garden
or woke him up with their singing in the mornings. He felt that the
best way to deal with such 'bad behaviour' was to smack the
children. In addition he felt that it was totally wrong simply to
sacrifice oneself to the child's behaviour and, for example, chose
not to eat with his daughters because he found their table manners
unpleasant.

(ii)   A further image related to the definition of children as 'learning' beings was that they needed boundaries to be set for them. Children were perceived as not knowing the 'adult' boundaries of behaviour. They 'needed' to be taught these not only for the peace of mind of their parents but also for their own psychological development. Barbara Johnson illustrated both aspects of this image. Speaking about how she and Ian viewed themselves as being fairly authoritarian with their children she said:

> So in a way, [we're] repressive. [*Ian:*   Mmm, it is rather] But we rationalise it very neatly by saying 'well these kids have got to live with us, so if they don't suit us THEY'VE got to change because WE were here first!' (F)

In an earlier interview she said about Dr Spock:

> . . . far too permissive. I don't think you can give children complete freedom. They NEED some kind of, well, they need very STRONG guidance and discipline because otherwise they're completely at a loss. (I)

Even those parents who maintained that they did *not* believe in restricting children, still established certain kinds of boundaries. They would, for example, maintain that children needed *some* behavioural boundaries for their own safety. Thus all of the parents justified those actions which, in effect, prevented children doing exactly as they wished.

The legitimation of such parental behaviour, which was often implicit in respondents' accounts, was the belief that, without boundaries, children were potentially anarchic and oppressive. This was often expressed in terms of clichés such as 'give them an inch and they'll take a mile', or 'give a child enough rope and he'll eventually hang himself.' Children were perceived as 'needing' boundaries otherwise they would make life unbearable for themselves and others. Being a parent was sometimes described as a sort of constant battle against the breakthrough of this anarchy and oppression. Most respondents described instances of their children destroying parents' belongings, disrupting social situations and defying any kind of rational parental action. Such instances were often put forward to legitimate restrictions which parents attempted to put on their children. Again, however, this vague image allowed for considerable variation in practical interpretation.

(iii) General images of the mental characteristics of children were qualified in practice by personality images of the *particular* child. In one sense these images were 'grounded' in that parents were constantly learning about the child's personality by seeing him/her in different contexts. In another sense these images were 'abstract'. A child might be defined as having a certain kind of personality or personality characteristic. Some children were, for example, defined as 'determined' or 'shy' or 'adaptable'. The parent subsequently developed his/her behaviour towards the child in terms of his/her interpretation of that 'abstract' image. Sometimes a particular image provided a subjectively satisfactory level of understanding of the child and therefore reduced the felt need to develop other more grounded understandings. Much parental behaviour was subsequently legitimated by reference to that particular personality image. David and Marjorie Russell gave a good illustration of how images of their children's different personalities led to their reacting differently to the *same* item of behaviour.

> *David:* Kathleen has to be treated with more sensitivity, she's less easy to understand than Timothy.
> *Marjorie:* He accepts things as they ARE, Kathleen's, Kathleen doesn't really, she doesn't accept things.
> *David:* A fit of temper's a fit of temper as far as Timothy's concerned, but em you would tend to think as far as Kathleen's concerned that a fit of temper is a symptom of something which is more, em, which is deeper and under-lying. I think you would have to search for causes with Kathleen rather than anything else. (F)

Here the image of children as beings to be 'understood' was further qualified by the personality image that one of the siblings was more sensitive than the other.

(iv) All of the couples tended to put forward very similar general images of a child's basic emotional needs. Although there was no question specifically directed to this area, parents regularly referred to such images when talking about how they felt children should be treated. Three main sets of needs were repeat-edly mentioned: love and affection, security and stability, and consistency. Again, of course, although such images could be seen as commonly held underlying assumptions, people varied considerably in how they thought these should be put into practice. In addition, many coping mechanisms came into operation when parents felt they might be violating what they perceived to be these basic needs.

Love and affection as a basic need was such a fundamental image that it was generally only referred to in an offhand and totally taken-for-granted manner. Occasionally, however, respondents stressed that they felt it important to manifest their love to the child so that he/she should know, without doubt, that the love existed. George and Helen Moffat had the following discussion in their joint interview:

> *Helen:* I mean I think the most important, the first thing after food a child needs is affection and I don't think, I think everything you do should be with a background of affection and if you don't give a child . . .
> *George:* Well, it's all affection isn't it?
> *Helen:* Yes, well I mean it's all caring. I mean if you don't care about a child you don't try and discipline it. But I mean . . . there's got to be an atmosphere of affection. I mean, lots of people clearly love someone else and they don't they can't express it at all, it's not completely, I mean a baby knows you love it because you feel it, but an older child expects more proof of your affection for it doesn't it. [*George:* Yes] I mean it's not an instinctive thing by any means is it? [*George:* No] (Jt)

A further point made by Barry Coulson leads on to the next part of the section. Like several other respondents, he indicated that if the love and affection were *shown* in the family, then this was a major way of satisfying other emotional needs. He said:

> I think affection is a very important, and for children to see affection and love between the parents is a good thing, it must give him a lot of feeling of security (I)

If two words dominated the interviews with this group of parents, these were security and stability. One could hypothesise at length on the reasons for this finding. Classic sociological theories about alienation, anomie, and the psychological effects of accelerated rates of social change, could all be applied. Here, however, the intention is simply to emphasise that these couples saw the satisfying of this perceived basic need as the major challenge facing them as parents. Having identified this objective they were far less certain of how it was actually to be achieved. Occasionally this uncertainty was voiced if parents sensed that they were somehow not succeeding in this aim. Barbara Johnson, for example, made the following observation about her daughter, Nicola:

> She's basically insecure, which I very much regret because, you know, security's the one thing you want to give your child and yet, you try and it still doesn't seem to work. (I)

John Clark said about his elder daughter, Louise:

> . . . and she's still a bit like this you know, if she wakes up during the night she just lets out a yell, she never, er. I don't know why, I mean, we've tried to make her feel secure, [laughs] whether we've failed somewhere I don't know. (I)

Again, couples usually saw this need as so taken-for-granted that there was no reason to explain it further. When explanations *were* given they were usually connected with ideas that people needed a secure emotional base on which to grow and develop. It was often implied that, without this feeling of security, the child might find itself in some way handicapped. Two quotations illustrate some of the meanings behind this image. Jim Robson argued:

> But I think insecurity, insecurity for a child is a catastrophe; and for an adult too, you MUST feel secure, a child must feel secure and if there isn't this security I think it's a terrible undermining thing for a child both in everyday educational things that, they're not secure, they don't know what's going to happen next. (I)

Nick Wilson gave his view as follows:

> In a situation where you have children is er, the one that they

they [parents] MUST provide is a degree of permanence and steadiness in the home. And I think this is, well I suppose it's just common sense to most people, but I'm SURE that children grow up better when they've got a stable, steady relationship of husband and wife close to them. (I)

The image of security as a basic need was such a vital factor underlying parental behaviour that it was constantly referred to in discussions about childrearing. The couples operated with such a wide variety of 'common-sense' notions about which actions would, or would not, foster this sense of security, that it is impossible to describe them all. Two examples are given, therefore, which deal with areas where parents particularly felt that their actions might threaten the child's emotional needs. The two areas which were often mentioned as especially sensitive in this respect were discipline and independence from parents. James Gilchrist felt that ill-feeling over disciplining should not be allowed to linger. He explained:

I don't like to put a kid to bed on a bad note because I would think that it would tend to make them feel insecure. (W/E)

Thus, the image of a child as needing security posed problems for most of the couples if they had to punish their children. Most explained that they felt firm action to be necessary at times, although they varied as to whether this was some kind of deprivation or physical punishment. All of the parents, however, described ancillary tactics which they hoped would make the child still feel loved despite these actions. Some couples, for example, had one parent carry out the discipline and the other then try to explain the reasons to the child. Others simply tried to ensure that a friendly atmosphere, with no rancour, was resumed as soon as possible after the disciplining had taken place. All of the tactics which were described aimed not to jeopardise the child's sense of security by making sure that the element of rejection, which is inherent in discipline, would be felt by the child only to be temporary and, ideally, clearly to relate to the particular item of offending behaviour.

Maureen Rankin illustrated the second area, independence from parents, when they were talking about their decision to allow the children themselves to decide when they wanted to go to nursery school. She said:

> If you push a child before he's ready then they're suspicious of
> you and they think that you're trying to get rid of them or some-
> thing, and you can give them a sense of insecurity if they think
> you're trying to get rid of them. You're NOT, but they think
> you are. And I think it's a problem that you don't really need to
> come up against if you just wait a bit, and em certainly with
> Lynne, I can't say for everybody, but it paid off to wait just a bit
> longer till she was ready. (W/E)

Here then is an excellent example of the interplay between
abstract and grounded images. This parent was concerned to
foster a feeling of security in the child. She tried to satisfy this
perceived need by certain specific actions. An ongoing grounded
interpretation of the child's reactions was, however, necessary to
sustain belief in the adequacy of her parental behaviour.
Throughout the fieldwork it was evident that this kind of belief
was frequently sustained through negotiation between the
spouses. As the child's definitions of reality were gradually
accorded greater legitimacy, he/she might also be *actively* included
in the negotiation processes.

The final much-mentioned emotional need, which everyone
claimed to be trying to satisfy but no-one felt he/she was
succeeding, was consistency. This was used as a blanket term to
cover all of the ways in which children might be subjected to conflicting treatments. Respondents stressed the importance of each
parent behaving in an internally consistent way as well as both
parents avoiding contradictions between themselves. Internal
consistency meant that the parent not only tried to react in the
same way to *similar* situations but also to try to avoid giving contradictory signals in *different* areas of behaviour. Everyone tended
to feel that this was all extremely difficult to achieve, primarily
because one's objectivity could so easily be swamped by personal
emotional reactions. Louise Wilson said, for example:

> Some days I would get very annoyed about something which on
> another day wouldn't worry me. And I try not to do this if I can
> because I think it's grossly unfair to the child who is too young
> to understand that people can go through good moods and bad
> moods. I think that basically a mother has to give the child the

sort of security which they need. (I)

The problematical nature of parenthood was here at a premium. Parents were faced with an immense range of actions and situations in which to be consistent. Various coping mechanisms were developed to sustain belief in this abstract image. Some respondents, for example, selected certain specific issues on which they tried *never* to fail. Breaking of promises to children was, for instance, tabooed by most of the parents. The notion of balance was also employed. A parent might claim for instance, that perceived failures in one area of childrearing were balanced by consistent behaviour in another. An extreme example was given by Ray Mitchell when Alice was commenting on the potentially harmful effect on their children of the large number of working hours he spent away from the home. He said:

> I don't know whether this is being overplayed a bit because you know, I think they would notice, you know if I, if they suddenly stopped seeing me once a year or something. But, you know, it's been more or less at this pitch most of the time [*Alice:* Yes] probably just em, a little bit less just over the past three months [*Alice:* But] than before, but I would have thought a child would probably respond far more to a CHANGE in circumstances. (W/E)

Here Ray maintained that time spent with the children was not important *per se*. In his opinion the vital factor was that he *consistently* gave them the same, albeit small, amount of time.

(b) Physiological images

The next part of this section which deals with images of the child's physiological needs, also raises some interesting points about the research process itself. Apart from their considerable references to sleep problems, respondents talked far less frequently than might have been expected about the child's needs, problems, and development in this area. Personal observation of friends and comments from colleagues would suggest that the use of physical images to account for a child's behaviour were implemented very much more often in everyday life than was indicated by the research. The 'teeth, tired, tummy' syndrome, for example, would seem frequently to be used as a first-line account. This perhaps means that respondents somehow felt that I wanted more from them than an understanding on that level. Equally, they might have felt that it was boring or uninteresting to me to hear about their child's bodily functions. Undoubtedly the kinds of under-standings employed by parents vary with the particular context. Physiological images were perhaps considered inappropriate when talking to a young unmarried interviewer who was only slightly acquainted with the children concerned. Another reason is also possible, drawing on the arguments being put forward in this book. By the time of the fieldwork respondents had been dealing with their own children for at least three years. Perhaps they had amassed such a subjectively satisfactory stock of know-ledge about dealing with the child's physical needs that they were quite confident in this respect, and did not see such needs as particularly problematical, or worth mentioning.

This suggestion is strengthened by noting that there were five cases where a physiological understanding was more frequently given. These were of children who had a specific physical ailment: asthma, digestive problems, eczema, febrile convulsions, and a severe scalding. Two examples illustrate the way in which parents drew on physical images in these cases. Margaret Barber said:

> And the main thing I think has affected the difference between them as babies has been their digestion, Mary has an excellent digestive system and Karen, poor child, has a rotten one and this you know, is a large part of a baby's world. (I)

Mary Clark said about Louise:

> She suffers from bronchial asthma which is a problem, and we think half of her problems, not PROBLEMS, but half of her little tantrums and her funny ways are caused by this because when she's WELL, she doesn't have any funny little ways. (I)

It seemed, therefore, that if a child had been diagnosed as in some way physically problematical, then parents would resort to this kind of image to understand the child more so than if he/she was considered basically healthy. The exception to this was if the child's sleeping habits were causing difficulties. This was frequently so oppressive and apparently insoluble to the parents themselves that it was very dominant in their images of the child.

(c) 'Incomprehensible' images

There were often instances when parents were unable to develop subjectively satisfactory images of the child's needs or wants.[7] Thus, although there was an underlying assumption that understanding the child was fundamental to parenthood, it was also felt that, at certain points, this became impossible. Also, whilst respondents claimed that they were concerned to develop and understand each child's personality, they were at the same time trying to develop a degree of felt predictability in his/her behaviour. Most parents, for example, expressed similar kinds of sentiments to the following from Barbara Johnson. She said about 'being a mother':

> It's been a most wonderful experience, you know, at the same time, most interesting experience. I would say fascinating, it's fascinating to study children. And yet it's very difficult too because while you're observing them and also appreciating them, you're also having to live with the little wretches. (I)

These couples faced the problematical situation of trying to bring up a child who was sufficiently socialised to accept common definitions of reality, but yet retained the individuality on which they placed high value. Some of the problems that this potential contradiction might cause for parental behaviour were indicated by Hannah Gilchrist when she criticised the childrearing activities of a friend. Speaking about his elder daughter, she commented:

> From really a tiny baby, em, she's really been smacked, something which I think is very wrong, but em, he's very loving in another way. I mean they've got to have discipline but they're only children. You've got to let them have their childhood, you can't force them all the time. (F)

Problems involved in developing subjectively satisfactory images of the child's needs and wants were illustrated by parents

describing their reactions to specific items of the child's behaviour. The most recurrent example was their description of
'temper tantrums'. My respondents were usually totally unable to
form understandings of these, and tended to relegate them to the
sphere of the 'incomprehensible'. This, it could be argued, was
basically because a 'temper tantrum' was a piece of behaviour
which was difficult to understand, except in terms of innate drives.
These, of course, were essentially what parents were trying to
direct by socialisation. When their efforts were challenged in such
an overt manner, the simplest solution was to define the behaviour
as 'incomprehensible' (and therefore unmanageable?).

The importance of the interpretative activity behind parental
behaviour was highlighted when responses to 'temper tantrums'
were described. Parents related how they had been totally unable
to remedy the situation, or had 'lost control' of their own tempers,
since they could not understand the child. Subsequently, they
expressed considerable feelings of mortification that they had
been unable to cope, as the child's behaviour had seemed so
irrational. Reactions varied from (i) defining their own parental
behaviour as unsatisfactory, because they could not understand
that particular item of behaviour, to (ii) simply defining the child
as a 'difficult personality' whom *nobody* would be able to
understand. In the first situation the coping mechanism of phase
or stage was usually employed. In the second situation, described
by two respondents, outside help had been sought. In both of
these cases the children were then defined as having a 'certain
kind of personality', in formal psychiatric terms. The parents
accepted these definitions and maintained that they were better
able to deal with the child since they now 'understood' the reasons
for the frequent 'temper tantrums'.

In this section I have outlined some of the abstract images of
children's needs and wants which these parents were using in
their everyday decisions about child management. Respondents,
however, legitimated their parental behaviour not only in terms of
general ideas about children and their needs and wants, but also
in terms of their future development into adults. Implicit in this is
the underlying assumption that the child will grow and change.
Physiological and mental growth is one of the few certain factors
to which these parents could orient their behaviour. In the next
section I shall present the kinds of projected images which
emerged from respondents' accounts.

IV   PROJECTED IMAGES OF CHILDREN

Many images of children were put forward which related to the future. These also had considerable effect on the current activities of the couples in my group. Such images are closely connected to underlying assumptions about family behaviour as a life-cyclically oriented reality. Some of these projected images were evolved in response to direct, open-ended questions, but many were expressed indirectly in the course of describing everyday activities. Three broad categories of projections will be outlined in this section. They are as follows:

(a)   Images of the future character of the child, and the implications for this of current parental actions and reactions.

(b)   Images of the parent's future relationship with the child.

(c)   Images of the child as a future member of society independently of his/her parents.

(a)   Images of the future character of the child

In the process of developing parental behaviour, respondents were also operating with images of the kind of person their child would grow up to be. In the final interview their attention *was* specifically directed towards such future frames of reference This was, however, to a large extent, the outcome of earlier observations that, during the course of the study, parents had frequently put forward projected images. An extreme example had, for example, been given by Anna Robson in her first interview. She said:

> I think I'm a typical mother in the respect that if I've watched them together in a group, I look for leadership, for instance in Martin and it's not there at the moment. And yet when he DOES show any tendencies, he's bullying. (I)

Projected character images were sometimes expressed in such specific terms but, most often, they took a much more generalised form. This quotation from Margaret Barber was a fairly typical example, she observed of her elder child:

When Karen's gone through some of her stranger phases, I've thought, 'what I would REALLY like are two jolly little extroverts who did everything at the right time and who slept fourteen hours a night.' And then I think 'no, because I would hate them to grow up into jolly little ordinary people'. (F)

Parents also frequently related their current actions to the projected images of their child's character. Sometimes this was simply *implied* and sometimes it was directly articulated as is illustrated by the following two quotations. Patrick Hislop said:

She [younger daughter] generally makes her presence pretty forcibly felt and er, I'm quite proud of that, except that *I* know it's gotta be watched and to that extent Anna gets trod on much more forcibly than Julie [elder daughter] ever had to be trod on. (I)

Madeleine Harris expressed her views as part of a much more integrated philosophy of character formation when she explained:

I don't WANT to be rigidly disciplinarian. I don't want to make lots of rules, I'd like to be flexible, I'd rather let them have their own way, I DESPERATELY want them to be independent sort of children, you know, I don't want to make them very closely dependent, you know, so I would encourage the things that weren't, you know. (F)

All of the parents perceived that this whole process of the effect of their current activities on the future character of their child was delicate and intricate. The uncertainty of the future outcome of their current parental actions was an issue which, in a general way, was referred to by everyone. Some interesting points arise out of the following quotation from Martin Chapman who observed:

I would say generally speaking that Anne tends to follow rather than be a leader, em, probably due to the way she's been brought up. Because ultimately, recently we've had to be quite strong with her because she's been a wee bit strong willed. And I think this is maybe em, this is where I'm maybe being a bit hesitant in trying to force her to do things because I don't want to curb her completely or else she's going to be just a follower all her life. I want her to be able to lead as well, when the time comes, if it's needed. (I)

This degree of self-consciousness about making sense of the child, and trying to be aware of parental actions and the child's reactions, was quite typical, although levels of articulation might vary. The, so to speak, 'monitoring' of the child's development was a taken-for-granted part of being a parent, as was a certain amount of self-consciousness about future outcome of present actions. (This was the case even if the self-consciousness simply resulted in the conclusion that it was impossible to sense the outcome!)

With varying degrees of explicitness, all of the parents implemented images of how their present actions might affect their child in the future. Again, in line with arguments elsewhere in the book, such projected images tended to be *ad hoc* and based on 'common sense' understandings or personal experiences rather than on any more formalised body of knowledge. Ben Pringle said, for example:

I mean I TEASE the children, I don't think it's wrong for them. I was teased incessantly as a boy and I don't think it does anyone any harm, in fact it makes them a little more pliable. (I)

Sometimes, projected images meant that respondents decided to abdicate the, as it were, 'control' aspect of parental behaviour. They legitimated this by maintaining that, in the long term it was in the child's own interests. Kathy Hislop gave a good illustration of this when she said:

I tend, on the other hand, if they WANT to do something that I either know they CAN'T do or is a stupid thing to do, to say, IF they're determined to do it, to say 'well go ahead and do it and you'll find out what happens'. And I still do this, obviously it's through laziness in that, em, I'm not prepared to maintain a firm stand and say 'no', but unless it's going to harm them, I feel, well, they'll learn by it. (F)

As the above quotation shows, reasonings behind parental acts were often multiple and interrelated. Equally, projected images were implemented for both the short term and long term. Generally, the reference to the future implications of present actions tended to be somewhat vague. Even if the parent felt quite strongly that one of his/her actions could have relevance for the child's future behaviour, exactly when and how this would be manifested was perceived as, by definition, unforseeable. General remarks such as the following from Mary Clark were typical. She commented:

> If you say you're going to do something then DON'T, then there'll come a time when they just won't accept anything you say. (F)

(b)   Images of the parents' future relationships with the child

Many of the projected images of the child were bound up with ideas about the future relationship between parents and children. As will be illustrated further in the following chapters, parental behaviour can be seen as emerging from a process of negotiation between the spouses. Part of this process involved the mutual legitimation of previous and intended actions. Just as this legitimating activity was integral to the spousal relationship, so it was also, albeit more subtly, a vital part of the parent-child relationship. The couples all hoped that their children would retain some form of contact with them when they became adult, and, presumably, left home. It was recognised, however, that in the twentieth-century context, this would be an essentially voluntary act on the part of the off-spring. Several parents went so far as to hope that their child would, in future, regard them as a friend or companion. Others simply hoped that, at the very least, their child would accept their frames of reference and share some of their basic ideas and beliefs. It was thus an aim that, in the future, the child would, to *some* extent, accept and even respect his/her parents and their views. The ability of respondents to legitimate their parental behaviour was therefore also relevant to the parent-child relationship inasmuch as it was hoped that the child would, in future years, be able to understand his/her up-bringing and a mutual respect might be achieved.

All of the parents put forward abstract images of the place of the child in their lives. They displayed a polarity of attitudes on this issue. This is best illustrated by some quotations. On the one hand people such as Martin Chapman saw their children as the focal point in their lives. He said:

We both agree that the children come first, that is a definite MUST. We both agree on that: the children come first, they're our main goal, our main objective is the children and they're our prime function, em, that's our main agreement. (I)

On the other hand, there were some who, like Nick Wilson, felt that:

I think the most important thing when you have children is that you shouldn't crucify yourself for your kids. And THAT I think is the major difference between OUR attitude and my parents' attitude, I don't know about your parents but MY parents certainly limited THEIR lives to a fantastic extent for the children. (F)

The Russells were perhaps representative of the middle ground of opinion, when they said in the final interview:

David: Well the children aren't the be all and end all here as far as we're concerned. I think that we, you know, we COULD do things ourselves, em, without the children quite happily; whereas some people tend to live purely in the children and em, even in the grandchildren if you like.

Marjorie: I think it places an ENORMOUS burden on the children for a start [*David:* It does, yes] when they're the sole focal point of interest for the parents. (F)

The final two quotations in particular were implicitly oriented to the underlying assumption of family life as a 'fairly' shared reality. It was also being acknowledged that living in a family was life-cyclical, and that parents could not take-for-granted a future relationship with their grown up child.

In this way, various projections were based on the fundamental image of the child as only a temporary full time visitor to the parents' lives. The image of the child as a future friend was something that several respondents claimed deliberately to be working

towards. The Davies frequently mentioned this and referred to it
again during their final interview. Andrew said:

> *Andrew:*   But I think what, em, what we've always said with,
> with our own family, what we would like to do is grow up
> WITH them MORE than what we've seen in our own
> parents, put it that way.
> *Judy:*   We don't want this gap of, you know, we want our
> family to come in and say 'look Dad, I've done so 'n' so' or
> 'look Dad I would like to go somewhere, are you coming with
> me?', sort of thing. (F)

Patrick Hislop put forward a similar viewpoint. During his first
interview, he said of his two small daughters:

> I see them both as being on fairly friendly terms with adults,
> myself and Kathy in particular, obviously, but with what I
> think of as a, as a friendship rather than necessarily a parent
> relationship. Which is something, this is something obviously
> that'll either grow or disappear as they get older. But this is
> something that we want, this is one of the reasons why we
> wanted the family while we were young; so that we would be
> more friends to them. (I)

Other parents, who made no claim to such objectives, still
hoped that their children would not diverge too greatly from their
own value systems. The Johnsons gave an example of this:

> *Ian:*   I hope that they share, share a lot of our values because
> they're gonna be living with us whether they or we like it or
> not for some time. And it would be a lot nicer [*Barbara:*
> More comfortable!] if they share a lot of our views and our
> interests. (W/E)

By and large then, these couples hoped that, through common
interests and values, their children would in future, retain a
relationship with them when they became adults. On a general
level, Louise Wilson articulated a view which would have been
echoed by practically every respondent. She said:

> Well I just somehow think that one of the nice things about

having a family is not that you should just enjoy your family when they're up to about the age of four. I think it should be a sort of dynamic thing which goes on for the whole of a life-time. (F)

(c) Images of children as future members of society

The final category of projected images involved respondents' ideas about the place of their children in society in the future. All of the parents were making everyday decisions about their child-rearing activities with at least some regard to the fact that the child would not always have the parental buffer against the outside world. In line with arguments elsewhere in this chapter, they were, at the very least, aware that whereas *they* would accept and understand their child and so allow it leeway, *others* might not share such an attitude.[8] Again, this involved both short and long term projected images. The Jeffreys, for example, had the following exchange during their final interview. Marjorie had just said that she hoped their boys would be decent citizens and not cruel, and maintained that they were kind at the moment. Andrew argued:

Andrew: Yeah, well that's true to some extent except that if Michael thinks he'll kick our cat, he WILL.
Marjorie: But he's three.
Andrew: He's three, well OK, you've got to accept that he's three.
Marjorie: Well people WILL accept that he's three, but it's when they get a little bit older that people start going on about what traits they've got, isn't it, when he's a bit older. (F)

No matter how highly couples valued originality and individuality in their child, they also perceived that he/she was going to make his/her own way in society, and felt that, as parents, they should be aware of this. Louise Wilson, for example, said that she worried about her elder daughter, Jane, for the following reasons:

She has inherited ENTIRELY Nick's [husband] complete, well, shyness doesn't worry me, but, em, his independence, to an extent that I think it would be completely undesirable in a woman at a later age, that's all. [and she went on later] I think that maybe she'll go out on such a limb that she's gonna find it rather difficult to have a totally happy future life with other people, and I think you have to live with other people to a certain extent in your family life. (F)

Other respondents also expressed their perceptions of those specific personality traits of their children which might cause them personal difficulties in the future. Often, however, the projected images of their child in future society were expressed in a much more general way. The following two quotations illustrate quite clearly how parents were making everyday decisions about their child's upbringing which were, at least in part, derived from such projected images. One example was given by John Clark when, in his first interview, he explained why he was anti Dr Spock. He said:

Some of it I think in my opinion is not really for the benefit of the child in the long run. You can't allow children to virtually dictate how the house is to be run, you've got to try to more get the children to fit in with what's there already. (I)

(At this point, I probed as to why he felt it was not for the child's benefit in the long run.) He continued:

Well it's not good to be giving in to them all the time I think. Because when they do grow up a bit they then find out that they can't get all the things they want, then they'll take it much harder. (I)

In his first interview Jeff Harris talked about his aversion to 'way out' schools as follows: He explained:

And I'm not so sure that very progressive schools are not, you know, bringing up children to fit into a society that doesn't exist. Not that fitting in makes em, I mean it isn't just so much you know, making the hand fit the glove sort of thing, but rather finding a compromise situation where you don't attempt to create tensions which are unnecessary. And er I feel that sometimes this could happen in a VERY progressive school. A certain amount of discipline doesn't hurt anybody [laughs]. (I)

Here then were two examples of respondents legitimating their current parental behaviour in terms of images of the child in future society. They were quite typical statements. Respondents attached meanings to their parental behaviour both in terms of their immediate relationship with the child, and their ideas about society in general. Hence, several of them felt that 'progressive' childrearing was, by and large, disruptive in the home and ultimately disadvantageous to the child him/herself when he/she had to make his/her own way in a non-'progressive' society. Such views of children and society were put forward to legitimate the use of firm discipline and of making sure that the child did not get all his/her own way.

V   SUMMARY

In this chapter I have argued that the images which parents formed of their children had considerable implications for all of the everyday decisions and behaviour involved in bringing them up. The couples were faced with an enormous number of stimuli from their children and, as in all kinds of social behaviour, they formed typificatory schemes as part of the process of deciding how to act. By and large this was carried out subconsciously and unreflectively; and a major aim of the study was to uncover some of these taken-for-granted images.

I divided the images of children which emerged during the interviews into 'abstract' and 'grounded' categories. This was simply an analytical procedure since the two categories were, in practice, inter-related, with each continuously modifying or reinforcing the other. Abstract images discussed in the present chapter, were derived essentially from the individual's social stock of knowledge. Grounded images, to be discussed in the following chapter, were developed out of the parent's ongoing biographical experience. Both sets of images were sustained through the processes of negotiation between family members.

I described three main categories of abstract images. Firstly, the parents in my group held general images of children and childhood. Secondly, they described a variety of abstract images of children's needs and wants. Thirdly, abstract images related to the child in the future, and their relationship with him/her, also influenced respondents' current behaviour.

These abstract ideas and beliefs about children were shown to have an effect on parental behaviour. However, perhaps of even greater significance for everyday decision making about all of the minutiae of childrearing were the 'grounded images' which I shall now consider. These are more particularistic and are derived from the individual's ongoing biographical experience, the reality of which is, however, constructed in continuous interpretative exchanges among family members.

6 Making Sense of my Child: Grounded Images of Children

I INTRODUCTION

How people behave as parents is affected not only by their abstract ideas about children in general but also by their everyday experience of looking after each particular child. In fact, in terms of the assumptions about family life held by the couples in my group, it could be argued that, for them, this biographical 'knowledge' was crucial. The stress which these parents laid upon 'understanding' their children, and upon family life as a learning and developing situation, meant that their 'grounded' images of children had an extremely influential effect on their behaviour.

Grounded images were developed from respondents' perceptions of a particular child and its behaviour in many different contexts. The first section of this chapter is concerned with 'comparative images'. These directly reflect the underlying assumption that family life is a shared reality since they deal principally with the meanings attached by parents to the structural fact that there were *two* children in the family. The second section is called 'contextual images'. These emphasise the indexicality of the process of developing parental behaviour. Respondents constructed and legitimated their own behaviour with reference to their interpretations of the various contexts in which the child was perceived as acting.

II COMPARISONS

This area of images was concerned with the basic fact that the couples in my group each had two children. These parents were very conscious of the ways in which having two children affected their dealings with each individual child. They also formed many explicit images about the relationship between the two children themselves. Such ideas were often consciously used either as bases for actions or as legitimations. I shall argue, however, that out of these ideas arose further actions and images which were much more implicit and tended to contradict underlying assumptions about fairness in the shared reality of family life.

(a)   First or second born

There were a range of images of children associated with their being first or second born. These dealt essentially with parents' relationships with the child. At some point all respondents in some way talked about how the second (and presumably subsequent) children were treated differently from the first. This could be seen as stemming from three main interrelated factors which were as follows. Firstly, (i) the parents had experience of one child already and felt more confident in their actions; secondly, (ii) the second child inevitably received less of the parents' attention since another child was already in the family; and thirdly (iii) the second child could never be such a novelty as the first.

(i)   As parenthood was viewed as a situation of learning, all of the couples talked about how, having experienced the first child, they reacted differently to the second. Basically, they felt, on reflection, that they over-reacted to the first child and fussed over him/her too much. Three-quarters of the couples directly related past and present difficulties with their first child to their own inexperienced parental behaviour. The different images of first and second children were especially highlighted by those parents whose second child was still a baby at the time of the fieldwork. Before the child could communicate verbally, the interpretative activities of the parent were even more vital. All of the couples who had a baby at this stage made points similar to the following from Judy Davies. She said:

This is how I've got Ian [second child] onto his three feeds [*Andrew:*   Much quicker] quicker because I was frightened to lift Robert [first child] and feed him, in case it threw him off his routine. Well it doesn't really because after all, all of a sudden it just clicked with me, well he's a human being, if he loses sleep at one time he'll make it up the next time and what I feel with Ian is, I've HAD to do this otherwise I wouldn't, I would never have finished. (W/E)

All respondents made similiar comments to this in a completely taken-for-granted manner. The social construction of parental behaviour involved, therefore, developing and sustaining the belief that, as parents, they 'knew' what they were doing. The development of such a feeling of confidence in one's actions was a crucial factor behind the different parental attitudes towards the first and second child.

It seemed, for instance, that the first baby was seen as much more fragile, dependent and difficult to interpret. The second child was perceived differently largely because parents *felt* more knowledgeable, and were better able to develop subjectively satisfactory reasons for his/her behaviour. Jean Coulson gave a typical version of this situation when she said:

I think you know, the fault of many parents is that, you know, you over-protect your first child and it's trial and error, em, I don't think you can help that really. I think you're a very clever person that does. And *by the time you come round to the second one, em, you tend to relax a bit more and realise that they really are quite strong and capable of getting on on their own.* (I) [my emphasis]

In this complex process the respondents were not only forming images of the child but also of themselves as parents, and this also affected their behaviour. Several mothers in particular, who had feeding or sleep problems with their first babies talked of feeling upset and ashamed that *they* personally were unable to deal with the situation. They concluded, looking back, that at a certain point the difficulties had simply been compounded by their transmission of feelings of agitation to the child. The Rankins, both of whose babies they *now* maintained had had infant colic, provided considerable insight into the definitional processes involved in such interactions. Derek explained:

We didn't get much sympathy from the doctors. They just er, well obviously with Lynne being the first baby we didn't get much sympathy, they just thought that she [Maureen] couldn't cope with them. Other people tend to think as well, you know, their babies'll sleep but ours wouldn't sleep. And of course with Lynne we thought it was us, obviously, Maureen thought it was us. The second one arrived and he was even worse and we realised it wasn't, it was THEM, the babies. (I)

Both of the Rankin babies had been problematical in that they cried a very great deal. With the first child Maureen had had to resort to the image of the child as having 'incomprehensible' needs and wants. This was perceived by herself and others as a failure to fulfil the basic tenet of parenthood: that she should 'understand' her child. When their second child behaved in exactly the same manner, the Rankins developed the much more subjectively satisfactory physical image: that both of their children had had severe digestive problems (infant colic). Thus, while they were both equally tired by the sleeplessness of the second baby as compared with the first, Maureen was nowhere near the brink of 'nervous breakdown' which she claimed to have reached the first time.

This example also illustrated the process of negotiation between spouses and the importance attached to learning about children through *personal* experience. The first baby had done most of its crying when Derek was at work. Maureen maintained that, consequently, he had not appreciated fully the seriousness of the problem. She felt that he also thought that the problem lay in *her* inability to cope. The second baby, however, cried all the time that Derek was at home. Maureen defined Derek as then 'understanding' the situation. Subsequently they became mutually involved in 'finding a solution'. This solution, in analytical terms, was the sustaining of the belief that the children had physical ailments.

(ii)   Couples also talked about seeing the second child differently because he/she was not the sole object of parental attention. All of the parents had been concerned about the reaction of the first child to the arrival of the second. This led most of them to be very conscious of the first child when dealing with the second and therefore, in some way, to behave differently towards him/her. Thus, from the start, the second baby had to share its mother's attention. For example, whilst the baby was being fed the elder child might share its mother's lap or be told a story. The majority of the parents said that they were conscious of potential problems with the first child and described ways in which they had tried to avoid these. Several mothers, for instance, related how they had tried also to include the first children in activities centred on the babies. Barbara Johnson had been very aware of this situation and described as follows how she had dealt with it. She explained:

And I was SO afraid of jealousy arising IN her as a result of her brother coming along, that I more or less, em, well I think I gave more conscious attention to her, my attention when it was HERS was consciously directed to her. Whereas before obviously the attention she got was a naturally arising one, just by her very presence. But when HE came along I felt that the attention had to be directed TOWARDS Nicola, and I feel that he probably was a bit deprived. (W/E)

Several respondents also felt that it was the best solution all round if the new baby *appeared* to get less attention so that the elder child did not feel deprived in any way.

In this way, parents felt that they inevitably perceived the second child differently because their actions and reactions took place within a different socio-psychological context, i.e. that another child had always to be considered. On a general level, Jeff Harris's observation would probably have found agreement among the other respondents. He observed:

Ian being younger, em, for Ian there IS a problem in that he's got to, as it were, carve out his own place. Somehow with Frances being here first she almost had it guaranteed, and Ian hadn't that. And, so the DIFFICULTY is to try to see exactly how best to, as it were, insure him his place. (F)

Perhaps more crucially, however, parents seemed to feel that the second child was inevitably different directly *because* his/her family situation was not the same as that of the first child. People identified these perceived differences in a variety of ways. Louise Wilson said:

The other one is a holy terror but this is a second child syndrome and this arises entirely from the fact that mother has another child to think about and therefore doesn't scream and shout at the younger one or stop them doing what they shouldn't. (I)

There were varied opinions within my group about whether the different situation affected the development rate of the second child. Interestingly, polar conclusions were sometimes justified by appealing to the same cause. Anna Robson and Kathy Hislop, for example, claimed that their second children had made much more rapid progress in every way than their elder siblings because they had been stimulated by the first children. Derek Rankin on the other hand, felt that Jonathon's slowness in walking and talking was because everyone, and especially his older sister Lynne, was able to sense what he wanted and get it for him. Here again we can see an excellent example of the importance of studying interpretative activity. Respondents all assumed that second children would be affected by the presence of the first. They then used their very different practical interpretations of this structural fact to form understandings of the second child.

(iii)　The parents in my group also saw the second child differently inasmuch as he/she was not so much of a novelty. They said that this was not simply a factor of the degree of parental experience, but was connected also with a decrease in the amount of active interest in the minutiae of the child's activities and development. This was reflected by the fact that all of those respondents who claimed to have kept detailed records about their first child, said that they had not done so, or only minimally, with the second. Another example of this arose out of the fact that all respondents had one child of approximately three years. Whereas everyone whose *elder* child was the three year old was able to describe him/her in considerable detail, this was not always the case if the three year old was the younger. Out of the twelve families who fell into this *second* category there were five in which one or both parents felt that there was little to say about the younger child, as his/her personality was only just beginning to show. Of course it might very well be that these five couples found equally little to say when their *first* child was that age. Observations of the ten couples in the *first* category, however, made this seem somewhat unlikely. Again, it could simply be a function of those particular five children but this also seems unlikely as the other three year olds provided much for their parents to describe, no matter how their personalities or development were perceived. It seemed therefore, that the first child, as an infant, was viewed very much more as an object of interest and discussion than was the second.

Several respondents made explicit or implicit criticism of this very fact. Some people expressed this by laughing at themselves, in retrospect, for being so absorbed in their first baby. Others wished that they had been able to put the baby into what they *now* saw as the proper perspective which they considered they had achieved with the second. About a quarter of the parents were directly critical of their own behaviour. Mary Clark, Elizabeth Vaughan and Kathy Hislop all felt that they had created difficulties with their first children simply by being *so* interested in them, and giving them far too much attention. John Clark made the following comment:

> It's quite funny the difference between them. Louise is, whether it's the fact that she was the first one and got too much attention I don't know, but she, she moans a lot when she's, when she wants something, instead of coming and asking reasonably for it. (I)

Several parents commented that they wished that *all* children could be treated like *second* children. Implicit in this seemed to be the notion that, although the child should be understood, too great a preoccupation with him/her was, in fact, disadvantageous. This was a further indirect example of the underlying assumption that children needed boundaries.[1] Somehow, one of these boundaries was the amount of parental attention they felt was *good* for the child. The demands of *two* children were seen as an automatic deterrent against *one* child having too much attention.

One of the most explicit assessments of the fundamental differences in images of the first and second child came from Ian Johnson. This long quotation is presented in its entirety as it emphasises basic points which were made or implied by most of the respondents. He said:

> *Ian:* It's a bit unfortunate in a way that he's been the second child because you tend to take much more notice at the time, although you always forget it, of the first child and their development. We were always looking at the way Nicola was developing and noting when she said her first word, and when she drew her first pictures, and when she managed to put a shape into a box, this sort of thing; and trying to work

out whether this was advanced or retarded or about average.
But em, Thomas tends to do these things and you don't
notice them. One day you suddenly notice them, and notice
that he's been doing them for a long time, and you didn't
notice because he's a second child and the novelty's worn off,
and well, probably that's just as well for him, people not
taking as much notice.

K.B.:   Why do you think it's just as well for him?

Ian: Well because I think an obsessive interest in the
development of the child is a bit unhealthy, em, if you show
too much interest in them, I don't know why, it makes them
too full of their own self-importance, makes them feel that
they're the important, the focal person of the household. (I)

(b)   Interactions between siblings

Many images were also formed through parents' perceptions of
the interactions between their two children. These were used not
only to gain further understandings of each individual child but
also as guidelines for parental behaviour when dealing with both
children together. *In this way, parents were forming images of the two
children by seeing the behaviour of each within the context of the other.* They
tended to stress the interdependence of the children, and how each
perhaps behaved differently if the other was not there. Images of
each child were also formed from observations of how they treated
and reacted to each other. The Robsons, the Hislops and the
Jacksons for example all felt that the gentle and kind characteristics of their elder children were confirmed by their reactions to
their much more dominant and aggressive younger sisters.

Images of the children's personalities and development were
also formed by comparing their reactions to situations when they
were together or alone. By this process, Patrick Hislop and Louise
Wilson had arrived at rather similar conclusions about their
apparently very forceful younger daughters. Patrick Hislop
observed to his wife Kathy:

In the sort of, the older child situation, particularly the strange
older child situation, where em Julie, Julie is still the leader.
[Kathy agrees] Anna in the domestic situation is able to take
over, and also in the sort of familiar LOCAL surroundings, is

able to take over, but when I think they get outside that, Julie is still the boss. (F)

Louise Wilson said:

> On the other hand, she's terribly dependent on both Nick and myself because she has spent a lot more time with us. And er of course she's always got her sister there and on occasions when Jane isn't there she becomes quite shy and very lost. (I)

(c) Implications

These were some of the ways that this group of parents formed comparative images of their children which were used as bases for their parental behaviour, and as legitimations. Although the points discussed so far were usually explicitly articulated during the interviews, there were certain implications which were far less apparent both to respondents and, at that stage, to myself. These were primarily related to contradictions between the underlying assumption that family life was a situation of learning, and images that each *individual* child should be understood. The crucial point is that the elder child provided the first major acquaintanceship of the parents with the bulk of childrearing activities and experiences. This knowledge, once acquired, was rapidly absorbed and taken-for-granted. Consequently, in terms of everyday management, the second child was much less of an unknown quantity and parents had greater confidence in their ability to make sense of him/her.

This would seem to imply that parents developed understandings of the first child much more in his/her own right than they did of the second. This did not mean that the second was any the less valued as an individual personality. Rather, it is suggested that less time and mental effort was devoted to identifying and dealing with his/her everyday needs, since experience with the first child could be drawn upon as a cultural resource. Philip Barber gave an illustration of this kind of process when he said:

> *And you don't worry, you've been through all this, the kind of worries over every little detail with the first one. And you've learned, where to draw the line,* you know, what's a cry that really needs attention, and how

long it can go on before you really need to do something serious about it. You've learned all these things. (I) [my emphasis]

This implicit tendency to treat the second child differently (i.e. the same!) was also shown in another way. Parents frequently explained an item of the second child's behaviour in terms of phases which the *first* had also gone through. Similar images of phases and stages had perhaps also been implemented when there was only one child. It is suggested, however, that a felt lack of direct experience with the first child meant that this was done much more tentatively, and that then this notion had simply been used as one of a large range of possible explanations. With the *second* child it seemed that the image of phases and stages was very readily and confidently applied, and, consequently, more varied ways of 'making sense' of the child were not resorted to so frequently. Everyone made remarks such as the following by Andrew Jeffreys to his wife:

You did say that Michael's sort of a bit of a monster in his own way at the moment, but Brian wasn't very much different three years ago. (Jt)

The vital qualifying point, however, was that respondents were making judgments and reaching decisions on the basis of ill-remembered information. As previously discussed, the parents sometimes discovered that their working model of the first child had been 'inaccurate'.[2] Such semi-intuitive models were, however, in constant use as basic working formulae to deal with second children. Even when the inadequacies of this process were appreciated, the fact that it provided such great reassurance to parents meant that it continued to operate. This can be illustrated by a conversation between Eric and Carol Burns during their joint interview:

Eric: Well, I wouldn't have thought he [John, elder child] was as determined as Alison anyway. She shows it more anyway.
Carol: Well given their age difference anyway [*Eric:* Well, em] and er, they're very determined when they're beginning to realise that they're a person, at two and two and a half they assert themselves tremendously at this age, [*Eric:* Mmm] which is very normal and er, they just see how far they can go.

[Eric agrees] John CERTAINLY had that period and because he's nearly six, he STILL asserts himself, but he can be reasoned with [*Eric:* Mmmhm] you know, it's just different ages but you're er, you know, now you have an OLDER child in the [*Eric:* Oh yes] you can compare.

Eric: Yes, it's very difficult to tell with the first one.

Carol: And you can look back.

Eric: Well you can't really look back cos you don't remember.

Carol: You can't look back but you do have this comparison before you now, so obviously you can compare. (Jt)

A further instance of implicitly different treatment was given when couples frequently talked about having made mistakes with their first child which they were determined not to make with the second. Thus, although they stressed that the situation and personality of the child affected their parental behaviour, they had nevertheless, by the second child, developed in practice considerable constraints on their perception of courses of action. No matter how well intentioned their motives, parents were tacitly assuming a similarity of the needs and wants of the two children by using a consciousness of their perceived errors with the *first* child to avoid problems with the *second*. Their beliefs in equal treatment and individuality were thus being implicitly undermined by this acquisition of a taken-for-granted stock of grounded parental knowledge. This observation has fascinating wider implications for decision making situations generally. It seemed that, for these families, personal experience of one particular situation was quite likely to achieve precedence as a decision making resource over any 'rational' assessment procedures.

Images of the second child also led to implicit redefinitions by the respondents both of the first child and of themselves as parents. What might, for example, have been a tentative assessment of the first child was sometimes reinforced when the second arrived. Sometimes parents had *thought* that the first child was particularly 'good' or 'bad' in some respect but did not feel sufficiently knowledgeable to reach a firm conclusion. Perceptions of what the second child was like in that respect often led to a firmer definition of the first, since a directly experienced relative standard was now available. A simple illustration was that a child who had seemed at the time to be very active and a poor sleeper was often *categorically* defined as such when the younger sibling

exhibited a different pattern of behaviour in that respect.
Elizabeth Vaughan provided a further example when she said:

> We often say that having Catherine makes you realise how
> awkward Jenny is because we used to say, em maybe they're all
> like this, but now that we have Catherine we know that they're
> NOT all like that. (I)

Finally, the use of comparative images of children seemed to
lead to inherent modifications in ideas about being a parent. An
increase in definitional confidence has already been suggested.
Respondents described several ways in which their experience
with the first child led to an increased self-confidence in their
dealings with the second. The feeling that, by the second child, a
stock of taken-for-granted knowledge had been amassed, led to a
completely different level of parental self-assurance. Barbara
Johnson illustrated this when she said about her second child,
Thomas:

> He was difficult from the word go, he wouldn't sleep and em,
> fortunately he was my second child, I think I would have
> worried myself to death if he'd been my first. (I)

It can also be suggested that being able to compare reactions of
two children to their actions, led respondents to a slightly different
parental outlook. A fundamental dilemma in the process of
making sense of the child was whether or not to attribute causes of
perceived problematical behaviour to parental actions, or to the
child itself. It seemed that respondents were very quick to blame
themselves in retrospect for problems with the first child. My
impression was, however, that with the increase in definitional
confidence there was a greater tendency to assign causes to the
second child itself. A danger inherent in these changes was the
potential tendency to take for granted the fundamentals of their
parental approach and, with this greater rigidity, to assume that
problematical elements required modifications in the child rather
than in themselves.

III   CONTEXTUAL IMAGES

Having suggested that some images of children might imply a

tendency to inflexibility in parental outlook, another area will now be considered which, in some ways, acted as a counterbalance.

This further way in which the parents made sense of their children was the formation of contextual images. There is some overlap between the points in this area but for presentation purposes, I have divided them into 3 main categories. These are called (a) social, (b) temporal and (c) genealogical images. Again the material included in each category reflects the points which were most stressed by the respondents. Future researchers will undoubtedly identify images in other groups which will both amplify and contradict my own observations. Presented here, however, are those contextual images which seemed relevant in the construction of parental behaviour of the twenty-two couples in my own group.

To a certain extent, what is basically being discussed in this area is how these parents drew upon environmental and genetic images in understanding their children. Although they were not specifically asked to consider the environment versus heredity issue, it was apparent that they were as varied and as ambivalent in their views as most other human beings, including the specialists! The basic pragmatism in the development of subjectively satisfactory images meant, however, that my respondents were able to hold what specialists would see as theoretically contradictory views with the greatest of ease. This was essentially because the process of understanding and making sense of their child involved drawing on a repertoire of images, some of which might be given greater weight than others, in certain situations, and at different times.[3]

(a)   Social contextual

Three main sets of images will be discussed in this section. These were the kinds of images to which respondents most frequently referred. Basically they formed images of the child and its behaviour in the context of what could be seen as overlapping sets of social situations. These were: (i) the particular social situation in which the child was immediately involved; (ii) the family situation; and (iii) the wider social context. It must be recognised that the images to be discussed were very much more complex than these three simple categories suggest. While the quotations are principally to illustrate the images, it is hoped that they also give some indication of the complex interactive and definitional features of the process of image formation itself.

(i)   Firstly, as part of the process of understanding their child, the parents in my group frequently referred to the importance of considering the immediate situational context. By this they meant either the physical or social context, or a combination of the two. Everyone either explicitly or implicitly made distinctions, for example, between the child in its home and non-home context. An extension of this was their image of the child in familiar and unfamiliar surroundings and situations. This had a considerable impact on their behaviour. Some parents, for instance, confidently planned all sorts of activities since they saw their child as responding well in unfamiliar contexts; others approached such situations with great trepidation.

Contextual images were also used to broaden their basic understanding of the child. The Hislops, for example, had the following conversation about their two daughters in their joint interview:

Patrick: One's an introvert, the other's an extrovert.
Kathy: Yes that's what it really boils down to, although Julie's not really such an introvert as she makes out.
Patrick: No, it's all relative, it's not all the time.
Kathy: She's fine on her own, without anybody there, she'll talk, but then so is Anna, she'll talk much more if I'm not there, to strangers. (Jt)

Social situational images of this kind were also implemented to make sense of specific items of a child's behaviour. The features of the relevant social situation were frequently examined if, for instance, a child was perceived by the parents as acting 'out of character' or 'unacceptably'. By putting the child's actions within their situational context, parents were doing two main things. They were reassuring themselves that the perceived aberrant behaviour firstly was comprehensible and secondly did not require them to make any more general reassessment of their view of their child. Barry Coulson's observation that their elder child had been a nuisance during a recent visit to a friend was revised when Jean put forward a contextual understanding. Barry explained:

Barry: . . . he was a pest really, he was going upstairs, he was [*Jean:*   I don't know what he was doing upstairs] you know, I don't know, you see this is.

Jean: You see, this is, I think where you probably couldn't see HIS point, in that you obviously wanted to talk to Mike [Barry's friend] but I suppose Matthew [child] wanted your attention you know.

Barry: Yes, I think that's it, you see, the other kids had gone so he had nobody to play with. (W/E)

Of course, the parents did not always see their child's behaviour as generated simply by the social situation. Equally often they put forward an image of the child as asserting his/her personality and manipulating the situation. A good example of this occurred during one of the interviews with the Pringles. It was quite late in the evening when their younger daughter came downstairs, appearing at the living room door, demanded a special drink, and refused to go back to bed without it. After much gentle persuasion she got what she wanted and went back to bed. Ben commented:

Ben: She's got courage anyway, if you [K.B.] weren't here she'd be absolutely killed for that you know.

Sheila: I'd grab her and dump her on her bed. [laughing]

Ben: She would cry for a second and then that would be it, but she knows when to sort of perform, you know, she knows [laughs], we won't make exhibitions of ourselves if we've got visitors. (W/E)

(ii)   Secondly, understandings of the child were developed by considering his/her behaviour in the context of other family members. A more complex point is intended here than simply extending the previous section and seeing the family as one kind of social context. This, of course, is *part* of the process but the aim is to highlight the definitional intricacies involved by considering the form which it often took during the interviews. This kind of image usually arose if Parent A was either being somewhat critical of a child, or was suggesting that an item of the child's behaviour was incomprehensible. Parent B then tended to suggest that the behaviour had to be seen in the light of Parent A's image of, and behaviour towards, that child. Parent B might also make a similar response but refer it to the sibling definitional context. Essentially, it is being suggested that respondents developed contextual images of their child's behaviour by seeing it as a response to the images and behaviour of other family members. Some illustrations should clarify this intricate but very basic point.

Examples of images of the child in the context of a parental definition came from the Hemingways and the Wilsons. Alan Hemingway tended to be critical of his two children, stressing that they had very strong and determined personalities. His wife, Dianne, felt that he defined their daughters as demanding and badly behaved partly because he expected too high standards of them, and reacted accordingly. Here the Hemingways could be seen as involved in the negotiation of practical interpretations of the abstract boundaries of behaviour 'needed' by children. Dianne felt that she allowed the children more leeway than did Alan, and that she therefore had fewer confrontations with them. She disagreed with his abstract image of how children *should* behave, and maintained that they were only hard to deal with in the context of his 'unrealistic' expectations.

Louise Wilson told of how her two daughters seemed to dislike each other intensely, and also expressed worries that they would end up with no relationship at all, as had her husband and *his* brother. Here projected images were also important meanings behind her parental concern. The following conversation took place in their final interview when Nick maintained that Louise was accentuating the situation by developing this image of the children's relationship:

Louise: But em, they're just going through a stage at the moment where they *loathe* each other.
Nick: Egged on by Mummy.
Louise: Why?
Nick: Cos you set off every day to look for the loathing in the two children.
Louise: Well it's not difficult when they come in with sort of bite marks and nip marks all over them. [*K.B.:* Do they?] Oh, little girls are horrid.
Nick: Louise was encouraging them to escalate the war the other day by encouraging the one to thump the other. [all laugh]
Louise: Yes, well I got this half strangled child saying 'Jane [elder sister] *squeezed* me! [laughs] and I said 'well, thump her

one'. So now they thump each other and then come to me crying afterwards, so it's just a waste of time altogether, but I'm
sure they'll grow out of it. (F)

This quotation also provides an excellent illustration of the vital
importance of interpretative acts of parents. Nick completely disagreed with Louise that there was anything 'out of the ordinary' in
their daughters' fights. He defined it simply as sibling rivalry over
scarce resources, and refused to give it the status of a problem or a
worry in his discussion with Louise. She, however, had tried many
tactics to lessen the amount of fighting and ill feeling whereas Nick
simply ignored it.

A similar kind of family definitional process also took place with
reference to images of the child and its behaviour formed through
making sense of the sibling relationship. An excellent example
came from the Johnsons when, in a particular instance, they
concluded that it was only possible to make sense of one child's
behaviour by seeing it in the context of the actions of the other
(and the mutual sibling images involved). The incident took place
when Barbara was at work and the children were being looked
after by their home-help (Mrs Smith). Nicola, the elder child, had
been behaving badly by trying to put a door handle in her mouth,
and defying Mrs Smith to do anything about it. When her brother
Thomas tried to persuade her to stop doing this, lest she hurt
herself, Nicola punched him hard in the face. On arriving home,
Barbara had found it difficult to understand this unusual and
callous action, and had been very angry with Nicola. When Ian
arrived home, however, he put the following somewhat different
interpretation on the incident:

Ian: He'd said what he [Thomas] had to make Nicola cross
     and he'd said it in such a way that to an outsider like Mrs
     Smith [*Barbara:*   And me!] or to Barbara [*Barbara:*   Not an
     outsider!] it would seem that he was being genuinely solici-
     tous, but in fact he was [*Barbara:*   Doubly crafty] being
     slightly derisory, not in, not in the tone that he used, but
     Nicola, Nicola would have known that he was, he was
     mocking her, or sort of kicking her when she was down I sup-
     pose, that's the nearest.
Barbara: Embarrassing her [*Ian:*   Yes, yes] because she was
     defying Mrs Smith, KNOWING, that she was being

naughty in her defiance. (F)

(iii)   Thirdly, parents formed images of their children in the wider social context. By this two main points are suggested. In the first place, respondents formed images of their child's reactions in extra-familial contexts. In the second place, they formed images of how the child was viewed by others in these contexts. In both of these ways, parents were continuously forming contextual images of the child which helped them to make sense of his/her present behaviour. They could also draw on these images to help them make everyday decisions about possible courses of parental behaviour.

The couples in my group were concerned to have information about how their child behaved and reacted in social situations where they themselves were not present. Reports of playgroup leaders, schoolteachers and other parents were often related to me. Whether or not these reports had been actively sought by the respondents, they were rapidly assimilated and evaluated as part of the parental process. In fact, they often drew on these somewhat scattered and superficial comments either for reassurances that all was well with their child, or for hints that something might be wrong. The Pringles, for example, related frequent reports about how their daughters fared at playgroup. During their final interview, they spent a lot of time trying to make sense of their younger daughter, Helen's behaviour which, at that point, had been reported as being somewhat introverted and 'out of character'. Ben's comments illustrated the extent to which they acted on these reports, when he said:

> Helen seems to have been going through a bad spell at school. [*Sheila:*   God!] Her teacher seemed to think that she was getting idle and not bothered with things you know. To the extent that Sheila took her to the Doctor and she was put on an iron tonic which has er, not really, I don't know, she's been very much better recently, hasn't she? (F)

A slightly different example came from the Vaughans. They, in fact, observed their daughter's reactions in the extra-familial context of the Sunday School prizegiving. Subsequently, they felt the need to modify their image of Jenny when her behaviour in that situation was not as they had anticipated. They made the following remarks in their final interview:

> *Roy:* On Sunday there was the prizegiving in her Sunday School and she was in her element in the class, you know, quite proud of herself and sort of joining in with all the other children cos that was the first time that I had seen her like that, you know. You'd [to Elizabeth] maybe seen her at play-group or that but em, I hadnae really seen her up until Sunday, taking part in anything just herself, you know. I enjoyed seeing her.
>
> *Elizabeth:* Cos I said to Roy 'just look, I bet she'll not go up for her prize'. You see, this is it, where you can be so wrong about them. (F)

Images were also formed in the context of how *others* perceived the children. Most of the parents, however, felt it difficult to answer the direct question 'how do you think other people see your children?' except in the most general terms. About a third of them said that, in any case, they either did not *care* what others thought of their children, or else were only concerned about the opinions of *valued* outsiders. This, however, was where a semi-structured multi-interview methodology proved its worth and elicited much more valuable information than had the simple direct question. Throughout my meetings with the couples they, in fact, *frequently* referred to other people's remarks about their children. This was especially the case with the mothers. It is not being suggested that this kind of contextualising activity had a clear-cut *direct* effect on respondents' images of their children. There was, however, such a distinct awareness in this respect that some indirect reassessment or confirmation of images was undoubtedly taking place. In terms of my analytical perspective this can be seen as an important way of sustaining belief in their images. When an image was perceived to be confirmed by outsiders, this enhanced its subjective satisfaction. A simple example was that I was told by three different couples that their child was kind and thoughtful. They all substantiated this by relating how the playgroup leader had told them that *their* child was always the one who took a newcomer under his/her wing. Equally, if the parents heard of any behaviour defined as violent or odd, this generally led to considerable reflection about the child.

Two somewhat contradictory sets of images of children were, in

fact, being held concurrently. On one hand, these parents generally placed a high value on developing individuality and originality in the child. On the other hand, they also expressed an
awareness that the child would have to make its own way in wider
society and face any problems which might result from its
'individuality', increasingly without themselves as buffers. Either
explicitly or implicitly, they acknowledged that outsiders had no
reason to understand and accept the child in the same way as did
the parents.[4] It would appear, therefore, that a degree of
sensitivity to the opinion of outsiders was, for these respondents,
one of the ingredients of parenthood. This had subtle, indirect
effects on their images of children and parental behaviour.

An example of this kind of process was given by Madeleine
Harris. Their position was particularly sensitive in this respect
since they were the only non-British family in the sample. They
talked at one stage about their awareness of differences in
manners and conventions, such as terms of address. Madeleine
spoke as follows about people's reactions to her elder child's
calling them by their christian names:

> Well, I suppose she could pick up Auntie whatever, but I think
> that it would be so strange she wouldn't bother about it. As I
> say, this kind of thing. It's more a matter of behaviour and also I
> think in some sense I feel sometimes that people feel that they're
> typical wild American children, you see, no manners, this sort
> of thing. And sometimes it hurts because I don't want it to carry
> over to the children in how they're accepted or rejected, but
> there again I don't WANT to stress these things. (F)

(b)   Temporal contextual images

Respondents not only made sense of their children by considering
everyday, ongoing social contexts, they also developed images
which referred to their own previous parental actions. The most
frequent instance of this has already been discussed. This was
where parents formed images of their children's current
behaviour as being contingent on their own inexperienced
treatment of them at an earlier stage.[5] John Clark said, for
example:

I think to begin with, we probably gave in too easily, this is what did the trouble, whereas now we're trying to stop it because it was just getting to the stage that, as soon as she went out the door, she'd start whining until she came back in again and she'd still be whining. (I)

Similarly, parents sometimes related an item of their child's behaviour to something which they had unthinkingly said. This area of images tended to be forward as well as backward looking. The main underlying reason for not mentioning certain subjects in front of the child was that it might have some deleterious effect on him/her in future years. (Here again was a projected abstract image.) Even when their children were still quite young, some of the parents related their behaviour occasionally to a previous parental remark, now perceived as unfortunate.[6] The Harris's gave a good illustration of this in their final interview. Madeleine said about her elder child:

Mostly any SERIOUS talk we had about them was after they were in bed or some such thing but, you know, often we would say something to each other about them, or remark about something that they had done, while they were still around. But she was OBVIOUSLY, you know, becoming very aware not only of what she was doing but of OUR reaction to what she was doing, [*K.B.:* Was she?] and began to, you know, size it up and em . . . as I'm saying, the kind of self consciousness that I wouldn't like to see happen too much. (F)

This quotation also again highlights the interpretative activities of parents. Here Madeleine Harris related the development of self-consciousness in her daughter to some chance overhearing of occasional comments. The Harris's accorded legitimacy to this 'understanding'. Subsequently they altered their communication process, by becoming very much more careful about what they said in front of their daughter.

Images of the child related to temporal contexts were also formed in a much more immediate way. All of the parents related their attitude to the child, and the child's attitude to them, to the amount of time which they had together. Three main ways in which temporal factors affected images of the child were constantly mentioned. Firstly, that at the stage of very young children, the mother was perceived as having to spend too much time with them. The beneficial effects of each having an occasional break from the other were frequently mentioned. Judy Davies felt, for instance, that one effect of being constantly with the child was the undermining of the pleasures of the relationship. She said about her three year old son, Robert:

> I think we generally get on quite well together, we enjoy each other and, I think I'm enjoying him much more now that he's sort of off my hands more, you know, I'm having time during the day to watch him, just quietly when I'm doing things. (I)

Secondly, it was frequently remarked that, during the week, the father had very little time with the children, and that this led to his having a different kind of relationship with them from that of the mother. This point will be elaborated upon in Chapter 8. The main point to be made here, however, is that respondents often related aspects of the father's images of children to this temporal context. Thirdly, distinctions were made between quantitative and qualitative temporal contexts. This was usually expressed by contrasting 'passing time' (which implied simply mutual co-presence) and the more active 'spending time' (which implied more dynamic interaction). Here we can see a further example of the social definitions of time. [7] The meanings attached to time, as opposed to the quantifications of time per se, were vital factors involved in the negotiation of parental behaviour. All of the parents in my group operated with the underlying assumption that a child needed to have time actively 'spent' on him/her in the way of specially focussed attention. They saw this as very different from simply being with the child and 'passing' time. They frequently said, however, that the simple rigours of everyday living led them to neglect this perceived need. Kathy Hislop said of a neighbour who gave a lot of time to playing with her baby:

> She seems to be very patient and obviously devotes time to Gillian, which I envy because I felt when mine were that age they should have had more time devoted to them, but, I was just never in the frame of mind, well not NEVER, but, didn't feel in the frame of mind to do it [laughs]. I'm only glad now that mine don't NEED so much time devoted you know, to teaching them, showing them things, because they can do it themselves. (F)

Simplistically, this third point can be related to the previous two as follows. Most respondents claimed that the quantitative limitations on the father's time with the children meant that, in effect, he consciously gave them his attention and 'spent time' with them when it *was* available. (This, at any rate, was how they felt the situation *should* be!) On the other hand, the mothers tended to feel that *their* time was *not* so clearly delineated and that it took a sort of conscious effort to 'spend' as opposed to 'pass' time with their children. Helen Moffat commented:

I think your child deserves your whole undirected attention, it might just be for ten minutes, but for PART of each day that it's just you and she doing something, well not even doing something, or talking. (I)

Some of the ways in which mothers created a belief for themselves that they *did* 'spend time' with their child are discussed in the following chapter.

Lastly, by far the most frequently implemented temporal contextual images of the child related to notions of phases and stages. For all of these couples such images seemed to constitute a range of understandings of their child which provided a very high level of subjective reassurance. In the interview situation, the basic procedure was that they tended to focus on an item of the child's behaviour (usually something viewed as problematical) and then they resolved it subjectively by maintaining that it was a non-permanent phenomenon. This was done in two main ways. On the one hand the particular item of behaviour was defined as a temporary manifestation common to most children or 'well known' in child development. Dianne Hemingway said, for example, of her 18 month old daughter:

Joanne, she's still quite clingy to me, but I think there's a lot of children her age are. (I)

On the other hand, the behaviour was seen as a temporary attribute of that one particular child in the context of his/her ongoing development. Shirley Jackson said, for example, about Elaine:

Her temper tantrums are getting less [laughs] which is because she's not so frustrated. I think most of her temper tantrums before were coming from the sheer frustration of not being able to do what the [others], because it was always older children that she played with, and not being capable of doing what THEY were doing. And I think most of the temper tantrums stemmed from that. (F)

Whichever way the behaviour was defined, the process could be seen as another way of making sense of the child. Simplistically, certain items of behaviour were being assessed in order to decide whether or not parental intervention was required and, if so, what form it should take. By forming images of the child which related items of behaviour to this temporal context, respondents were coping quite effectively with the vast uncertainties involved in parental behaviour. By defining behaviour as a phase or stage they could either feel justified in simply 'riding the storm', or else reassure themselves that any interventions were merely palliative gestures in an inevitable course of events.

Some further comments are necessary about this process. Firstly, although a few respondents had actually read about theories of child development, the majority based their images on vague and impressionistic information. In many ways this lack of formal knowledge was a great subjective advantage because it enabled these parents to develop very flexible ideas about the ages at which certain phases were supposed to occur. Dianne Hemingway, for example, was quite happy with the following images of her younger daughter, Joanne:

But if you speak to other parents of three year olds, *well Joanne's at the age now, one and a half*, they're all terribly irritating cos they're at, what do they call them, the negative age. (W/E) [my emphasis]

Another example came from Hannah Gilchrist, who felt that the fact that her three year old needed a light in her bedroom was nothing to worry about. She explained:

I think this is a phase children go through because em I see this house across here, em, their hall light's on all night. Their boys are five; and a friend of mine that has twin boys, their light's to be left on and they're four. (W/E)

Such an open-ended definition of phases gave parents considerable leeway in deciding whether or not positive action was necessary. The Mitchells' problems with their elder child, Rachel,
provided a good illustration of this. After a considerable time of
seeing her difficulties as a phase, they eventually decided to seek
outside advice about her clinginess and behavioural upsets. They
reflected on their previous reasonings as follows:

Alice: Well mainly we'd let it ride because I felt sure that
time, time would cure it. [*Ray:* Mmmhmm] But as time
hadn't seemed to make a GREAT deal of difference, and em I
knew she was YOUNG and so on.

Ray: You were getting a bit screwed up about it that was all.

Alice: Yeah, but well, em, I expect if in ANOTHER year it
was STILL as bad, we'd take more advice and so on. (W/E)
[Interestingly the specialist's advice was to regard the problem behaviour as a phase!]

A second relevant point is that everyday parental behaviour
was constantly grounded in ongoing interpretations of the child's
behaviour as being either a facet of his/her personality, or simply a
phase or stage (or sometimes both). The Johnsons, for example,
had the following discussion about five year old Nicola:

Barbara: She's priggy, she doesn't like certain sorts of
disorder, and if she sees, I don't mean PHYSICAL disorder
though, I mean people not conforming to the rules and
things. [*Ian:* Yes] She's a very self-righteous person and if
she sees people em, which she sees often because her brother
is SO different from her, she gets very indignant and out-
raged and upset in general.

Ian: It's perhaps partly to do with her age though, because
kids of that age tend to be a bit priggish. [Barbara agreed]
(Jt)

Such a facility of being able to understand behaviour by seeing
it as a phase or stage seemed to be acquired primarily through
experience. Here again we see the practical implementation of
underlying assumptions that family life is a learned reality. As
discussed earlier. respondents tended to look back on their initia-
tion into parenthood as being characterised by an over-attention

to the slightest whimper.[8] It seemed, to a certain extent, that such a preoccupation with the quirks of one particular child gradually lessened as parents became more confident in forming contextual images such as phases or stages. This ability to see the child in a wider context led most couples, by the time of my fieldwork, to claim that they had developed a less fraught and somehow more resigned general view of the child's development. They tended to talk about this in two main ways. Sometimes, they referred back to their reactions to their first child and commented on how they were now reacting differently with the second. Colin Duncan gave a good illustration when talking about his reactions to his younger child Sarah. He said:

> *Colin:* You realise right away that, it must just be this age band that she's in you know, why she's reacting like this, or acting like this. And em, we DO tend to treat some of her, och I call them problems, differently you know. Cos you know it'll only be a wee while and she'll grow out of it. And we learnt this from Alistair, [elder child] but unfortunately [laughs] he got the rows.
>
> *Mary:* Just lack of experience. (F)

At other times, parents simply made general statements about the inevitability of both problematical and pleasant phases in their children. John Clark made a fairly typical statement in his first interview when he said about being a mother:

> I suppose you've definitely gotta be a bit of a psychologist yourself, try your best to, by whatever means you have, to help the children to grow up happy. But er, it's a losing battle, I think, because whenever you think you've found the answer to whatever ails them, it just starts all over again. (I)

(c)   Genealogical contextual images

Another way in which the parents in my group made sense of their children was to put them into the context of their own person-alities and lives. At an early point in the fieldwork respondents were asked to describe the ways in which their children were like or unlike themselves and their spouses. Reactions to this question varied. Most of the respondents gave their replies without challenging whether or not this was a valid frame of reference for them. Of these, a few related a large number of intricate points of similarity and dissimilarity. The majority of this group, however, (about half of the total sample) simply explained one or two points which they spontaneously felt to be relevant. By and large, people saw their children as having physical and personality points of similarity to and difference from *both* parents. Five couples, however, (each spouse independently of the other), said that they perceived one or both of their children as having many facets which strongly resembled one or other of the spouses. The Johnsons were one of these couples who identified strong likenesses. Barbara said for example:

> You see I'm a very jealous person, feel CONSUMED with jealousy sometimes. And it's a horrible feeling, and I realise now in Nicola, you know, see it in Nicola that I was jealous as a child too and that she's SO like me I can't BEAR it for her because you make yourself very unpopular and very em, very unattractive (W/E)

Interestingly, however, it must be noted that even if spouses agreed that such strong likenesses existed, their interpretations of these images did not necessarily lead to similar parental behaviour. Ian Johnson gave a hint of this when he said:

> I think Barbara feels despondent because she's, Nicola's so like HER in temperament so she can see, em, she sees all the worst side of it. Whereas I, I just don't take as gloomy a view, don't know why. (W/E)

On this particular point the Johnsons provided a typical example of the negotiation of parental behaviour. They agreed that Nicola's temperament was like that of her mother but constantly debated how, as parents, they should react to the child. Ian evaluated the 'problems' of the particular temperament as being less serious than did Barbara. The eventual way in which each 'managed' the child was the outcome of this interactive and evaluative process. They agreed that Ian usually 'dissolved' the tense situations between mother and daughter which arose when Barbara was defined as over-reacting to her daughter's temperament.

The reactions of the relatively few respondents who expressed
reservations about the 'like self/or spouse' question were, in themselves, interesting. Two people simply said that they found it
difficult to describe such things because they just did not think
about the child in that way, seeing him/her as an independent
individual. Another respondent maintained that she could only
answer the question with reference to her spouse, because she was
able actually to observe him and the children. She felt that it was
impossible for an individual to perceive him/herself sufficiently
accurately to make personal comparisons with his/her children.
Six respondents qualified their replies by saying that they would
describe those characteristics which seemed to be childlike
manifestations of the adult concerned. People who said this then
tended to make comparisons by referring to what they *thought* they
and their spouses had been like as children. Finally, two respondents claimed that it was impossible to compare a child with an
adult because their personalities were at such different stages of
development. Many of these reactions were thus implicitly based
on the abstract image that children were different from adults.[9]

Thus a few respondents had some reservations about forming
understandings of children by referring to the personalities of the
parents. Despite this, however, during the course of the interviews
it was apparent that these respondents also tended, in practice, to
implement such images if other ways of making sense of the child
were not proving satisfactory. The essential differences within this
group of parents were not so much that some people avidly embraced such genealogical contextualisations and others did not,
but rather that some felt them to be more subjectively satisfying
understandings than did others.

IV   SUMMARY

In this chapter I examined some of the 'grounded' images of their
children which respondents developed in the course of their
everyday parental experience. Such images were particularly
powerful factors behind parental behaviour since they reflected
respondents' views that family life was a learning and changing
situation.

Firstly, I looked at these parents' 'comparative' images of their children. It was evident that the structural fact of having *two* children to bring up affected parental behaviour towards each individual child. For example, the way in which parents 'made sense' of their child and its behaviour was affected by whether he/ she was first or second born. Examination of another group of comparative images showed that parental behaviour towards one of the siblings was affected by an awareness of the relationship between the two children themselves. Thus, images of the two children were being formed by seeing the behaviour of each within the context of the other. For instance, parents used their ideas about one sibling as a standard from which to judge the other.

Secondly, parents developed detailed understandings of each individual child. These I called 'contextual' images. They made sense of their child by placing him/her and his/her behaviour in the context of overlapping sets of social situations: the particular social situation immediately involved; the family situation; and the wider social context. Parents also formed 'temporal' images by locating the child and its behaviour in the context of previous events. Finally they developed 'genealogical' images which involved seeing their children in the context of their own personalities and lives.

All of the images of children discussed in the previous two chapters were regularly used in the negotiation and legitimation of parental behaviour. However, up to this point in the book, I have made only passing reference to the distinction between the parental behaviour of the spouses. In fact, despite respondents' claims to a degree of equality in parental roles, the interviews revealed some fundamental differences between motherhood and fatherhood. It is to this I now turn in the following chapters.

7 Being a Mother

I INTRODUCTION

It is often claimed that in recent years there has been a trend towards greater equality between men and women in family role behaviour. Although there have undoubtedly been considerable developments in social attitudes towards the position of women generally, my study casts doubts on the extent of real change in the organisation of family responsibilities.

In this chapter and the next I examine the pictures of motherhood and fatherhood which emerged from the couples' accounts of their normal daily lives. The development of parental behaviour is treated as a reality continuously being negotiated by family members. The underlying assumptions and images of children described in earlier chapters are crucial factors in this process, since, it is argued, they play an important part in blocking any radical alterations in parental roles.

The majority of the couples in fact themselves maintained that being a mother and being a father were essentially similar activities. However, as they talked about their family lives, it became evident that whilst these couples were concerned to sustain their belief in mutual involvement with the children, they were in effect describing two very different kinds of parenthood. Those developments which *were* taking place in these families were concerned more with sustaining such beliefs about joint parenthood, rather than actually constituting practical attempts to create objectively equal arrangements.

It is important to remember that the following discussion deals with one particular stage in the family life cycle. All of the families had at least one child of pre-school age. The respondents themselves held the underlying assumption that their family lives would change since they viewed being a parent as a dynamic situation which altered with the changing contexts of the family life cycle.[1]

The main factor characterising respondents' perceptions of being a mother with pre-school children was her greater commitment, at this stage, to childrearing. In this chapter I concentrate mainly on the meanings attached by the couples to this 'objective fact'. Such meanings resulted in rather different precepts behind the negotiation of maternal and paternal behaviour. I group respondents' views of being a mother into three main categories: (1) context, (2) knowledge and (3) responsibility and availability. Most attention is devoted to 'context' since this seemed to be the most important set of meanings. 'Knowledge' and 'responsibility and availability' are more or less corollaries of this main point. Again, it must be stressed that in everyday life these categories were by no means as distinct as my analysis suggests. Also, although all of the parents made reference to these meanings during the interviews, this was done with varying degrees of explicitness.

II CONTEXT

During the interviews husbands and wives frequently commented, favourably or critically, on one another's parental behaviour. However, such exchanges were often qualified by the acknowledgment that *individual patterns of behaviour were being developed in the context of differing overall relationships with the child*. No matter how great was the father's involvement in backstage negotiation, it was the mother who was predominantly in the front line in the ongoing childrearing activity. The mother's greater time commitment meant that, at this stage, she and the child had to relate to each other through the full gamut of events of every working day. Much of the present chapter focusses on the meanings attached by parents to this basic situation. In the following sections I examine the issues of discipline and the division of labour to illustrate how the different contexts in which mothers and fathers related to their children affected their parental behaviour.

(a) Disciplining children: an example

The importance of the different contexts in which maternal and paternal behaviour were being developed was often taken-for-granted until problematical issues arose. One such issue was the disciplining of children. What respondents actually *meant* by the term 'discipline' was, in itself, very varied and complex. Simplistically, two main views of the concept of discipline seemed to exist concurrently. Firstly, disciplining involved teaching the child ideas about 'right and wrong', as each parent defined it, and enforcing these by means of varying punishments. Couples saw this as being for the benefit of the parents as much as for the children. One respondent referred to it as 'civilising' the children and making it possible to live with them. Often this view was legitimated by reference to images of children such as their defined needs for 'boundaries'.[2] Secondly, it was seen to involve encouraging the child to develop an internal 'sense' of discipline, *self* discipline. By this respondents meant fostering the growth of a certain rational and reflective awareness of self and others. Projected images of the child were often put forward to support this view.[3] These parents tended to see 'reason' and 'example' as the mean ways of instilling this awareness. As Helen Moffat argued:

> . . . all discipline is finding your own discipline, isn't it? I mean if children haven't got their own discipline, it doesn't matter what external disciplines are imposed on them, they're going to rebel. But if they've got a sort of reasoning in them that this is a sensible thing to do and I've got other people to think of not just myself, well, I think this is important. (I)

Before embarking on the main part of the discussion it is important to note the overall picture of the disciplinary activity of parents which emerged from the interviews. The mother was presented as the main agent of discipline in the child's life. Judy Davies' view of being a mother was typical in this respect. She commented:

> I think [she has] more parental control than the father because the mother's with the children an awful lot more than the father is. (I)

Although most of these parents mentioned disciplining as constituting an important feature of 'being a father', no-one suggested that this should be put aside as *his* responsibility. In fact the notion of 'wait till your father comes home' was frequently abhorred. Rather, it was defined as important simply that the father supported the supposedly mutually agreed line, and reinforced discipline on important matters.

The meanings behind these views can be examined on two levels. Firstly, respondents themselves emphasised that the constant presence of the mother meant that she was *inevitably* the main disciplinarian. The Gilchrists, for example, discussed 'being a mother' during their joint interview. Hannah said:

> I think it's a lot more involved than a father. I mean, for half an hour each night when you come in, you can hardly teach her what's right and what's wrong, cos at that time of night she's tired and she's ready for bed and *she's a different child anyway*. (Jt) [my emphasis]

Several respondents pointed out that it would be practically impossible for the father effectively to lay down rules about disciplining if the mother did not wish to abide by them. It seemed, however, that the fathers were very much involved in the backstage negotiation of disciplinary behaviour. Ian Johnson said, for example, that he found it difficult at times to support Barbara because he felt that she was too harsh in her methods. Although he used the coping mechanisms of the 'attribution of permanency' to alleviate the tensions of his critical feelings,[4] he also exerted pressures on her to modify her behaviour, as the following quotation illustrates. He explained:

> I disapprove of this but she keeps saying well this is the way she IS, and she HAS these great mood swings. I think she's a very good mother in lots of ways, she does a lot FOR them and she's a very loving mother. And I think, well, if that's the way she is, well, even though I don't like it, I reckon I'll have to sort of put up with it. Well, what I do is, if she goes on a bit too far I try and make her feel guilty like I did with this dislocation thing. [Barbara had dislocated Thomas's arm by pulling him away from something too roughly.] If I'd been a perfect husband I'd have said 'well, just forget about it, it was an accident, don't blame yourself'. But I tended to be a bit reproving and I was rather cross about the whole thing: just to make it sink into her a

bit more that she IS a bit too rough with them. (I)

Secondly, the *overt* rejection of the father as the main disciplinarian can be seen as another aspect of sustaining belief in mutual
involvement with the children. As will be shown in Chapter 8,
couples employed many tactics to sustain this belief. In line with
this argument, it would have been perceived as detrimental to the
father-child relationship which they were attempting to create if
they defined the child as seeing the father principally as an agent
of discipline. As Martin Chapman remarked:

> So I'm not seen [by the children] as an ogre, you know, 'wait till
> your father comes in' sort of thing or 'wait till I tell your father'.
> We don't carry that policy out so, I don't have to BE an ogre,
> except when it's necessary when I'm there at the time. (Jt)

The couples in my group saw disciplining children as a particularly sensitive area of behaviour. They gave frequent instances
of disagreements between themselves. I would suggest that disagreements were perceived as especially problematical because
they threatened the image that the child *needed* consistent parental
behaviour.[5] Analysis of these disagreements (both reported and
witnessed), showed the complexity of meanings being negotiated
behind each disciplinary act. Spouses argued with one another
about many aspects of the disciplinary process including, for
example: (i) the method of discipline, (ii) the choice of behaviour
worth disciplining, (iii) interpretations of the child's reactions to
each parent's disciplinary behaviour and (iv) interpretations of
the context in which the 'misbehaviour' took place. Each of these
sets of meanings will be introduced and discussed in this chapter.
Examples (i), (ii) and (iii) are treated as most relevant to the
section on 'context', whereas example (iv) is incorporated into the
next section entitled 'knowledge'.

(i)   *Methods*

Legitimations of the disciplinary methods of the mother, whether
these were perceived as harsher or more lax than those of the
father, were often related to their overall context. Mary Clark
said, for example:

If Louise does something naughty I SHOUT, and John says I
don't treat her nicely. So I used to flare up, and the usual *you
don't know what it's like having a child from 6 o'clock in the morning till 7
o'clock at night* AND up through the night. You NEVER had to
get up through the night. (I) [my emphasis]

Roy Vaughan also reacted against his wife's occasional severity
towards their elder daughter, but again felt that this had to be seen
within the context of their total day together. He explained:

She's got the children all day and maybe I'll come in at night
and she'll tell Jenny 'go through there now', sort of in a quick
voice. And I could maybe say 'dinna talk to her like that'. But I
don't because I realise *she's had them all day* and you don't know
what's happened during the day you know. (I) [my emphasis]

Several husbands felt that their wives were not strict enough
with the children. They defined their *own* attempts to invoke
discipline as more successful because they were more forceful, or
more consistent, in their methods. Again, the wives tended to
counter their husbands' arguments by putting forward a contextual legitimation. The Burns's, for example, had the following
argument during their final interview:

Carol: But they get so, *seeing me every twenty four hours or whatever,*
it's just this constant voice coming at them 'don't do this,
don't do that'. It just rubs off, they don't even look at me now.
[my emphasis]

Eric: But that's cos you don't mean it. [laughs]

Carol: You know, I mean it as well as I CAN, but you know,
you're asking me to do the impossible. [*Eric:* Not really]
Then YOU'RE not taking your part in their disciplining.

Eric: Well they do it when *I* tell them to do it but I have a bit of
difficulty sometimes because they're so conditioned by it.

Carol: It's IMPOSSIBLE, Eric.

Eric: No it's not impossible, it's traumatic initially [laughs]
I'm sure.

Carol: For everyone, you know.

Eric: More especially for YOU, more especially for you than
them. (F)

Unlike Carol Burns, who would not concede that Eric's methods were any better than her own, Dianne Hemingway felt that her husband was much better able to deal with her elder daughter's moody behaviour. She saw Alan as firmer than herself and more determined to be 'in control'. He replied that he simply practised 'diversionary tactics' to get his own way with the child. Dianne, however, felt that, in the everyday course of events, she seldom had the time to apply such methods. She said:

> If I'm doing nothing else, you know, if I've got a few hours that I'm dealing specifically with them, I WILL go out of my way to take her mind off it. But if I'm working to a tight schedule, you know, I have to be out at a certain time and I've got to do this n' that before I go out, I just, there isn't time. (W/E)

In these ways, negotiation of the mother's disciplinary methods acknowledged that her reactions to the child took place in a different context from those of the father. This was in part, I suggest, because the amount of time, and the context within which she related to the child, led to the development of different images of children. Several mothers for example described how they 'enjoyed' the children more when they saw less of them. Meanings attached to the different contexts were also illustrated by accounts of the alterations in the *father's* disciplinary methods when he was placed in what was perceived as a similar situation.[6] It was often mentioned, for instance, that fathers changed their attitudes towards disciplinary methods when *they* had to deal with the children for full days, either at weekends or on holiday. Martin Chapman said:

> I maybe see them [his children] for about half an hour in the morning, at the most two hours at night. So I see them for about two and a half hours a day from Monday to Friday, so I'm bound to have a very lenient attitude with them. But it's different when I'm here all day. If we're cooped up in the house, you know, if it's a day when we can't get out. (W/E)

Here Martin acknowledged that he had a different image of the children's 'misbehaviour' dependent on the amount of time spent in their presence, and on the environment in which they were relating to one another.

Several other fathers also maintained that they were less patient with the children, and much quicker to reprimand rather than persuade, at these times. James Gilchrist, for example, had been much criticised by Hannah for his 'soft' attitude to their elder daughter and his inability to smack her. Towards the end of the fieldwork, however, he found himself at home for a few weeks between jobs. During this time he was much more sensitive to Susan's misbehaviour, and began to reprimand her more frequently and more severely. Ben Pringle found that *he* became much more erratic in this disciplining of his daughters when he was with them for full days. He and Sheila had the following conversation when Sheila remarked that she was pleased to hear him say, '*on record*', that he *too* could be erratic. She felt that he usually maintained that it was *she* who was the failure in this respect. Ben replied:

Ben: No, well if I HAVE said it was you, it's for your own good, and the fact that you have had to, you know, look after them throughout the day. And you keep sort of er, you DO keep sort of asking me 'where the hell am I going wrong?' and 'why do they exhaust me so?' And I try and point out to you the fact that you must, you know, you must be less erratic in your treatment of them. But this doesn't eradicate ME from blame because I'm just as bad.

Sheila: But you shouldn't be because you don't see them for as long as I do.

Ben: No, but I mean when I've had them for a whole day. (Jt) [my emphasis]

(ii) *Definitions of behaviour worth disciplining*

Thus it can be argued that, in the negotiation of disciplinary methods, it was taken-for-granted that the mother acted in a different context from the father. Implicit in this was the assumption that methods differed according to the amount of time spent with the child. Disciplining children also involved decisions about which aspects of behaviour merited a reprimand. Respondents frequently maintained, for example, that the mother had gradually become accustomed to not noticing every little 'misbehaviour' of the child. They said that the mother simply did not have the time or the energy to deal with *every* issue. Many of the fathers were presented as more likely to focus on these 'little things', and to take more forceful stands over issues which the mothers had decided to ignore.

For the Jacksons, Wilsons and Moffats, one such issue was behaviour at table. All three couples related their disagreements on this matter to the differing perspectives from which the mothers approached the problem. Not only did the mothers have to face the situation more frequently, but they also saw it as of minor importance compared with the many other behavioural problems with which they constantly dealt. In my terms, the mother's perspective also differed because she was better able to develop subjectively satisfactory contextual images of the child's behaviour. She defined the behaviour as less problematical because she had wider direct experience than did the fathers of the similar behaviour of other children.[7] Louise Wilson described their own particular situation in the following way. Speaking about Nick she said:

> . . . in some ways I think he's stricter, well he's just less used to your own children, this is basically what it is. I think he in some ways expects more of them than I would ever expect them to do. You know, their bad table manners annoy me but they IN-FURIATE him. [*K.B.* Do they?] Oh, he can't eat with them. And he certainly does hit them a lot more for a lot less than I would do, although I certainly smack them. I think in general he tends to be a lot harder with them physically than I would be, but then every other husband I've seen has done this. (I) [Note coping mechanism at the end.]

Helen Moffat said that she had become so used to the noise at table that she was able to ignore it. She described, however, a recent row where George had become furious with the children over this issue. In her terms, this was because he had been working away from home for a few evenings and, on his return, the noise had seemed even more oppressive than usual to him because it was less familiar.

(iii) *Interpretations of the child's reactions*

A further way in which couples attached meanings to the different context in which the mother's disciplinary behaviour was developed was by reference to the child's reactions. Here parents constructed temporal contextual images of children to legitimate their actions.[8] They 'made sense' of the child's perceived different reactions to the mother's disciplinary efforts from those of the father by relating them to the amount of time which each spent with the child. However, although such images were *usually* put forward to legitimate the greater obedience obtained by the father, some respondents also used them to legitimate the opposite situation.

As will be elaborated further in the following chapter, the couples in my group maintained that the unequal amount of time spent with the child led to his/her perceiving each parent differently. They constructed images that, for example, the child perceived the father's authority in a different way from the mother's. The actual exercise of this authority was also held to have a different subjective meaning to the child. Alan Hemingway felt, for instance, that the child had more opportunities to learn about the mother's reactions compared with the father's. He used this image to legitimate his greater success in getting their younger daughter to go to bed. He explained:

> My thoughts are that she thinks of me as a bit more strict, and she HAS to go to bed for me. I know that probably won't last but she knows, probably because she's had more chances of getting round Dianne, she can do that. She's not really had the chance with me yet. (W/E)

Helen Moffat expanded this kind of point further when she maintained that the regularity of the mother's discipline ultimately resulted in its having less emotional meaning to the child. She said:

> If HE's cross, if I'M cross with her it's just 'oh', you know, mummy again, but if HE says anything she's heartbroken. (I)

By contrast Elizabeth Vaughan, Hannah Gilchrist and Alice Mitchell all felt that their husbands' disciplinary efforts made less impact on the child than did their own. Their husbands agreed with this view, and either said that they thought this unimportant or that the mother was *inevitably* more influential in the childrear-

ing processes. These alternative images of the child's different
perceptions of his/her parents' discipline relate to my earlier
observation that respondents defined the mother as the main
agent. These three respondents said that their children took little
notice of their fathers' discipline because they were not with them
enough to be trained in this way. Also, they constructed an image
of the child as having learnt to perceive the mother's methods as
punishment. The more lenient approach of these three fathers was
defined by their wives as ineffective. They all maintained that the
children either ignored or defied their fathers' disciplinary efforts.
Elizabeth Vaughan said that Jenny would obey *her*:

> . . . probably because she knows that if she doesn't em, I'll give
> her a good smacking, which her daddy doesn't do. I could say
> he's only done it a couple of times, em, I've maybe had to say to
> him 'for goodness sake give her a smacking'. So I think she
> knows that she'll get away with it, so she doesn't seem to pay
> much attention. (I)

Hannah Gilchrist felt that, in some ways, the different contexts
in which the child related to the father impeded his attempts to
discipline. Like most of the other parents she emphasised that, in
the lesser time the father spent with the child, he was seen by him/
her as 'fun'. James agreed, but said that he still felt that, as a
father, discipline was an area in which he *should* be involved.
Hannah replied:

> But it's difficult really because you can only be involved at the
> weekend and *at the weekend you're there and it's a game*. If you take
> them swimming it's a special treat and anything you do is, you
> know SPECIAL. But every day a mother's got to be there and
> teach her right from wrong. (Jt) [my emphasis]

To a certain extent the images of the child's reactions which
these three mothers developed highlighted the ways in which the
rest of the couples were maintaining belief in *mutual* involvement as
parents. In the negotiation processes they too acknowledged that
the mother, being the main agent, had greater overall control over
the ways in which the child was disciplined. Barbara Johnson
said, for example:

She's a bit of an anxious child, possibly because we've been fairly severe with her. And yet we've, well of course ME mostly, and Ian's agreed. I THINK he's agreed, whether he's done it for the sake of peace I don't know, i.e. followed my general sort of trends. It's usually the mother that does most of the disciplining anyway. (I)

I would suggest that one way in which this view of the mother's greater influence and involvement could be modified was by parents constructing an image that the father's disciplinary acts, although objectively fewer, had nevertheless a greater subjective effect on the child. The Johnsons also illustrated this attribution of meaning when they discussed the matter during their joint interview. Barbara said:

Barbara: I feel that a child will probably respect in the final analysis the father's authority above the mother's authority because the mother [pause].

Ian: Well because he exercises it less frequently.

Barbara: Yes. The child, I think children in general see the mother as less authoritarian.

(b) The division of labour: an example

A second illustration of the way in which respondents saw maternal behaviour as being developed in a different context came from their accounts of the division of labour. As will be elaborated in the next chapter, fathers were only very infrequently placed in the position of concurrently managing children and ongoing household matters.[9] This was so even in the case of the most actively involved husbands, who claimed that, when they were at home, they helped out with whatever needed to be done. In fact, this situation usually resulted in the separation and sharing of household and childcare/management tasks. The classic example was the early evening routine. Most couples described how, if both of them were at home, one bathed and dealt with the children whilst the other cleared away the debris of the evening meal. Thus, if the fathers were dealing with childcare, their wives were carrying out the other pressing domestic tasks. This meant that paternal behaviour was usually being carried out in a different overall context from maternal where, most of the time, childcare and domestic tasks were faced concurrently.

My couples' accounts of their division of labour were characterised by the frequent acknowledgement of this different context. Often, for example, wives reminded their husbands of this if they felt that husbands were being in any way critical. Andrew Davies was, for instance, telling me that he was doing much more domestic work since the arrival of their second child. He and Judy then had the following exchange:

> *Andrew:* I spend my day off in the kitchen, that's what *I* do. If I'm not cooking, I'm making up feeds.
>
> *Judy:* And then of course, as *I* say to him, 'well try doing that AND washing, housework, feeding, cooking – you wouldn't last a day.' (W/E)

Similarly, Martin Chapman remarked on how much he *enjoyed* looking after the children and did not find this to be as hard work as Sylvia maintained. Sylvia replied:

> I was just saying that when I DO go out and come back, em, he's always saying how EASY it is to look after the children. But this is because he just looks after them, you know. He's not having to wash dishes and cook and go to the village shopping, WALKING, not by car. You know, if you go into the village it's either a morning wasted or an afternoon wasted. (W/E)

Husbands also made reference to the different contexts in which the wives related to the children. Sometimes they did this directly, using verbal acknowledgement of the wife's more demanding situation as a coping mechanism. Often, however, the reference to the different context was indirect. George Moffat, for example, pointed out jokingly that he was never asked to do the dishes any more. When I asked why, he replied:

> I think it means that if I'm not doing the dishes I've got the kids, you see, jumping all over me or away out for a walk or something. And that lets Helen get them done in half the time, under probably about half the pressure. (I)

The couples perceived the more diffuse interweaving of the

mothers' general housework and childrearing commitments as resulting in difficulties which were not faced so acutely by the *fathers*. Two main problematical areas were mentioned most often. Each can be related to underlying assumptions about family life and images of children. Firstly, being a mother was defined as potentially having considerable implications for the woman's overall personal existence and development. This was not necessarily the case for the man.[10] Here respondents' accounts reflected their assumptions that family life was cyclical; that children were only transient but potentially overpowering family members; and that individuality should not be swamped in the shared reality of family life.

Secondly, and of particular relevance to this section, the mother's situation of having to relate to the child within the context of her other work commitments was perceived as having special problematical features. The main difficulty was that the images of children which were held by these parents involved attaching high priority to understanding them, and interpreting and dealing with their needs and wants. For these couples, therefore, children were *not* beings to be ignored. The other demands of the mother's work situation meant however, that this was an ever present possibility. In addition, respondents' projected images of children led the mothers to be very aware of the degree of priority which they attached to the child in the context of their other work commitments. Here, images of the potential impact of parents' present actions, and the desire for the future friendship of the child, were especially pertinent. Marjorie Russell's statement was typical. She said:

> You're torn between the housework and the children, and ideally the children should always come first. But in practice, if you've got visitors coming that night or something, the housework comes first and the children get left along the line somewhere. But whether this does them any harm or not I don't know. Because if they get TOO much attention, they won't learn to be independent, it's hard to say. (I)

The latter part of this quotation also provides interesting illustration of the use of needs and wants as coping mechanisms. The uncertainties involved in developing parental behaviour, and the many possible ways in which perceived needs and wants could be satisfied in practice, led to the continuous pragmatic selection the most subjectively satisfactory image at any one point in time.

The wives' working days were intimately connected with child-rearing. For these parents this was seen not just as administering everyday physical needs but also as catering for emotional and psychological needs. All of the wives made this latter point, even if this took the form of expressing guilt that they did not accomplish it adequately. Kathy Hislop put forward her view of this dilemma as follows, she explained:

> When you're a housewife you get used to doing certain things in the house and when you become a mother suddenly these have to be put in second place and the children sort of take over in importance to, well to the housework very often. Em, especially when they're younger, and in the winter when they can't get out, can't amuse themselves, and there's ironing to be done and washing to be done. Or, there's things that you would like to do, just for the sake of doing them, in the house, which you can't do because there's a child needing amused. And, because you're a mother you feel that, well the child isn't just THERE. You don't feel that you've done your duty em keeping it in clean clothes, keeping its face clean, feeding it. I think it does involve giving up a certain amount of time to the child and, I suppose, developing some sort of relationship and, well, teaching it. (I)

Like all of the mothers, Kathy maintained that the way to satisfy the emotional and psychological needs of the child was to 'develop a relationship' with him/her. Again, using respondents' terminology, this involved 'giving time to the child'. By this they meant some form of special *directed* attention, such as conversing with the child, teaching, or entertaining him/her. 'Conversing' was perceived as a self-conscious activity focussed directly on the child. This was defined as qualitatively different from the ongoing exchanges intrinsic to child management. Similarly, although by giving up paid employment for a time all of the wives had acknowledged that they would be constantly available to the child, they made further *qualitative* assessment of this 'availability'. Simply to 'be there' was not perceived as adequate in terms of their abstract images of children. 'Being there', although helping to satisfy the child's needs for security and stability, was defined as only a small part of the necessary total relationship.

Paradoxically, it was seen as in some ways easier for the *father* to feel satisfied with the quality of time which *he* gave to the child. Again, the way in which respondents attached meanings to this time was connected with the different contexts in which they saw maternal and paternal behaviour as being developed. The father's 'being with the child' was an activity *separate* from his defined work commitment. In addition, it was objectively less than that of the mother. In many of the families, therefore, the time which he 'gave' to the children was often institutionalised into special 'time with Daddy'. Analytically, this was a further mechanism for sustaining belief in mutual involvement with the children. Although, like the mother, the father might be engaged in activities not even directly related to the child, respondents imbued this 'time' with greater significance. Many, for example, described how the children were encouraged to be with the father after he arrived home in the evenings. They might be in his company when he changed his clothes, sat down to relax, or assisted with some of the evening chores. If the children were with the *mother* in similar circumstances, such 'time' tended to be much more taken-for-granted and not defined as 'given'. As is discussed later in this chapter, respondents constructed images of the children as defining the father differently from the mother.[11] In part such images were the meanings which they defined the *child* as attaching to the different amounts of time which he/she had with each parent.

Some of the wives had developed their own subjectively satisfactory means of sustaining belief that they 'gave time' to their children, despite their current work commitments. Like the fathers, they did this by also institutionalising some time especially for the children. One respondent had a 'minimal housework' day each week, when she devoted her time entirely to the children. Others tried to work into their weekly routine a regular event especially *for* the children, such as a visit to the swimming baths. Here again we can see the importance of gestures as coping mechanisms. It was not the *amount* of time 'given' to the child but the assessment of its quality which was relevant for the maintenance of belief. In this respect some of the wives said that it was important to 'give' just a few minutes each day of direct attention to the child. This might comprise reading a story after lunch, or simply sitting down and conversing with the child. The impression given by most of the wives was, however, that they felt under constant pressure adequately to deal with the many demands of their domestic lives without neglecting this qualitative aspect of childrearing, and vice versa.

The following comment from Mary Clark was typical. Here she was justifying to her husband the fact that she and her elder daughter frequently got on badly with one another. This usually occurred, she maintained, because it was practically impossible adequately to satisfy the child's demands for attention whilst dealing with the household chores. She explained:

> . . . during the day, if I didn't have to do any cooking, or cleaning, or laundry, or ironing then Louise and I would get on quite well together really. The days when I've got nothing to do such as, well yesterday and Wednesday, I'd nothing very much to do, we got on beautifully, there was no problem. I sat and drank cups of dirty water and artificial mince, and there was no problem. But as soon as I stop to do housework then the trouble begins. She comes to the back door and she cries and she lies down on the floor because I can't just drop everything. Every-time I put my hands into water, she WANTS something which, I'm sorry I can't do it. (Jt)

Although this respondent was facing particular difficulties in dealing with her three year old, many other parents described a similar clash of activities. Sometimes mothers succeeded in organising some suitable alternative entertainment for the child whilst they were busy with other things. Most often, however, they tended to feel that they simply concentrated on one area of responsibilities rather than the other, and they expressed guilt if the childrearing aspect was taking second place. (Interestingly, guilt was seldom expressed by those respondents who had decided that 'the house came second'.) A final interesting corollary was that the mothers expressed guilt when they rejected the child's demands for attention. It was, however, perceived as much more legitimate if the fathers came home from work and were too tired adequately to respond to the children.

III KNOWLEDGE

Related to couples' perceptions of the different contexts in which maternal and paternal behaviour was developed were their views that the mother had more extensive knowledge of home and family than did the father. I would suggest that not only was this knowledge viewed as more extensive, but also that the *directness* of its acquisition meant that it was accorded greater legitimacy in the negotiation processes.[12] Here then are further practical interpretations of underlying assumptions about parenthood as a situation of learning, and the high value attached to direct experience. In this section I shall consider some of the ways in which the meanings attached to knowledge affected the development of parental behaviour. The practical contradictions of a belief system which held that parenthood was a learning situation, but also one which was mutually and 'fairly' shared, will again be evident. These contradictions stemmed from the fact that the mother was in a more constant learning situation than was the father. In the family, just as in other social institutions, knowledge implies influence. The mother's greater knowledge and influence in the development of parental behaviour inevitably affected the extent to which it could be seen as 'fairly' shared.

(a) Knowledge and practical childcare

Dealing with the practical aspects of childcare was perceived by these couples essentially as a learned skill. It involved not only knowing *how* to do things for children (abstract images) but also how best to do things for that particular child (grounded images). In an earlier section on comparative images I suggested that the parents developed a greater definitional confidence that they 'knew' how to deal with the second child.[13] Many looked back on their problems with the first child as being due to a lack of knowledge and direct experience. Similar beliefs about knowledge characterised the ongoing division of practical childcare between spouses. Possession or lack of knowledge were frequently put forward to legitimate the mothers' and fathers' activities in this area.

(i) Firstly, mothers were defined as having had greater opportunity to learn the skills of practical childcare. The majority of respondents claimed that mothers were better or quicker at, for example, dressing and undressing children, changing nappies etc., simply because they had had more practice. The physical care of very small children and babies was viewed as especially problematical. Here perceptions of the father's greater size and gaucheness were frequently added to his lesser knowledge to further legitimate the mother's 'superior' childcare ability. Respondents related 'explanatory incidents' of fathers putting on nappies inadequately so that they slipped off.[14] Other incidents were related of fathers perhaps putting odd combinations of clothes on to the children. Stories were also told of fathers 'forgetting' to brush the children's hair, or not taking out ribbons, when they undressed them. Only in two cases were the fathers defined as equally knowledgeable about the overall practical care of small children. Even these two fathers, however, claimed other gaps in their knowledge. They said, for example, that they did not *know* where clean clothes, nappies etc. were kept, and which items of clothing the mother wished the child to use. Ian Johnson said:

> I still tend not to dress the kids unless the clothes are put out because I find when I DO dress them their clothes aren't there, and it takes me a half a bloody hour to find them.

Barbara replied:

> Well that's because you won't find out where they're kept. (W/E)

In part the definition of the mother's greater knowledge of practical childcare stemmed from an initial image of the fragility of small babies. Philip Barber gave one of the many examples of this when he said:

> I mean, there IS a skill in just knowing how to handle a very small baby. It takes a little time to develop it and if you're not in the HABIT of doing it it's, you're not quite so careful or safe as you might be. (I)

As the mothers had been with the babies constantly, they had had to overcome their initial apprehensiveness in this respect. It seemed from respondents' accounts, however, that fathers had had the *choice* of whether or not to attempt the various tasks. Few of the fathers had bathed or dressed the babies regularly. Most, though, had made a token effort which sustained the belief that they *could* do it if they *had* to.[15]

This initial predominance of the mother in practical childcare tended to be self-perpetuating. The usual legitimating procedure was as follows: the mother 'knew' best how to carry out the tasks; therefore she was more efficient than the father; therefore it was in everyone's interests that she should continue. In most of the families, therefore, the wives still continued to dress, or supervise the dressing of both children even when both parents were present. As Elizabeth Vaughan commented:

> I'm always moaning you see that there's three of me. Roy'll come through and say 'well I'm ready then' and I'm just in the middle of getting one of the kids ready. And then I've still got Jenny and then I've got to stick something on myself. (W/E)

Thus the couples in my group defined the mother as having more extensive knowledge of practical childcare. She was perceived as having acquired this essentially through her greater direct involvement with domestic and family matters. This meant that, in many instances when fathers were dealing with childcare, they only carried out *part* of the total task. Mothers continued to be involved in a 'supervisory' capacity. The classic example was the bathing of the children. Although in several families this task was frequently relegated to the fathers, they seldom carried out the *entire* procedure. As Helen Moffat remarked:

> If he's in in the evenings he's quite happy to fling the children in the bath when I'm doing the dishes. *As long as I don't expect him to clean the bath or pick up the children's clothes.* (I) [my emphasis]

(ii) Secondly, dealing with children's practical needs also entailed sustaining belief that the parent 'knew' what the child wanted. This was especially problematical when dealing with a baby who could not communicate verbally. In such a situation of extreme uncertainty several respondents resorted to the belief in a 'maternal instinct' to provide a subjectively satisfactory legitimation of their practical decisions.[16] However, even when their small child was able to communicate verbally spouses continued to interpret and negotiate with one another the validity of these claimed needs. Again, the mother's knowledge was perceived differently from that of the father. Margaret Barber maintained that Philip played a very large part in practical childcare. Nevertheless, during their joint interview, she qualified these views when she said to Philip:

> I dare say that on some matters I would make a decision (about a child's needs) before YOU did. But probably because I knew them, knew certain aspects of them better, I mean their eating habits and so on. (Jt)

The mother's greater time commitment was perceived as enabling her to have a wider fund of direct experience on which to draw when interpreting the child's practical needs. She was also better placed to put forward subjectively satisfactory grounded images of the child to legitimate her behaviour. These were two of the factors which, I would suggest, resulted in her interpretations either being overtly accorded greater legitimacy, or simply in their being tacitly taken-for-granted in the negotiation processes.

Thus the evaluation and attribution of knowledge was one set of meanings being negotiated in the development of parental behaviour. Respondents' accounts indicated that one way in which this affected actual behaviour was that, when several things were happening concurrently in the domestic situation, such as preparing to leave the house together, it was the mother, rather than the father, who tended to carry out the majority of *childcare* activities. Another example was the return home as a family following an afternoon out shopping or visiting. Exceptions to this were those tasks which had been imbued with special significance for sustaining belief in father involvement. Here the concurrent evening tasks provided a typical example. The father was frequently engaged in special tasks for the children, such as bathing them or reading a story. Even in this situation, however, the mother's overall domestic knowledge meant that she tended to continue to be involved, and in overall control.

(b) Knowledge and disciplining

The different meanings attached to the 'knowledge' of the mother were further illustrated when respondents talked about disciplining children. Here I shall take up the final point (iv) concerning the meanings attached to discipline, which was introduced earlier in this chapter. In the development of disciplinary behaviour the definition of 'misbehaviour' was also contextual. The use of comparative and contextual images of children played an important part in this process. The couples in my group saw the mother as better able to make sense of the child in this way since she had wider direct experience. In this section I shall show how the mother's disciplinary behaviour was legitimated in terms both of her greater contextual knowledge of the child, and of her wider experience of success and failure in this respect.

This must first be placed against the background of the parents' accounts of the disciplining process itself. Analytically this can be seen as a direct reflection of underlying assumptions about family life as a shared learning situation. Respondents saw the development of 'successful' disciplining as a process of 'trial and error'. They felt that, not only did the *parents* have to work out effective tactics, but also the *children* had to learn to see such acts as a punishment. Thus the development of subjectively satisfactory disciplining was an ongoing interpretative and negotiated process.

The couples related many instances of trying out a repertoire of parental reactions to the child's misbehaviour. Some said that they had discovered one particular method which they defined as invariably successful. The Johnsons, for example, discovered that they could persuade Thomas to stop misbehaving, or to obey their instructions, by counting up to three. The Coulsons, Robsons and Davies's all maintained that the only effective way to stop 'naughtiness' was to send the child to his/her room. Most parents, however, described how they went through a repertoire of reactions, dependent on their perceptions of the seriousness of the misbehaviour, and on the overall context in which it occurred. Usually they tried methods defined as progressively harsher until the desired end result was felt to have been achieved. Dianne Hemingway said:

> We try explaining, you know, saying 'no you mustn't, no you mustn't' two or three times. Try explaining, and if that doesn't do any good then I just smack her, or smack her and put her out of the room. (W/E)

Occasionally, couples said that none of their disciplinary tactics had any effect. This obviously jeopardised their beliefs that parents should be able to manage and understand their children. At this point they usually, therefore, resorted to coping mechanisms such as 'phase or stage' or 'defining the problem as immutable'.[17] These were put forward to legitimate their stated solutions, which were either simply to live through the problematical behaviour or else to work out how to avoid the inevitably tumultuous scenes. Louise Wilson explained:

> I've tried everything. I've tried bribing her, I've tried being nice to her, I've tried being terribly cruel to her, I've tried shutting her up, I've tried hitting her. And I can truthfully say there's not one thing that makes any difference whatsoever [laughs]. She just sort of comes round in her own time. (W/E)

The mother's more extensive knowledge of these repertoires had two important effects on the development of parental disciplining: (i) firstly, the father approached disciplining the child in the context of the mother's related experiences with him/her; (ii) secondly, his definitions of what constituted 'misbehaviour' were, in part, dependent on knowledge of the ongoing relationship between mother and child.

(i) The father had to take into account the prior 'trials and errors' of the mother. The mother was perceived as the main agent of discipline. This meant that she made the majority of initial definitions of what constituted 'misbehaviour', and also made the initial attempts at remedies. She therefore 'knew' more about the situation, and was often able to 'tell' the father whether or not a projected course of action might succeed. No matter whether the father accepted or rejected the mother's frame of reference, his view of the situation was in part being structured by *her* information. One such typical exchange about disciplining came from the Burns's.

Carol: Everything I say to him [elder child] he contradicts or alternatively ignores it.

Eric: Doesn't do that to me.

Carol: Best of luck to you then because at the moment it's a very trying business.

Eric: It's a bit of a problem getting him to bed and that. I think it's a question of spare the rod (and spoil the child!). I think if you were physically violent to him for a couple of times it would sort him out.

Carol: No, no. I've had that physical violence stage with him when he kept on, you know, doing jobbies in his pants. It doesn't improve anything. (F)

(ii)   Definitions of what actually constituted misbehaviour were also, in part, contextual. In order that the father could fit in with the mutual disciplining of the child, he was reliant on the mother's knowledge of these ongoing contexts. This point is akin to Cicourel's empirical observation that it was almost impossible for a researcher to 'make sense' of the tape-recorded remarks which a mother made to her child during an average morning. This was because many of the remarks were indexical, that is, contained complex references to contexts only experienced by the mother and child.[18]

The mother, at this stage, was involved with the child in more numerous and varied situations than was the father. In this respect her contextual knowledge was much greater. Parents described many instances of the father not 'knowing' that the child was, or was not, allowed to behave in a certain way. This was often simply because this was an arrangement made between mother and child during the day. Similar gaps in the *mother's* knowledge occurred much less frequently. Sylvia Chapman said, for example:

But at the same time, em, if I think that Martin was unjustified in giving her [Anne] a row, I'll say 'oh it was an accident'. Or if he hasn't perhaps seen ALL of what's happened or that, and he'll say 'oh well I didn't know that, I'm sorry'. (W/E)

The Barbers, like all of the other couples in the group, saw their children as being able potentially to exploit such parental incon-sistencies and, as Philip put it, 'to play one of us off against the other.' Respondents' accounts indicated that this occurred very often because the father had inferior contextual knowledge. The Barbers discussed this as follows with reference to their elder daughter:

Philip: It's just that there are sometimes little arrangements that you have with her that I don't know about.

Margaret: Yes, during the day for instance, there might be certain things that I would allow and Philip might have said 'no'. [*Philip:*   And she goes to you, you see.] So in fact there IS a dilemma there because I can't say anything to Karen, I have to say to PHILIP, 'look, she's normally allowed to do so n' so.' But this is just one of the hazards of being an absent father by day. (F)

(c) Implications

In this section I have argued that, at this stage, the mother was perceived as having a larger fund of directly acquired knowledge about the child than did the father. This was taken-for-granted by couples in their negotiation of parental behaviour. The implication of this is that the mother had a subtle influence over the development of the husband's paternal behaviour, since she was his major source of information about the child and its world. In this way the mother was continuously exerting a greater effect on the father's behaviour than vice versa. These effects were manifested in various ways. As was discussed in Chapter 6, the formation of social contextual images of children constituted an important element in the process of understanding and making sense of the child. It seemed that the husbands in the sample saw their wives as having greater opportunities to form valid images, they felt themselves to be less directly 'informed', and therefore tended often to concur with their wives' interpretations of the child.

Frequently this was illustrated by the husband either referring to his wife for some information or conceding that her opinion on some specific issue was likely to be more accurate than was his own. At other times these feelings were presented as a generalised view of the parental process. An example of this was given during the final interview with the Johnsons when they were considering how they had arrived at their ideas about dealing with the children. Their discussion was as follows:

Barbara: I think they just emerged sort of naturally.
Ian: Sort of, em, well I think they probably . . .
Barbara: We didn't have any great sort of think out session did we?

Ian: Well I think they probably emerged through you, [*Barbara:* Yeah] and I was quite happy to acquiesce because YOU were the prime bringer up of the children. [Barbara agrees] I mean inevitably because I'm not here all the time and Barbara, well for the first two or three years of their life, she was here all the time. (F)

Only occasionally was the mother's greater knowledge challenged. This was usually where the father had been accorded some special intuitive knowledge of the child. Sometimes, for example, he was considered to be more 'on the child's wavelength'. Usually, however, the mother's wider experience of the child enabled her to make a more subjectively acceptable legitimation of her decisions or actions.

IV RESPONSIBILITY AND CONSTANT AVAILABILITY

For these couples being a parent involved understanding the child and administering its needs.[19] Their accounts indicated that, at this stage, they defined the mother as taking the greater direct share of this responsibility. Although, as will be discussed in the following chapter, they sustained belief in father *involvement*, it was nevertheless taken-for-granted that the overall everyday *responsibility* lay with the mother. Margaret Barber saw it in the following way, she said to Philip:

The only moment in my life when I feel FREE is when I'm asleep I reckon. [Philip laughs] Because even when someone else is looking after them, with the exception let's say of when you're looking after them, or when Mummy's looking after them. If it's someone else is looking after them, you [I] still feel responsible for them. (Jt)

In this section I shall describe some of the ways in which the mother's assumption of everyday responsibility affected the negotiation of parental behaviour. Examples are taken from the division of labour and the organisation of 'leaving the child'.

(a)   The division of labour: an example

The underlying assumption that family life was a 'fairly' shared
reality led the majority of couples to stress mutual responsibility
for the familial division of labour. The interviews revealed,
however, that, in practice, the wife took overall responsibility, and
the husband was regarded as the 'helper'. Being a 'helper' meant
that the husband was (or was not!) incorporated into the ongoing
organisation being administered by his wife. He was, in part,
reliant on her for information about the current state of that
organisation, and its participants, in order to 'know' what to do. It
also seemed that being a 'helper' involved a greater exercise of
choice and preference. This exercise of preference was incorporated into the negotiation of parental behaviour. It was, for
example, taken-for-granted that the wife would, by and large, look
after all of the children's needs; whilst the husband would *choose* to
look after some of them *if* he was present, and willing and/or able.
If the husband was absent or chose *not* to do certain things, then
the responsibility again reverted to the wife.

Paradoxically, one way of illustrating the effect of the assumption that the *wife* had overall responsibility is to show how the
husband's relationship with the child was differently managed. The
wife had a diffuse, overall responsibility for childrearing and
housework. By contrast, childrearing activities seldom became as
totally interwoven with the husband's domestic commitments. He
tended to have much more specific and well defined spheres of
involvement in the total domestic division of labour. Simplistically, the father was usually doing something with or for the
children; *or* he was carrying out a task in which it had been
negotiated between the spouses that the children *could* be
involved; *or* he was engaged in some well-defined domestic task
separate from the children.

A brief examination of the final alternative illustrates the
greater structuring and segregation of the development of
paternal behaviour, and, by implication, the mother's taken-for-
granted position of responsibility. Respondents' accounts indicated that when, for example, the husband was engaged in some
well-defined domestic task (or doing some 'job-connected' work at
home) the wife often made sure that the children were either kept
out of his way, or that they were removed if they impeded his progress. The usual explanation of this was that the husband might

be carrying out 'dangerous' jobs such as woodwork or cleaning windows. In contrast, the wife generally had to organise *her* 'dangerous' tasks concurrently with child management.

The Chapmans said, for instance, that they usually had to remove Anne from Martin's company when he was doing jobs around the house. They recounterd a recent occasion when Martin had become angry when he was unable to make progress owing to the child's presence. The conversation went as follows:

Sylvia: When Martin's here I'M just not wanted (by Anne) you see. But Martin gets annoyed because she's always on his tail. But, er, she'll have nothing to do with me; it's because she's got me all week and her daddy's here at the weekend.

Martin: But there again, I've got to get things done and I don't get any opportunity to get them done [*Sylvia:* I know], because she's following me around like a shadow. (W/E)

Alan Hemingway also said that he became upset when the children impinged on his activities. During their final interview he complained strongly that a whole day had just passed when all of their efforts had gone into looking after and entertaining the children. Dianne reacted sharply against this and said:

Dianne: Yes, but you spent the whole morning doing the car and *nothing stopped you.* [my emphasis]

Alan: No, I wouldn't have let it stop me. But it only didn't stop me because you were around to attend to all those screams and yells. (F)

Occasionally, some of the husbands made sure that their *wives* were allowed to get on with a task, unimpeded by the children. This seemed to be regarded, however, as more of a special situation. As such it was usually given particular emphasis during an interview, rather than being mentioned in a taken-for-granted manner. Analytically, this could be viewed more as a 'gesture' which sustained belief in a fairly shared reality.

(b) Constant availability

A corollary of this taken-for-granted overall responsibility was the premise that the mother was constantly available to the child. The parents in my group maintained that, at this particular stage when the mother was dealing with the majority of the child's basic needs, he/she continued to make demands of the *mother* even when the father was available. Anna Robson said:

> But Jim's lucky. For instance, I can get a sewing machine out on a Sunday because I think 'that's good, Jim's here, *that's a diversion for both of them*'. They don't go to him with their skinned knees, they still come to me. And Jim goes on merrily tuning the car or whatever he's doing. They never bother HIM (I) [my emphasis]

Similar examples were given by those couples who stressed that the child favoured his/her father and tended to spend a lot of time with him. Mary Duncan said:

> They like to be with him all the time you know. I mean, I'm just not here, em, *apart from if they NEED anything*, you know, if they want a drink or a biscuit or anything like that. (W/E) [my emphasis]

Margaret Barber saw Philip as equally able to deal with the children's needs and wants. She felt, though, that the children had learned to turn to their mother because of the different context in which the relationship had developed. Like most respondents she maintained that the child also tended to turn to its mother at times of *special* need, such as illness. She said:

> Quite often in times of stress a child will turn to the person that usually deals with the stressful situation. Karen tends to turn to ME at the moment and want ME. I personally don't think that's because she loves me more than Philip; it's just because I'm here more often I usually deal with it presumably more or less to her satisfaction. (I)

Thus couples defined the child as seeing its mother as more constantly available. This feeling of always being in demand was, in fact, perceived as oppressive by many of the wives. Marjorie Russell spoke as follows about the kinds of pressures she felt that the children exerted on her behaviour:

They absolutely HATE it when Mummy's not there. If Mummy's at the kitchen sink, that's fine, they can go and play. But if I for any reason go and lie down, that's not the same. They can't, they don't like THAT. They like Mummy to be THERE AND AWAKE, and to pay attention to them; and THEN they can go away. (I)

Two implications follow from these examples. Firstly these respondents seemed, in part, to see the constant availability of the mother (in their *current* situation) as satisfying one of their basic images of the child's needs: that of security. Secondly, it is important to note that they maintained that this kind of pressure to be 'available' was not experienced in the same way by the father. On an analytical level, this was supported by their grounded image that the child *itself* made fewer direct demands on the father, and was therefore less dependent on his *constant* presence. The effect of these images on everyday familial behaviour seemed to be that the father was less likely, therefore, to feel constraints on his activities. He was also better able to retain spheres of activity into which the child did not encroach. Thus the negotiation of parental behaviour has also to be seen within the context of the parents' images of the ways in which their children saw *them*.

(c) Delegation of childcare: an example

Beliefs about the mother's overall responsibility and availability were also reflected in respondents' accounts of the delegation of childcare. This applied to their organisation of 'leaving' the child, whether it was a matter of the occasional babysitter, or a permanent substitute whilst the parents were engaged in other activities (most especially when *both* had jobs).

Most of the times that one parent wished to carry out activities away from the home, the child was 'left' with the other parent. For these couples, joint activities away from the child were much rarer than were individual activities. The majority of them simply saw this as the most convenient way of carrying out non-domestic activities. A regular and *frequent* organisation of babysitters was not seen as an attractive proposition because it cost money, or time (return 'sits'), or obligation ('taking advantage' or friends/relatives). A minority of couples put forward images of children to

legitimate the fact that they were seldom 'left'. Usually these
images were grounded in their experience that the children were
unhappy if their parents were not available, or simply that the
children were somewhat afraid of non-familiar people. 'Explana
tory incidents' were often related.

The organisation of babysitters was usually, however, taken
for-granted as being the mother's responsibility. It was predomi
nantly the wives who both made arrangements for a babysitter to
come, and who also returned the babysitting service if necessary
Only one couple said that they shared return babysitting equally
depending on whoever felt like going. In the majority of couples
the husband either *never* went babysitting or went only under
special circumstances. Examples of these were if it was to be a
particularly late 'sit'; if the other household had a television; or i
the husband would have more peace and quiet to work or study in
someone else's house. The apparent lack of 'fairness' of the situa
tion was usually qualified, however by respondents maintaining
that the husband was *willing* to go. This can be seen as another
coping mechanism to sustain belief in fairness in the face of a
practical violation.

Context and knowledge were the usual legitimations put
forward to account for the wife's organisation of babysitting. They
said that: (i) she knew the other families and sitters better; (ii) the
other children were more familiar with the wives; and (iii) many
people preferred *women* to 'sit' for small babies. Here also then one
can see how images of children's needs and wants affected the
division of parental labour.

Context and knowledge were also used to legitimate the wife's
organisation of more permanent delegation of childcare, such as
nursery schools or childminders. It appeared that the mothers not
only did the actual organisation of these matters, but that they
also made the initial observations about when the child would be
able to cope with the situation. Here again the mother was per
ceived as in a better position to make such decisions because of her
greater knowledge of the child and its world.

It would appear that, once established, this basic situation is
rather difficult to change. As the Rapoports found, even in the
dual career family, the wife tended to take greater overall respon
sibility for childcare (and its delegation) than did the husband.[20] I
have argued that, in part, this arises from taken-for-granted views
that the mother has overall responsibility and is more 'available'

to the child. 'Leaving' the child is, therefore, more problematical to the mother.

Looking to the future, most of the wives anticipated returning to paid employment. (Some of them in fact did this during the field-work). One of the major considerations about a suitable job was whether or not it would fit in with the organisation of the children. By that point in time the husbands would be well established in their own working routines. It was, therefore, not seen as viable to start from the basic premise that childcare could be organised around the jobs of *both* spouses. By the end of the fieldwork, eight of the wives were either involved in, or seriously considering, some form of paid employment. In every case the organisation of alternative methods of childcare was seen as the wife's responsibility. This alternative method of childcare might involve employing childminders, swapping childminding with other working mothers, taking the children with her to work, or working only at those times when the husband was able to look after them.

Although it was, by and large, a mutual decision that the wife should work, it was she who tended to express worries that *her* absence might cause problems for the children. The absence of the father was, by that point, taken for granted. Barbara Johnson, who, at that stage, was perhaps the most determined of all the wives to have a second career, said that she would feel bound to give this up if she perceived that the substitute care of her two and a half year old son was unsatisfactory. Carol Burns, who worked night shifts as a nurse, felt it necessary to convince her husband (and herself) that the bed wetting and clinginess of their three year old daughter were not sufficiently serious to warrant her giving up her job. She and Eric had the following conversation during their fourth interview:

Carol: Going to somebody else's, em, even with me there, em, she clings to me in case I'm gonna vanish. So I don't know if it's because I'm working and she disappears on a Thursday [i.e. when a friend looked after the child to enable Carol to sleep].

Eric: Och, she's always asking for you at night, em, I mean if she appears, I mean she knows fine where you are!

Carol: Mmmm, but I don't think it's upsetting her.

Eric: Well she does trot round to come to bed with me occasionally.

Carol: Yes, but I mean once she's in bed with you she's fine.
There's no 'mammy, mammy' misery. I mean I don't think
it's worth giving up work for that. (W/E)

V   SUMMARY

In this chapter I examined various characteristics of being a
mother, as presented in the couples' accounts of their daily lives.
The special features of being a mother were separated into three
categories: context, knowledge, and responsibility and availability. These features both describe and explain why, for these
couples, motherhood remained distinctively different from fatherhood, despite the various gestures which they had developed to
emphasise the claimed jointness and equality of their parental
behaviour.

Firstly, I argued that the mother developed her parental
behaviour in a different subjective context from that of the father.
This stemmed from her being predominantly in the front line in
looking after the children. She had a much larger time commitment to the children than did the father, and, consequently, a
great *direct* involvement developed.

A second area of difference was that couples viewed the mother
as having a more extensive knowledge of home and family than
did the father. Such knowledge was felt by the couples to be
important because it was *directly* acquired, and thus was accorded
considerable legitimacy in the negotiation processes. The meanings which couples attached to this knowledge had a considerable effect on the development of maternal and paternal behaviour.

The final main characteristics of motherhood were responsibility and constant availability. My couples' accounts showed
that they saw the mother as taking the greater direct share of both
of these features of parenthood. The mother had the overall
responsibility for the organisation of home and children, with the
father being regarded as 'helper'.

Thus, some doubts have already been cast on the *actual* similarity of maternal and paternal behaviour. Being a mother had,
for these couples, some important distinctive features. The same
was true of fatherhood, and it is to this that I turn in the next
chapter.

8 Being a Father

I think fathers should be very involved with the children, and I think the time for them to be involved is right from the word go. I think, if they're going to get on well with their children when they are older, they've got to start right from the beginning and develop the relationship at the same time as the mother develops a relationship. Maureen Rankin (I)

I INTRODUCTION

The theme of this chapter is the problematical nature of father-hood. It was evident from my interviews that whereas many fundamental aspects of 'being a mother' were taken-for-granted, this did not apply in the same way to 'being a father'. No matter how dissatisfied the wives might feel about the adequacy of their parental behaviour, they had, nevertheless, negotiated with their husbands a subjectively satisfactory base of early motherhood. At this stage this comprised, in essence, an involvement on a general level which was 'proved' by being constantly available and responsible for the children, and thus in a continual learning situation. The parents in my group defined this basic situation of being at home with small children as extremely demanding but vital in the context of present day British society.

Fatherhood was not perceived as having this fundamental and unchallengeable base. In order to sustain their underlying beliefs about parenthood, these couples did not consider it adequate for the husband simply to earn the money and act as a male presence in the household. Being a father was perceived as entailing also a direct involvement and active interest in the children. Therefore the problematical nature of being a father lay in negotiating with the mother a mutually satisfactory degree of *direct* involvement in home and family life, during the non-job time perceived as available. Although, within the group there was variation in the kinds and range of 'appropriate' behaviour being negotiated, respondents held very similar everyday images of fatherhood. More importantly, they had similar myths and coping mechanisms which enabled them to sustain belief in the reality of the paternal behaviour which they were creating.

Spouses negotiated with each other mutually satisfactory arrangements which enabled them to maintain belief in the *direct* involvement of the father. In terms of actual behaviour this involvement varied both between couples, and within each family over time. The crucial factor in the process of belief maintenance was the ability to draw on various spheres of behaviour at different levels, all of which provided 'proof' of involvement. These will be discussed in this chapter. Importantly, it was *not*, however, perceived as necessary for the father to participate fully and constantly in *all* of these spheres. Rather, it was a matter of his participating sufficiently regularly in those particular spheres which spouses had identified as relevant to their own family situation. (Or, alternatively, being able to rationalise his temporary non-participation, in which case beliefs could be suspended!) In other words, for father involvement to be subjectively satisfactory it did not tend to be measured against some abstract set of behavioural ideals. It was negotiated and evaluated in terms of the paternal behaviour perceived as appropriate by the spouses within their own special situation at any one point in time.

II   PERCEPTIONS OF THE DIVISION OF LABOUR

A brief description of respondents' general perceptions of the overall division of labour provides background to the following discussion of the different levels of father involvement. Basically their accounts provided a picture of the division of labour as a flexible and dynamic entity. During the course of the multi-interview study each couple described many changes in their everyday administration of home and family. They saw these changes as being related principally to (a) alterations in the extra-familial commitments of group members and (b) to differing perceptions of children's needs.

(a)   The majority of respondents (including both husbands *and* wives) reported, for example, changes in their paid employment commitments, or routines, throughout the months spanned by the interviews. All of these had necessitated re-arrangements in the domestic routine. Usually the result was simply an increase in the wife's overall workload or organisational activities since, as I argued in Chapter 7, she tended to have the taken-for-granted major responsibility for domestic matters. Five of the husbands, though, reported doing slightly more childminding as a result of their wives' commitments. By and large, however, the majority of changes affected the wives predominantly, and stemmed from their husbands spending more time at work. Husband involvement in home and childcare was thus seen as fluctuating and problematical.

(b) The division of labour was also described as changing in response to developments *within* the family. Differences in this respect were described between the pre-children, one child, and two children stages. Images of children played an important part in the legitimation of these changes. Couples claimed that the husbands had been more involved with practical *household* chores before children, when both spouses were working.[1] Once the woman was at home with one child, most respondents then saw it as either desirable or inevitable that she took the main responsibility for carrying out household chores in addition to her childcare activities.[2] Also, at first, images of the fragility of small babies were used to legitimate the more peripheral involvement of the father in childcare. As the first child grew older most of these parents defined the husband as becoming more involved with him/her. Gradually, more practical 'gestures' were carried out by the husband, which supported this belief. As is discussed later in this chapter, further changes occurred with the addition of the second child.[3]

Alongside changes in family commitments and structure, couples also perceived their children as developing and altering. Their images of these developments often led to revised definitions both of the child's needs, and of the father's ability to deal with them. A frequently cited example was the greater willingness of the father spontaneously to become involved with childcare on a regular basis once the child was no longer seen as 'a baby'. Marjorie Russell said:

I think men like them when they're a wee bit bigger to handle and so on, and a bit more independent and able to say what they want. (F)

Carol Burns echoed this when she said that Eric did more for the children now that they were no longer 'babies'. She said to Eric:

> I think you are doing more now because *the children are becoming more people*, and are more communicating with you. Whereas before they were, you know, a bit lumpy. (Jt) [my emphasis]

Also, as the child became better able to do things for itself, the father might become more involved in a supervisory capacity. As David Russell said of his three and five year olds:

> . . . take bathing as an example: I just throw them into the bath and let them get on with it themselves, you see. I never do that [wash them]. I mean, that's up to them. Or I just leave them to soak and take them out. (W/E)

It seemed, therefore, that, not only did the changing image of the *child* affect the division of labour, but also that the image of the father's ability altered. The progression to his being regarded as having acquired 'adequate' knowledge was more gradual than that of the mother. His opportunities to provide 'practical proof' of ability were less relative to the mother. At the same time, however, that the father's fund of directly acquired knowledge was defined as increasing so his childcare abilities became more taken-for-granted.

III   FATHER INVOLVEMENT

There were three principal overlapping areas within which spheres of paternal behaviour were being developed. These were (a) dealing with general domestic and family matters; (b) nego-tiating acceptable parental behaviour in relation to the mother; and (c) developing a direct relationship with the child. The first and second areas are progressively further removed from the situation to which, in theory, these couples attached so much im-portance. This was that being a parent was a learning situation characterised by direct personal experience. Even though the importance of (c) was stressed by all respondents, *most* spheres of paternal behaviour were directed towards (a) and (b). For the majority of the husbands, time limitations and personal choice led them *in practice* only to be minimally involved in the third area. The interest for this study lies in the ways in which a generalised belief in father involvement was sustained, and the kinds of direct relationships with the child which *were* developed.

(a) Dealing with general domestic and family matters

This was the widest area of paternal behaviour in which respondents claimed involvement. Being a father meant sharing overall responsibility for the administration of domestic matters, such as finances, care, education and development of children; and taking part in the organisation of family activities. Images of the child as being different from adults, and as having to be administered by his/her parents, were implicit in this view of fatherhood.[4] The underlying assumption that parenthood was a shared reality, meant that spouses had to sustain belief that the father also took part in this administrative activity.

This area of overall administrative activity was extremely broadly defined by respondents. They all sustained a belief that the fathers were involved. In practice, however, there was considerable variation between couples in the kind, and amount, of administrative activity actually undertaken by the fathers. This is an interesting area of behaviour, since there was often only a fine subjective distinction between passive and active involvement. All of the husbands were kept 'informed' by their wives, and claimed an interest in this everyday administration. All of the couples sustained a belief in this passive level of paternal involvement by claiming, for example, that domestic matters, especially those pertaining to the children, constituted a major part of their 'mundane' conversation. The variation lay in the extent to which husbands played an *active* part in making decisions, allocating priorities, and general organisation.

In addition, it was a crucial part of this practical involvement that the husband's activity was believed to be a vital ingredient by *both* spouses. His involvement remained more on the *passive* level if, for example, the wife regarded him simply as a 'sounding board' for the decisions which she had already made. The response of the wife was always vital, since it was *her* everyday existence which tended to be most affected by these administrative and organisational decisions. Also, the very constancy of her presence gave her considerable power over the choice of those activities or routines which were actually put into practice.

The different levels of involvement will be illustrated firstly by presenting the two extremes which existed amongst the couples in the group. The position of the majority of the respondents will then be discussed. Given the importance attached to the wife's greater experience and knowledge in the domestic sphere, the tendency was towards a general passive involvement, with occasional active interventions negotiated between the spouses.

Two of the fathers maintained that their involvement was demonstrated by their acting in a sort of 'overseer' capacity. For couples to sustain belief in this behaviour, the husbands had to be seen simply to be aware of, and interested in, the ongoing developments of home and family. They were required primarily to acknowledge and acquiesce to the decisions constantly being made by their wives. This extreme type was illustrated by Patrick Hislop when he spoke as follows about 'being a *mother*':

> *Patrick:* Being a provider of a stable home life and, much more so, influencing the children by example, em, much more so than the father.
> *K.B.:* Why do you see it as being much more so than the father?
> *Patrick:* Because the mother will inevitably be in much closer contact with the children. And this is obviously to some extent just because of my particular job, not just MY particular job, many fellows in my position because of the demands of their job, they are not in as close contact with the children as they could be or should be so that your presence is required only 'in extremis'. (I)[5]

In addition, Patrick perceived his wife's greater knowledge/involvement in domestic matters generally as justifying his own lack of direct administrative activity in those spheres also. Both of the couples who adopted this position perceived the mother as inevitably central in domestic matters, and, for them, this was a major legitimation in itself for the peripheral involvement of the father.

In addition they, more than any of the other respondents, stressed that women understood and dealt with children better than did men. Images of children were put forward to legitimate these beliefs. Roy Vaughan said, for example:

> I think, you know, the women handle them every day n' that, and the child gets used to the handling of the one person. And I think probably if I HAVE handled her, em, quite often the child wants her mother you know. She just, she probably feels uneasy with me handling her and I'd say [to Elizabeth] 'och you fix her up'. (W/E)

Both Kathy Hislop and Elizabeth Vaughan concurred with their husbands' views of fatherhood. The fact that this was a *negotiated* reality, in which images of children played an important part, was illustrated by the accounts of those parents who said that they and their spouses had *not* initially had such a similarity of views. Maureen Rankin said that Derek had helped out with the babies and done lots of things, '. . . he probably never thought he would do.' (I) Both of the Rankins now defined this as an essential way for the father to develop a relationship with the child. Projected images of the future relationship of father and child were used to legitimate his current *practical* involvement with baby and infant care.

Philip Barber said that he had come to view fatherhood in a similar way to this, but only with Margaret's guidance. He commented:

> I think probably the majority of men don't, they see themselves in the role of father as PLAYING with the children rather than, you know, nurse-maiding the children. And THAT was certainly MY kind of feelings as far as I'd thought about it. Margaret was very keen for me to be an active participating father em, in EVERY respect. So that I've been present at the birth of BOTH kids, em, and I read up the pamphlets beforehand; and we'd go to the hospital for the daddy's evening before the happy event and see a film of the birth. (I)

Philip Barber was, in fact, one of the three fathers whose views were in direct contrast with the Hislops and the Vaughans. These three maintained that their overall responsibilities were only *really* being met if there was a very active involvement in the ongoing administration. For them being a father meant a practical sharing of mundane decisions and organisation whenever one was available for participation. Nothing should be simply 'left up to the mother', except where time constraints made an effective sharing impossible. (Interestingly, the three fathers who believed most strongly in the importance of this practical overall involvement, were in occupations which had allowed them flexible time schedules.) This kind of attitude is again best illustrated with reference to childrearing. Philip Barber said:

> I think it's one's parental responsibility to SPEND time with one's children, and to sort out priorities like this in the early years in particular, when the child's development is progressing at a VERY rapid pace and so much of the basic pattern is being set. That it's a FATHER'S responsibility, as well as a MOTHER'S, to give the TIME that is required for looking after the children in a very practical way. (I)

The most frequent pattern seemed to be a combination of elements from these two extremes. Belief in father involvement in this area was sustained by similar mechanisms to those described earlier in the study.[6] Spheres of behaviour considered appropriate in their own family set-up were negotiated on a hypothetical level by spouses. Usually the behaviour was subsequently held 'in reserve', and only minimal practical applications were required to maintain beliefs. It was subjectively satisfactory simply to maintain that the father 'would if he could' or 'could if he *had* to'. In addition, temporal fluctuations occurred between passive and active involvement in this area. On occasions, for example, some fathers were completely absent from the home for a period of time. Since, however, this was usually because of job commitments, a belief in involvement was sustained at its widest level. The situation was interpreted as a phase which would be in the long term interest of the family.

A good illustration of the typical fluctuations between passive and active administrative involvement was given by Alan Hemingway. During the course of his first interview he initially maintained that parenthood was a shared administrative responsibility, but subsequently went on to allocate the major part of initiative in these spheres to his wife. He said about 'being a mother':

> ... very much the same [as being a father] I would think, in our

case. These areas are very definitely the problems that we share, em, the children. We don't slot one aspect of their well-being into my area and another into Dianne's, em, they're very much OURS in terms of these kinds of decisions. And that's one thing we talk about a lot. (I)

He also said, however:

Dianne's sphere of things, em, involves very much more the children, in terms of doing things with them and, and er trying to be original in what we do, and doing the things that we ought to do. And these are very much her areas of initiative, because she will always say before I ever get round to it, 'we ought to do such 'n' such with the kids', and we DO it. (I)

Other examples occurred when the husbands claimed an overall interest in the pre-school education of the children, but the wives made all of the practical decisions and arrangements. Sometimes, however, the fathers *did* become actively involved by, for instance, providing transport to an alternative playschool. Equally, if initial arrangements proved unsatisfactory, husbands *then* became more involved in the subsequent decisions to sort out the problems.

The various 'fall back' levels of involvement, and the narrow divide between passive and active administrative activity, made this area of being a father the easiest in which to sustain belief. The other two areas were *more* dependent on practical than hypothetical proof of involvement. For the majority of these couples, as long as practical administrative activity was undertaken when it was perceived to be appropriate, then this area was very much taken-for-granted in the negotiation process. Most instances of lack of involvement were coped with by treating them as an inevitable phase or stage. Most of the time spouses had agreed (tacitly or overtly), or agreed to differ, on the spheres of behaviour perceived as necessary to demonstrate involvement in this area. This was, however, an ongoing debate, and often spheres deemed important were learnt as much by default as by positive discussion. An example of this was given by the Burns, when they talked about the choice of schools for their elder child. Carol had looked round various schools and felt that Eric should do likewise because, 'if he's gonna be any help to his child he should know how they do

things in his school.' (F) Eric maintained that he *was* considering
the matter, and that he had amassed information through hear-
say. This, however, was not adequate *practical* proof for Carol, and
she was, therefore, strongly critical of Eric's apparent lack of
involvement.

(b) Negotiating acceptable parental behaviour in relation to that of the mother

This second main area of 'being a father' entailed sustaining belief
in involvement through the relationship with the mother. Here
paternal behaviour was perceived as (i) supporting the mother in
her childrearing activities; (ii) relieving her of practical and
psychological pressures when present; and (iii) acting as substitute when she wished to have time away from home and family.
The father was very reliant on cues from the mother in this area.
His spheres of behaviour were developed very much in the context
of the mother's information about herself and the children. The
father was vulnerable in his personal evaluations of the everyday
family events since he was in fact absent from a great deal of the
childrearing activity. Therefore, although he might criticise
aspects of the information relayed to him, he was unable to challenge its validity, since the mother's account was his prime source.
In addition, he could never be certain that he had grasped 'the
total picture', since, inadvertently or deliberately, the mother's
account was bound to be selective. As the transmission of information is essentially an interpretative act, the mother's images
and assessment inevitably played a highly influential part in the
development of paternal behaviour.

(i) Support in childrearing activities

The different contexts within which maternal and paternal
behaviour was developed[7] seemed to affect the overall attitude
which each spouse took to the other's parental acts. To put it
simply, the husbands tended to adopt an 'understanding' attitude, whereas the wives were more 'critical'. This was shown in
the many situations where one spouse was unhappy about some
aspect of the other's childrearing behaviour. In these circum-

stances it could be seen as constructive and legitimate for the wife, drawing on her wider knowledge, to 'advise' her husband on the most appropriate course of action. In some ways the wife pointing out the husband's childrearing 'mistakes', and explaining them, was a short cut to passing on 'knowledge' about the child. It was, in fact, often rather difficult for the wife to stand back and allow the husband to learn through his own experience and 'make his own mistakes' with the child. This was very interesting, because it implied that when the wife had achieved a certain level of subjectively satisfactory competence in childrearing, it then became more difficult for her to accept others making what were defined as 'mistakes' with the child. Barbara Johnson expressed her own awareness of this dilemma as follows, she explained:

> There are one or two areas where we haven't actually agreed, aren't there? [*Ian:* I suppose there must be.] I, I'll say 'oh for goodness sake', you know, I might get a bit cross about the way he's handling a situation because I don't agree with it. But it doesn't OFTEN arise, and when it DOES arise, well, I feel I've got NO right because they're HIS kids as well as mine and who am I to say how he's gonna handle the situation? (F)

During the course of the interviews instances were often described where the wives had felt impatient with, or overruled, their husbands' childrearing activities. Husbands, however, usually tended to mute their own criticisms by qualifying them. On occasions when a husband was too overtly critical, the wife tended to counter defensively, and claim as legitimation the context in which she had to act. A typical example of this was for her to counter that the criticism was unjust because the husband was not subject to pressures of home and children every day of the week.

Therefore, an important way in which couples sustained belief in father involvement, without disrupting the assumptions of fairness and equality, was for the husband to adopt a supportive and understanding attitude to his wife's childrearing activities. Analytically, another interpretation of this could be that the husband's awareness of his lack of *directly* acquired knowledge led him to be tentative in his criticisms. Any critical comments were usually couched in an acknowledgement of the arduousness of the wife's situation, or that the husband's inferior knowledge might have led him to an incorrect conclusion. Roy Vaughan said, for example:

> I wouldn't like to do that every day you know, and so I can understand how she feels when I DO come in at night you know. It's quite a job for a woman really, two children. So I wouldn't condemn her at all, you know, just she maybe gives them a row, but they must be due or she wouldn't give it. (I)

Thus, images of children's needs and wants were put forward with the qualification that their practical interpretation had to be seen in the context of the parent-child relationship. Roy might *believe* his children needed 'fair' treatment but he acknowledged that constant interaction with them could undermine this. Ian Johnson maintained that he was aware of violating this kind of background supportive involvement at times when he felt Barbara was being too rough with the children. Even *his* very frank comments were, however, presented not as a criticism of her childrearing methods, but rather as an acknowledgement that she occasionally gave way to the strains of being tied at home with the children.

At other times husbands supported their wives' childrearing activities, because, even if they felt critical, they were aware of their own relative lack of knowledge. This was well illustrated when the Coulsons related an incident which had occurred during a visit to some friends. They had decided to leave their elder child with the friends whilst they went out for the evening. Their child cried and protested to his father that he did not wish to be left. Against Barry's wishes, Jean insisted that they ignored his protests and went out, maintaining that this was not serious and that the child would be perfectly all right once they had left. Events proved Jean to have 'assessed the situation correctly' and Barry commented:

> So, you know, he realised that I was soft like that, and latched on to it like a rocket. Whereas Jean identified it, and he didn't go to her, because he knew she would recognise that he was being a bit of a fraud; and *I* didn't, and it really annoyed me. [Jean laughs]. But, you know, I mean you've got to leave children from time to time, er, and they ARE going to be upset. I don't know why, I just felt terribly sorry for him. I felt, to my way of

thinking he was desperately upset. *I didn't know he was such a good actor.* (F) [my emphasis]

When jointly faced with a childrearing situation requiring immediate action, it was often impossible for the husband to amass the amount of relevant information which the wife could take-for-granted. The wife was defined as more informed, and therefore more able to make a mutually acceptable, (or more readily legitimated), spontaneous decision. Exceptions to this sometimes occurred when the situation concerned was well known to both parents. In such circumstances the husband's actions had perhaps been accorded some special legitimacy. He was, for example, perceived as being 'more comforting', 'more effective', 'firmer', or 'more on that particular child's wavelength'. Most frequently, however, greater legitimacy was accorded to the wife's childrearing decisions and behaviour, with the husband expressing *his* involvement by acting in a generally supportive capacity.

(ii) Practical and psychological relief

Father involvement was also expressed by relieving the mother of some of the practical and psychological pressures of childrearing when both parents were present.[8] Although, for all of these couples this was an important element in the construction of 'being a father', the amount of 'practical proof' required to sustain such beliefs varied considerably. For some couples, such relief was little more than an extension of the supportive behaviour; for others, it entailed the father working alongside the mother in a well defined range of activities. The extent to which involvement could be demonstrated *indirectly* through the relationship with the mother was illustrated by Louise Wilson when she said of the father:

. . . at the younger stages of their [children's] lives, they're very much less important, em, except I think that they, em, give the mother a feeling of security. And if the mother is feeling insecure then she can transmit it to the children. (Jt)

For all respondents, beliefs in the underlying assumptions of

fairness and equality, and of mutual involvement with th
children, were sustained by reference to this sphere of paterna
behaviour. To cope with the fluctuations in availability of th
father, couples emphasised the voluntary aspect of his domesti
activities, and stressed that 'help' was always given when reall
needed. Carole Burns, for example, commented:

> I think he's very good really, em, he comes in and sometime
> he's whacked cos he's had a very brain-filled day, which can b
> much more exhausting than pick and shovels. And er, the
> [children] just crawl all over him like ants, and he puts up witl
> it, which I think is quite good. (I)

Even at those times, however, when the father was perceived a
equally available, emphasis on his *voluntary* assistance tended t
continue. At weekends, for example, couples tended to continu
with a similar allocation of practical childrearing tasks to that o
during the week. In addition, most families tried to minimise th
mundane tasks typical of the weekday domestic routine. Th
majority of wives said that they tried to make weekends 'different
by doing only the most basic chores. Weekends were usually per
ceived both as a break from routine, and as an opportunity fo
leisure and relaxation.

The availability of the husband at the weekend was perceivec
as enabling activities to take place 'as a family', (such as visiting)
or facilitating activities where it was easier for two parents t
'manage' the children, (such as city shopping expeditions). Th
presence of the father was the main means by which norma
pressures on the mother could be relieved. The husbands tendec
to be 'involved' at weekends, but usually as part of a differen
range of activities, with relaxation often as an important aim
Voluntarism and 'opting in' were still highly relevant. Barr
Coulson, for example, said:

> And, em, I mean if you've got children, that's it, it's non sto
> work. I mean *I* participate when I feel like it, but if I feel lik
> burying my head in the newspaper I DO, or if I feel like ignor
> ing the disturbances that are going on, then I can do it. Jea
> sometimes will call upon, em, will say 'can you help me out', o
> something, and I can do it. And *I don't want her to feel that she has t
> do all the work* I usually help her more at weekends. (I) [m

emphasis]

As has been discussed, voluntarism *in itself* was a positive means of sustaining beliefs.[9] The issue of voluntarism, however, became complicated by the fact that many activities required knowledge about when and how they should be done. Here again, the position of wife as information agent was crucial. Even if husbands assumed a stance of voluntary availability, they could still, in effect, 'opt out' of practical involvements by asserting a basic lack of knowledge. Alice Mitchell said:

> Em, something, if it's very obvious that I'm very pressed em, he does it off his own bat; but most things, I mean, like most men he'll walk into a room just littered with toys at 6 o'clock, and say 'is there anything I can do?' (I)

Being a father was negotiated, therefore, in the context of less specific knowledge compared with that of the mother. In addition, stress was laid on voluntarism as an important means of sustaining belief in father involvement. In the light of these two points it was very interesting that a major way in which fathers 'proved' their involvement was by entertaining the children, or simply 'keeping them occupied'. This was an area of activity which fathers could carry out spontaneously and voluntarily, with the minimum of specific knowledge or consultation with the mother being necessary. It was also concurrently relieving the mother of psychological and practical childrearing pressures.

The father's practical involvement in childcare was also defined as changing in response to the perceived demands on the mother. (Again note the taken-for-granted assumption that this was life-cyclical.) The majority of couples said, for example, that after the arrival of the second baby the father tended to become more involved with the practical care of the *first* child. Colin Duncan provided a very typical explanation of this trend. He said:

> I would say possibly a father would HAVE to do more, you know. Perhaps with the one child he would take turn about *because he wanted to*. But I would say when the second child came along the father had more to do. He was more OBLIGED to do it, you know, it wasn't a case of just *wanting* to do it, obviously with the mother involved with the baby. (W/E) [My emphasis,

note assumption of voluntarism and 'opting in'.]

Those who said this did *not* happen in their families usually maintained that it was because the father had already been caring actively for the first child in a practical way. By and large, however, when the father was present he relieved the mother of the care of the first child, whilst she attended to the baby's needs. Images of children, notably the 'fragility of babies', meant that this particular division of childcare was taken-for-granted. Only on very infrequent occasions did the father take over care of the new baby in preference to that of the first child. At such times this was usually, in fact, a 'gesture' arising out of a comparative image of the reaction of the first child to the baby. The mother might 'give' the first child some specially directed time whilst the father dealt with the baby.

Regardless of the actual amount of practical involvement of the fathers, their being willing and available was, at times, perceived as vital relief for the wives from their constant childrearing responsibilities. The importance of the mechanisms for sustaining beliefs in this area of expression of father involvement was shown by its occasional violation. During the course of the research several families went through periods where the husbands were either working extremely hard, or were away on business. All made similar comments about the increased strain on the wives, which was shown in various ways, when the husbands had to withdraw from their usual activities in home and family.

The following statements illustrate some of the ways in which respondents saw the results of the suspension of husband support. David Russell commented:

> Oh well, when I'm away so much em, it makes you [to Marjorie] increasingly bored with a housewife's existence. [*Marjorie:* Oh yes]. The other day I came home and the atmosphere was pretty frigid. (F)

Helen Moffat said:

> Yes, the children miss seeing their father. They don't say they do but they become a bit difficult in the evenings when they expect he would normally be there [sighs]. Er, I feel tired, I feel as if they're never away from me just now, it's the weekends are

really terrible. (W/E)

(iii) Being a father as 'mother substitute'

A final means of demonstrating involvement through the relation-ship with the mother was that of being able to deputise for her when she wished to leave the children, or in times of emergency. Again, in order to sustain belief in this sphere of involvement, it was not necessary to establish a regular system of obligation but rather to create a situation of voluntary availability. For various reasons spouses tended to use one another as babysitters and childminders where possible.[10] When family life was perceived as entailing fairness and equality, and a mutual involvement with the children, it was important to maintain a belief that, just as the father was able to 'escape' from domestic responsibilities, so also was the mother. In addition these couples were dependent pri-marily on the human resources of their own nuclear unit. None of them relied on any regular help from the wider kinship groups either through choice or through geographical separation. It seemed that friends and neighbours were only used to a limited extent since most of them were similarly restricted by their own childrearing responsibilities. All of these factors resulted in an important element of fatherhood being seen as the ability to sub-stitute for the mother.

Interestingly, however, in order to maintain belief in father as mother substitute he needed only to deputise for *part* of the mother's usual activities. The main requirement was simply to mind the children. Some wives made elaborate arrangements, such as preparing food in advance, in order to assist their husbands with these substitute activities. Even when this was not considered necessary, domestic activities additional to the child-minding were usually defined as a welcome extra. Only partial substitution was necessary because the wives, even in their absence, retained overall responsibility and knowledge.[11]

Also, the standards of childminding did not need to be equal to those of the mother for 'being a father' to be subjectively satisfac-tory. Adequacy of parental behaviour was defined differently if it was carried out by the father. Here then was an implicit acknow-ledgement that definitions of children's needs were not *factual* but negotiable, and that there were therefore a variety of ways in

which they might be satisfied. The Duncans, for example, related
a story concerning one occasion when Colin had been left in
charge of the children for the day. It was treated simply as an
amusing illustration of the different attitudes of 'being a father'
that Colin had become so absorbed in digging the garden that he
had forgotten both to switch on the fire and lights in the house,
and also to give the children some tea. A similar belief in the
partial substitute activities of the father was illustrated by the
Wilsons when they had the following conversation about Nick's
childminding abilities. This occurred during their joint interview.

> *Louise:*   As far as the children are concerned I mean, you've
> done everything with the kiddies, you could look after a child
> as well as I could.
> *Nick:*   [laughs] Well not quite so well.
> *Louise:*   Oh you'd probably kill them off in the first half hour
> but, I mean, that would be your own personality problem,
> you could manage all the sort of necessities. (Jt)

Thus, although 'being a father' was perceived as involving
deputising for the mother, this activity did not need to be frequent,
or of an equivalent standard, in order to be subjectively
satisfactory.

(c)   Being a father in relation to the child

Finally, these couples stressed that being a father involved having
a *direct* relationship with the child. This area was especially
problematical since, compared with the mother, the father could
invest less time in such activity. This meant that much of the
father's direct involvement with the child tended, in any case, to
be mediated through the indirect understandings provided by the
mother, rather than through his own personal experience. Nevertheless, respondents defined the development of a direct father-
child relationship as crucial. Elaborate mechanisms were
developed to construct and sustain belief in its reality. It was
important that this area of activity was subjectively satisfactory to
the spouses since it was an expression of many of their underlying
assumptions about family life. Direct father involvement sustained, for example, beliefs about fairness and equality, and about

family life as a situation of learning.

In addition, an important aspect of the negotiation of parental behaviour was the ability to put forward subjectively satisfactory understandings of the child and its world. For these couples to define the father as actively involved in this process, his legitimations of past and intended parental acts had, in part, to be perceived as grounded in his *direct* experience. The importance of the direct father-child relationship was illustrated by Alice Mitchell when she discussed Roy's *non*-involvement. This dominated their negotiation of parental behaviour, since Alice was critical, firstly, that she had to carry out almost all of the childrearing herself, and, secondly, that her husband was relatively inept in this sphere. She explained:

> I find em the lack of regularity of the life and em, almost the lack of Roy being there to, to SHARE it very hard. (W/E) [and also felt that] If he was with them more, em, I think he would get to handle the children much more tactfully, em, more slickly you know. *I mean I didn't know to begin with but you quickly learn how to avoid the big scenes, em, how to distract their attention and so on, em, I'm sure that comes with just being with the children.* (I) [my emphasis]

Alice attributed some of her own, and the children's current problems to this lack of direct involvement, and expressed many worries about the children's future development if this 'inadequate' paternal behaviour continued.

This, then, was an area of activity which was accorded great importance, but was also perhaps the most problematical in terms of 'practical proof'. To a certain extent respondents sustained their beliefs by maintaining that the fathers *valued* the direct relationship with the child, and derived pleasure from it. The implication was always that, in the future or given more time, a greater involvement would be *desired*. Statements such as the following from Shirley Jackson occurred frequently. She said of 'being a father':

> I think, em, loving, really very much the same as what a mother involves. Er, loving your children, playing with them, spending time with them. I think Edward would like to be able to spend MORE time with the children, but unfortunately he isn't in, em you know, he isn't sort of nine to five. (I)

Only two fathers, however, actually claimed that they would like to be at home all day with the children. Even they subsequently qualified such statements by admitting that, like their wives, they found that, in fact, prolonged periods of direct involvement were a strain. Implicit in this view was the image of the child as demanding and potentially oppressive. Both mothers and fathers put forward many statements indicating that such images of children were affected by the amount of time which one had to spend with them. The images were thus contextual. John Clark, for example, said:

> I would like to be at home during the day to see the children when they're doing things. When I come home they're getting tired, they're just going to have their tea and off to bed so that [pause]. Although, at the weekends [laughs] I often think I've had enough of them and I'm glad to get back to work again. (I)

Again, the importance of sustaining the belief that being a father involved *enjoying* a *direct* relationship with the child was shown by its violation. If, during an interview, husbands *denied* valuing such involvement there were immediate reactions from the wives. According to Alan Hemingway, other people outside of the family often reacted similarly. He was unusual amongst the respondents in that he openly admitted a dislike of the extent of his direct involvement with his children. He described these reactions as follows:

> . . . the effect of having had two children, em, for the greater period of our married life makes me LONG now for a period without any more, particularly at that age. Em, because I used to say this so often you know, to people who were shocked, you know, they would say, 'isn't it lovely having children?' and I'd say 'no it's not', because I don't enjoy it as an exercise. And people of course take this the wrong way: they think I don't like the kids, which is a different thing altogether, of course I do. But the physical act of having the children about, and generally existing with them about, and, em, doing the things that they'd love to do, I do not enjoy. (I)

Occasionally, during the course of the interview, some of the other husbands commented, for example, that they only liked being with the children for short periods; that they often found their demands oppressive; or that they quickly became bored with entertaining them. Typically, their wives countered such statements by emphasising how well father and child got on with each other, and by reminding them of pleasurable times spent together. Such comments and reactions are treated here as an integral part of the process of negotiating paternal behaviour. Although varying *actions* might result from such an exchange, they were all directed at sustaining belief in the value of a direct father-child relationship. Some wives responded by reiterating that this was a vital aspect of 'being a father'; that his reactions were no different from her own; and that this was an area of activity which must be shared. Other wives responded by limiting the extent of direct involvement so as to maximise the positive value which the father might then attach to the relationship, and so encourage his continued participation. The importance of these illustrations lies not in the variation itself, but in the fact that the different responses were aiming to sustain similar meanings behind parental behaviour.

When the development of a direct relationship with the child was defined as a crucial part of 'being a father', the amount of time available for paternal activity acquired a heightened significance. The father had the problem of making time to 'get to know' the child, and this did not apply in the same way to the mother. As the mother was, at this stage, more constantly available to the child, she was perceived as being able to 'get to know' him/her through the whole variety of everyday interactions. The father, on the other hand, had more deliberately to set time aside, or organise his other commitments, in order to sustain belief that he was achieving this *direct* knowledge. In addition, underlying assumptions that parenthood was a process of learning, and images that children needed consistency and should be 'understood', implied that time had regularly to be 'made' for them. Also, the context of his relationship with the child was different from that of the mother, since she often played a significant part in organising the times when father and child could be available to one another. All of these elements behind the father's time with the child resulted in mechanisms to sustain belief that he frequently and actively 'spent' some of it on him/her.

A most significant example of a mechanism to sustain this belief was put forward by almost all of the respondents. This was the

situation of the father being left in *total* charge of the children and
household whilst the mother went out. Here a variety of beliefs
were in fact being sustained concurrently. First of all, this was
'practical proof' of his involvement and such an act supported the
validity of the important coping mechanism, voluntarism.
Secondly, the husband was seen to be 'spending time' directly
with the children. In these circumstances he *had* to learn about
them, and how to deal with them, directly through his own experience. Such experience affected the negotiation processes,
since it enabled fathers to form direct images with which they
might support or challenge the mothers' intrepretations. Dianne
Hemingway felt that, through having been left in total charge,
Alan had had practical experience of just how demanding their
children could be. She said:

> The moment that everything's untidy, em, he doesn't complain
> because he knows what it's like himself. You know, if HE'S had
> the children all morning and I've been out shopping, I'll come
> back and he'll say 'I haven't done anything at all, I've just
> looked after them.' (I)

This example provided a further illustration of the mother
exerting considerable influence over the development of the
father's behaviour. Paradoxically this occurred through her virtually abdicating her own perceived 'responsibility'. This meant
that, in her absence, the father had an opportunity to learn his
parental behaviour totally through direct, unmediated
experience.

The significance of the mother's influence was further
emphasised when she chose *not* to exert it. This was very much the
exception in the sample, and applied fully to only one couple. In
two cases, however, the husbands were left totally in control only
very infrequently. Kathy Hislop tended to leave practically no
childcare to Patrick. In addition, she seldom went out on her own,
or asked him to 'substitute'. She felt that children were the
mother's responsibility, and were of little interest to men. Consequently, Patrick was defined not only as inept at practical childcare, but also as being frequently unable to 'understand' the
children.[12] This was especially the case in the first interview when
Kathy said:

So I automatically did everything [with the babies]. I think, in a way, Patrick maybe missed out a bit when the children were babies. I think if I had let him do a bit more he would have seen a bit more what had to be done, as far as looking after the children goes. (I)

Interestingly, by the time of the final interview she had, occasionally, left the children with Patrick. Apparently, through their experience of this direct involvement, she had revised her image of his capabilities. She said:

More and more now, though, I realise that he's quite capable of looking after them on his own [laughs]. And at night time, if I'm going out, then I WILL leave them to be put to bed after I'm gone. (F)

It seemed, from respondents' accounts, that the fact that the father had less time with the children, than did the mother, in itself affected their images of one another. The mother also played a part in this process since, in his absence, she transmitted images of the father to the child. Personality variables aside, it seemed that the intermittent presence of the father led to the child reacting differently to him compared with the mother. The example has already been given of the child continuing to turn to the mother for comfort and certain kinds of assistance, even when the father was also present.[13] On the other hand, many of these parents felt that the intermittent presence of the father could lead to his being perceived by the child as a 'refreshment' from the mother. Several of them claimed, for example, that the elder child in particular tended to prefer the father's company when both parents were present. Jean Coulson's comment was typical of at least half of the respondents. She said of her elder son:

If we're both here he tends to go for Barry [husband]. But I think that's because I'm here all the time and it's great to have Dad at home sort of thing. (I)

It is also possible to interpret such statements as further mechanisms for sustaining beliefs in father involvement. The success of a *direct* relationship could be claimed to be undeniably 'proven' when the *child* chose to spend time with the father!

Even if the couples did not claim a special *personal* relationship between father and child, they still defined his intermittent presence as, *per se*, enabling a *different* relationship, compared to that with the mother. The fact that the father was regularly able to approach the relationship afresh, and unencumbered by the cumulative effects of constant interactions, established him as different from the mother. Whether couples maintained that he was seen by the child as, for example, more lenient or more strict, varied with the particular relationship. Elizabeth Vaughan said to her husband:

> You have more time to sit down with them and play with them and em, you sort of comfort them more than I do [*Roy: Do I?*] because, well you come home and you've got more patience and em, you can give them sympathy. (Jt) [My emphasis. The Vaughans here are negotiating their image of how the children see Roy.]

Alan Hemingway, however, gave this explanation for his being better able than Dianne to get the children to comply with his wishes. He said:

> I think er, they see less of me and what they do see of me tends to be fairly strict and I, I'm a bit more determined than Dianne really to get my own way. (F)

Thus, although descriptions of the differences were family specific, respondents tended to relate these special mutual reactions of father and child to the general point that their interactions were intermittent compared with those of the mother.

This point had many ramifications affecting the negotiation of parental behaviour between the spouses. As discussed earlier, the father was very reliant on the mother's understandings of the child since he was frequently unable to challenge her direct experience. Occasionally, however, a father was presented with aspects of the child which, intuitively, he found difficult to accept, since he had not himself directly experienced them. Nick Wilson, for example, found it hard to accept that his younger daughter was especially difficult to handle, since he had never witnessed her having a temper tantrum. These tantrums usually took place when Louise was shopping locally, and Nick was never present. Although he

'believed' Louise's accounts, he felt unable to offer any constructive suggestions since he had never experienced the situation. In
fact, when such perceived gaps in the father's understanding were
mentioned by couples, it was usually because the mother had
found the situations to be extremely problematical. The father,
however, had either challenged the mother's ability to handle it,
or had simply been defined as not sufficiently sympathetic. Derek
Rankin, for example, had not fully appreciated the extent to which
his first baby had cried, since this had occurred primarily during
the day when he was at work. Maureen felt that Derek had been
unable realistically to understand both her worries about the
baby, and the strain which she felt, since he had not been directly
involved. Also, different experience of the child sometimes led to
disagreements as to how easy or difficult he/she was to deal with.
During the negotiation process such disagreements were frequently related to the different amounts of direct involvement of
father and mother. Mary Clark claimed, for example:

> He [John] doesn't see Louise as as naughty or as bad as I do.
> But then he only sees her 5 to 6.30 every night, and on holiday
> he did say 'Mmm yes, she CAN be a problem'. (I) [Here the
> Clarks were negotiating the image of exactly how difficult their
> daughter was.]

All of the factors discussed in this section can be related to the
most frequently stressed aspect of being a father in relation to the
child. This was the definition of the father as a source of fun and
pleasure. Here the father was defined as providing enjoyment for
the child, both in his own right, and as a complement to the more
practical involvement of the mother. Helen Moffat argued, for
example:

> I think mothers and fathers do have different roles, and I think
> fathers are much more fun, and I think you get as much fun
> probably being a father. I think you get less of the draggy things
> like trailing them to the dentist when they don't want to go, you
> know, you can take them to the swings. And I think fathers
> SHOULD be fun, I think they should be light relief. But I
> think, because he's such fun and he's so precious, I think what
> he does, actually DOES with the children makes more im-
> pression. (I)

As mentioned earlier in the chapter, this was a sphere of activity in which the father could most easily and regularly provide practical proof of his direct involvement with the child. It was also one means of sustaining beliefs in fairness and equality in the face of the uneven availability of each spouse. The appearance of the father was defined as relieving the routine, and the constancy of interaction, for both mother and child. His 'non-work' time usually coincided with evenings and weekends, during which the wife was also trying to organise 'non-work' periods for herself. There was, therefore, a comparatively greater emphasis on non routine tasks and activities in which the father could take part. The different context in which paternal activity usually took place tended to enhance the 'pleasure' aspects of 'being a father'.

The intermittent presence of the father also facilitated the construction and maintenance of belief in father as fun and pleasure. Although it could also be used to add emphasis to his position as disciplinarian, the father's intermittency was most frequently used to establish a belief in the positive *affective* involvement between himself and the child. This process was a mutual definitional situation in which non-constant presence could be used as an advantage. Firstly, it meant that the father was potentially able to have a different perspective on the children from that of the mother. Ben Pringle commented:

> I would have said that *I* have enjoyed them more than Sheila has, perhaps because I haven't been here all the time you know being at work. And I wouldn't really say that they were a drudge, I regret that Sheila finds them that, but it's because she tries to be too good to them, you know. (I)

Secondly, the father's actions were seen by couples as being somehow defined differently by the child, since they were less frequent and less taken-for-granted than those of the mother. Such meanings were held to affect the father-child relationship, although varying results were described. Some respondents felt, for example, that one pleasurable gesture from the father, such as telling a story was, so to speak, more 'savoured' by the child. Others felt that the child made many more demands on the father than the mother when he was thus defined as a temporary source of pleasure. This long quotation from Martin Chapman provides excellent illustration of many of these points. He said:

I wouldn't say that em, the mother is seen so much as a source of pleasure as the father is. I think the, er, from the child's point of view, they don't see the father so much as the mother. And generally when the father comes home from work I'm quite pleased to see them, em, so he's seen more as a pleasure source than the mother is. So that, although the reason that he's not there all day, his authority is generally accepted because they get so much pleasure from the father that when he says 'no', they know that it means no. They don't take so much pleasure from the mother in the respect that they're in closer contact with her all the time. And when the mother buys them a bag of sweeties, it's not so much pleasure as when the father buys them a bag of sweeties. (I)

IV SUMMARY

In the previous chapter I argued that, for the couples in my group, motherhood had several taken-for-granted fundamental characteristics. In comparison the construction of paternal behaviour was a highly problematical exercise. Essentially this was because it was more difficult for couples to sustain belief in their much valued precept of the father having a *direct* involvement with the child. The present chapter was concerned with an examination of the different areas of father-involvement which were claimed by these parents, and a description of the ways in which they felt such involvement to be demonstrated.

Couples outlined three main areas of paternal behaviour. These were (a) dealing with the general administration of domestic and family matters (b) negotiating acceptable parental behaviour in relation to the mother and (c) developing a direct relationship with the child. Interestingly, however, in order for respondents to sustain belief in these levels of father involvement they did not see it as necessary for him to participate fully or constantly. Rather, it was a matter of each couple negotiating the kind of 'practical proof' which they found to be subjectively satisfactory. This was achieved by the father's participating sufficiently regularly in those particular spheres which spouses had identified as being relevant to their own family situation.

This completes my analysis of the parental behaviour of the middle class couples whom I studied. I have attempted to provide a detailed picture of this particular aspect of family life as it developed out of the interactions and mutual definitions of the members of these nuclear groups. The picture is complex but still tantalisingly incomplete; great scope remains for further depth research into families in Britain today. I hope that this book will further encourage empirically oriented researchers to take an interactive approach to the many issues remaining for study. In the following chapter I conclude by offering my views about some of the wider implications of my own research.

9 Implications – a Personal View

I INTRODUCTION

The main aims of this study were to describe the everyday parental behaviour of a group of middle class couples and to develop a grounded analysis of the important elements in this process. As far as possible I have tried to allow my respondents' accounts of parenthood to speak for themselves by using a style of analysis which, hopefully, has allowed me to examine critical features of their family lives without moving too far away from their original statements.

I have always been acutely aware of the problems involved in generalising from a small scale qualitative study and I agree with Lofland that:

> The strong suit of the qualitative researcher is his ability to provide an orderly presentation of rich, descriptive detail. He can move close to a social setting and bring back an accurate picture of patterns and phenomenological reality as they are experienced by human beings in social capacities. He can discover, document and render patterns of social action, and make the participants of a social setting live for us as human beings. But the methods useful in attaining these goals render him less equipped to achieve other goals. These other goals are the ones normally attached to the methods and stance of the quantitative researcher, the supported specification of causes and consequences' . . . [therefore] 'the analyst is well advised to phrase his conjectures in a qualified way.[1]

Nevertheless, if this book has had value for the reader, he or she will undoubtedly be making his/her own conclusions about its meaning for middle class marriage and parenthood now and in the future. In this final chapter, therefore, I offer my own views about the implications of this research for the women, men and children who live in families similar to the ones I studied. This is not just an academic statement as we now have a child of our own and, as a couple, have experienced many of the challenges and decisions which were described by the couples in my group.

II   THE DOMINANCE OF THE MOTHER ROLE

In the few years which have elapsed since the completion of the empirical part of this study the most pertinent changes which have occurred have been in social attitudes regarding the position of women. What was initially treated as the outbursts of a few 'women's libbers' has developed in the 1970s into a general debate about the role of women in society, and a greater awareness, reflected in law, of discrimination on the grounds of sex. I am, however, generally pessimistic about the extent of real change in the family lives of women. I hope that an important contribution of this present study is to help to understand why, although a greater 'consciousness' might now exist about the subordination of women in the family, the everyday existence of most women continues to be much the same as ever. One of the crucial factors is, I feel, the continued dominance of the mother role in the lives of women.

My study was carried out with a group of intelligent, educated and often well qualified women. Most of them had active plans for returning to some form of paid employment after the children were at school, and some of them returned to work during the fieldwork period. Only a very small minority seemed to have embraced domestication *per se* as the main focus of their lives for an indefinite period. Nevertheless, all of them had given up their jobs, if only temporarily, after the births of the children. In addition, their future work plans were being thought out in terms of arrangements which could accommodate their ongoing child-care responsibilities. Men might be 'involved' in taking a share of these responsibilities, but *their* work plans would not be fundamentally affected. Thus, my evidence supports and provides rather more detailed insight into the findings of several researchers that the woman continues to adopt the principal responsibility for childcare and organisation of surrogate childcare.[2]

This, it would seem to me, is one of the major problems facing those who would wish radically to alter the position of women in modern society. As Huber pointed out, 'only women can have babies, but the fact that women are also expected to rear them is a man-made decision.'[3] I make no attempt here to analyse how this situation has come about. My research has, however, allowed me to describe some of the practical reasonings of the actors involved in its perpetuation. It is perhaps these basic assumptions and interpretations which operate against fundamental change in the current arrangements for bringing up children in our society.

I do not feel that this situation is being perpetuated simply by the lack of alternative childcare facilities and the inflexibility of most work situations, although these definitely play some part. I suspect that, even if acceptable childcare facilities had *become* readily available, most of these women would have used them only as an *aid* and not as a total substitute. Equally, even if suitable full-time employment had been offered, most would still have chosen to work only part time, if at all. Their images of children's needs and wants were perhaps the chief impediment to radical change. The couples in my group believed that children should be 'understood', and that parenthood should involve the ongoing challenge of making sense of their child. They all felt that one of the parents should stay at home with the child in its early years. This was perceived as a vital way of satisfying the child's perceived needs for love and affection, consistency, security and stability. These parents did not even consider full time childcare substitutes. (The comment of one father seemed to reflect the overall view, he said, 'if they're gonna have kinks they may as well be *our* kinks'.) Each couple claimed that, in their case, (whether they felt this to be 'unfortunate' or not), the woman had been the obvious choice, in part because of her lesser earning potential. I say 'choice', but I suspect that this reflects respondents' *ex post facto* justifications, rather than this having been anything other than taken-for granted at the time of decision.

No matter what one might feel about the couples' interpretations of their situation, the fact remains that the woman rapidly became involved in a direct learning situation with the child. This seemed to lay the basis for subsequent decisions. Her situation was perceived as providing the most subjectively satisfactory way of developing the valid understandings of the child which were valued by the couples. She was also defined as being more directly knowledgeable about other aspects of the child's world. These images formed the basis of the mother's overall responsibility for the everyday administration of the child. They were supported by further images that the child itself came to rely upon and define the mother in a different way from the father.

Of course these parents had young and mostly pre-school children, and perhaps their own assumptions that family life would change through the years might result in a different attitude towards the mothering of older children. Certainly I expect that few of the women in my group will remain totally in the home for the full duration of their children's upbringing. However, the results of studies both in Britain and America indicate that it is a rare occurrence for a woman to pursue a career *full time, and* with her work being accorded equal importance to that of her husband, until her children are at least in their teens.[4] I can only conclude, therefore, that many of the assumptions underlying early motherhood in fact persist throughout the period of active parenting, and result in the woman continuing to be typed as mother first and person second.

Of course real social change takes time. Socialisation of the young to accept flexibility in gender roles will take at least one generation, and men as well as women will have to be willing to work towards changes in the organisation of parenting. However, I agree with the Rapoports that, for parenting to change, attitudes must also alter about the needs and wants of the children themselves. I would argue that it was the images of the 'psychological fragility'[5] of children which very much affected how the women in my group organised their family lives.

III   THE MIDDLE CLASS FATHER – MORE INVOLVED BUT STILL PERIPHERAL

Another crucial theme which has been stressed in this book is the interdependence of family roles. In a two parent family fatherhood cannot be understood simply in terms of the relationship between a man and his children, but must also be viewed within the context of the kind of mother role which has been developed. In this study I emphasised the problematical features of fatherhood and described paternal behaviour as a reality which was socially constructed within the family group. My discussion of the middle class father has necessarily to be seen in the context of the previous comments about the continued dominance of the mother role.

My study suggests that the discovery of highly participant fathers by other researchers has been something of an illusion.[6] The problematical nature of 'involved' fathering for my couples stemmed from the fact that the man spent the majority of his week out at work and could not, therefore, claim an automatic involvement similar to that accorded to the mother by virtue of her being constantly with the children. The couples in my group employed various mechanisms to sustain belief in the involvement of the father. One such mechanism was the assertion of voluntarism; that is, a willingness of the father to participate when possible. Belief was also sustained by the use of strategic gestures which did not need regularly to be demonstrated, and which often had greater subjective than objective significance for actual childcare. The kinds of questions asked by other researchers perhaps led them in fact to document how their respondents, like mine, sustained in these ways a belief in the 'involved father'.[7] And, of course, there could well be a wide discrepancy between beliefs of this kind and the *fact* of regular practical participation by the father in childrearing.

The Rapoports and their colleagues have made several important points about fatherhood which are relevant to the present study. They based their discussion of 'Fathers, Mothers and Others' on a 'selective review of the state of knowledge of the needs of parents.'[8] From this they concluded that the 'conventional model' of the conjugal family was often at variance with the experiential world of parents as people; and they suggested some of the new directions in which they saw parenthood as developing.

One of the trends which they suggested as perhaps emerging was the shift of fatherhood from a peripheral to a more central position in the existence of both the individual and his family. However, they qualified this suggestion by pointing out that:

Many fathers do not wish to share the load and are not convinced that it is essential for them to do so. Many writers and sociologists have put forward their accounts and analyses on the basis of an assumption that most fathers will not be either able to change or willing to.[9]

The Rapoports' concept of 'active' fathering is similar to the arguments in this study about 'direct involvement' of the father. My analysis indicates that it was important to the couples in my group to sustain belief in father 'involvement'. However, this was in practice 'proved' less by an equal sharing of tasks and responsibilities than, as stated earlier, by the strategic use of activities and gestures. There were, for example, different levels of childcare activities which couples claimed to be 'proof' of father 'involvement'. Some of these entailed a much greater active involvement with the children than did others. Also, it seemed that the *occasional* proof of willingness or ability to carry out childcare tasks was sufficient for respondents to sustain belief in the existence of 'active' fathering. In addition, strategic importance was attached to particular practical activities, such as bathing the child or entertaining him/her.

All of these observations lead me to conclude that the everyday behaviour of the couples in my group involved coping mechanisms which indicated that, in fact, the 'peripheral father' still persisted. In saying this I am not denying that there has been *some* change in the amount of participation by men in childcare activities. However, I feel that it is more realistic to view this, not as any considerable real change in degree of task allocation, but rather as a relaxation in traditional social prejudices about the kinds of childrearing behaviour considered 'appropriate' for a man and for a woman. Thus, although these fathers might well have been more involved with a wider range of practical care of their children than were those of previous generations, my analysis suggests that *equal* parenthood was far from being achieved. Fathers may now be more willing 'helpers' in the childrearing enterprise, but this is still optional for them, they remain peripheral with the overall responsibility remaining firmly with the mothers.

If real moves towards equal parenting are to occur then change is necessary in two main spheres. Firstly, an even more radical change in social attitudes is necessary than is indicated by the Rapoport's comment that:

> The myths of motherhood and the biological base for the domestic division of labour may have to recede further before fathering is actively sanctioned by society.[10]

I would further emphasise that attitudes must change towards the everyday basic allocation of responsibility for bringing up children. On the one hand *equal* parenting must mean that both fathers and mothers cater for the child's needs, are available to him/her where possible, and that their care is viewed as equivalent. On the other hand, it means that both parents should have equal choices about the freedom to carry out their own individual pursuits, with the overall *feeling* of responsibility for the organisation of childcare being shared between them. However, I appreciate that these are ideals which are almost impossible to realise without alterations in a second sphere, that of structural factors. Social changes, such as more flexible occupational arrangements for men as well as women, are essential if equal parenting is to be positively encouraged.

My study, however, does not encourage me to be greatly optimistic about the possibility of any immediate change, either in attitudes towards parenting or in social arrangements to promote equality between mothering and fathering. At present I am in continued agreement with Huber's assessment of the situation when she said:

> One basic theme pervades feminist literature: women are kept in their place by their responsibility for childcare and domestic work. This proposition implies that the problem is not only women's invisibility in market and political institutions but also men's invisibility in the home. Many men still see only one side of the problem: de-segregating the world of work, hard as that may be. The other side may be even harder: bringing men back in – to the kitchen, to the bathroom when it is time to scour the kiddies, and to the utility room which contains a fancy many-dialed machine that many men have not mastered. The most intractable issue is childcare – a problem of equality in parental responsibility that has hardly been addressed.[11]

IV THE POSITION OF CHILDREN IN FAMILY LIFE

Since I began this research there have been two important developments regarding analysis of the position of children in family life. The first is a general reappraisal of theories about socialisation which has resulted in the refutation of the myth of the passive child being socialised by responding to environmental stimuli.[12]

The second is a heightened awareness of the rights of children expressed in the development of protest groups and various kinds of children's organisations, also in some public debate about the topic. My study provides empirical materials which may be used further to reflect on the broader issues of how children are brought up in our society, and their part in the lives of those who bring them up.

In this book the importance of the influence of images of children on the development of parental behaviour has been stressed. The degree of emphasis which I have given to this aspect arose directly out of the content of my couples' accounts of parenthood. However, by concentrating on this topic my study has provided a useful general insight to help understand why parents bring up their children in different ways. Although I was able to draw out many points of similarity between my couples' images of children it was also possible to relate variations in their childrearing methods to differing interpretations of children. Further detailed work comparing such images amongst different social classes and in different cultures would undoubtedly further illuminate the often perplexing variations in childrearing practices.

My work has also provided some balance to the unidirectional model of socialisation which, until recently, had dominated studies in this area. Some sociologically-oriented researchers had earlier hinted at the importance for parenting of parents *interpretations* of their children,[13] but, in fact, it has been primarily in psychology that the interactive features of the socialisation process have been addressed most directly.[14]

An important contribution has also been made by the Rapoports in their analysis of the assumptions about parenting implicit in the work of various experts/advisors.[15] In this they too highlighted the importance of images of children, many of which were implicit in the works they examined. Interestingly, several of the assumptions which they examined were similar to those of my respondents. As the Rapoports themselves commented, debates amongst the various scholars involve issues which are often 'sophisticated expressions of many folk issues of the day.'[16] Thus, experts have stressed that, for example, care of children is not only physical but also psychological. They have pointed out that a neglect of a child's emotional requirements could be dangerous, as irreversible damage might result. More recently, the 'learning' aspects of childrearing have been stressed by experts.[17] The Rapoports concluded that such opinion has, until recently, placed the child's needs as paramount, with a concomitant neglect of the parents' needs, and, in particular, those of the mother. I would agree with this conclusion and find it reflected in my own research.

However, how does this apparent acceptance of the subordination of parents' needs to those of their children fit then with the current demands for *increased* rights for children? Once more I feel that the crux of the issue lies in our *images* of children. Parents' rights *and* children's rights *can* be maximised concurrently if it is accepted that children 'need' a greater element of independence and personal responsibility than, arguably, they have been accorded by recent generations of parents. For such developments to occur it would be necessary both to foster a greater degree of democracy in the parent-child relationship and also to make a detached appraisal of current views about the nature of childhood in Western society. In these ways, as the Rapoports stated:

> Beliefs and practices which may have a dogmatic certainty about them may be seen as myths of our time, variables open to study and possibly also change.[18]

V   IN CONCLUSION

I end this book on a note of qualified apology. The progressive reader will undoubtedly have noticed that all of my comments have been couched in the assumption that if change is to occur this must be within the framework of the two parent nuclear family. It is fashionable nowadays to conclude that the *only* solution to the problems and constraints of modern marriage and parenthood is to abolish the conventional pattern. I have not here indulged in such speculation for two main reasons. Firstly my own data concern the nuclear family and I feel that it is therefore appropriate to confine my comments to that area. Secondly, however, whilst in historical terms abolition may prove to be an adequate *long* term solution, and whilst I fully agree with current trends towards flexibility and experimentation in familial arrangements, I feel that abolition dodges the issue that in present day Western Society the nuclear family continues to be the overwhelmingly preferred domestic arrangement.[19] I therefore end by asking the reader to accept that I have confined my comments to the situation as it is, rather than how I might prefer it to be.

Appendix 1
Outline of the
Empirical Study

The fieldwork period in total lasted from mid-1971 to mid-1973. Twenty-two middle class couples took part in the fifteen months multi-interview study. Fifteen other couples, however, assisted with the preliminary research exercises. Prior to the study proper, three minimally structured discussion groups were convened, tape-recorded and analysed. Subsequently, a set of 'opening questions' was devised and practice interviews were carried out with five couples. These were also tape-recorded and analysed.

It was decided to focus on a small group[1] of middle class couples, each with two children. One of the children would be approximately three years old, and the other could be either older or younger. Three years was chosen as the pivot age for one of the children because, theoretically, they are, at that point, still the full-time responsibility of their parents. This 'control' ensured that all of the couples were still at the stage in the family life cycle of having at least one pre-school child. Three years also seemed to be an interesting age in terms of child development. The total dependency of infancy should be over and the child is acquiring a certain amount of independence from his/her parents, often challenging their authority.

When selecting middle class couples I defined socio-economic status in terms of the occupation of both husband and wife. Life style factors, such as home ownership and area of residence were also taken into account. In order to make contact with appropriate couples I approached playgroup leaders who worked either in middle class areas of the city, or in some of the new middle class estates nearby. These playgroup leaders acted as 'links'; they suggested the majority of couples who eventually took part, and they also made the initial approaches to the couples themselves.

Perhaps the most important 'control' of all was that both husbands and wives should be interested equally in participating in the project. This was crucial both because of my theoretical interests and for the success of the multi-interview study.

Twenty-two couples took part in a total of five interviews spaced out at approximately three-monthly intervals. The first two interviews were conducted with the husband and wife individually using the same basic set of 'opening questions'. These questions were very general and aimed to stimulate respondents to talk as easily as possible about their own particular family lives. There were usually a few weeks between these two interviews and the first spouse interviewed was asked not to tell the other anything which had been discussed. I am certain that this condition was scrupulously observed and, in fact, the secrecy element obviously provided some entertainment for the couples.

The third interview followed an experimental procedure. I left a tape-recorder with each couple and asked them to discuss the issues with one another. The questionnaire was essentially the same as in the first two interviews. My aim was to see how they described their family lives in each other's presence and without *my* actually being there. The success of these interviews was extremely varied, because some couples talked at great length whilst others spent only about ten minutes on the exercise.

The final two interviews were conducted jointly. Each was used to obtain accounts of events which had occurred since the previous meeting and to clarify points from other interviews. The fourth interview focussed primarily on obtaining detailed accounts of the family's previous weekend and previous evening. The fifth interview examined their images of children. During part of the final interview spouses were asked to write down their responses to various questions about the children. These were then pooled and discussed.

My analytical technique was simple and largely inductive. The themes which I noticed seemed to be those issues which were either most stressed or most recurrent in respondents' accounts. After each set of interviews I drew up lists of themes and ideas, made sure by cross-checking that these were representative of the group trends, and considered the cases which seemed to differ. At this stage I always had discussions with research colleagues and, further to this, I narrowed down some of the interests. I then went back to the transcripts and went through them in detail,

extracting stretches of conversation from each couple which
supported the themes. Interesting 'red herrings' *had* to be dropped
if there was insufficient support. As I explained earlier, emerging
issues provided some of the framework of the later interviews. As
with most sociological research the majority of analytical work
entailed refining, re-examining and ordering themes, always with
constant reference to the transcript evidence.

Appendix 2
The Families

All of these names are fictional. This list of pseudonyms is intended to help the reader to follow the detailed quotations. The ages of the children are as given in the first interview.

1	Philip and Margaret BARBER
	Karen (3½) Mary (6 months)
2	Eric and Carol BURNS
	John (5½) Alison (2½)
3	Martin and Sylvia CHAPMAN
	Anne (2¾) Judy (1 month)
4	John and Mary CLARK
	Louise (3½) Elizabeth (10 months)
5	Barry and Jean COULSON
	Matthew (3) Robert (10 months)
6	Andrew and Judy DAVIES
	Robert (2½) Ian (newly born)
7	Colin and Mary DUNCAN
	Alistair (5) Sarah (3½)
8	James and Hannah GILCHRIST
	Susan (3) Lucy (3 months)
9	Jeff and Madeleine HARRIS
	Frances (4½) Ian (2½)
10	Alan and Dianne HEMINGWAY
	Laura (2¾) Joanne (1¼)
11	Patrick and Kathy HISLOP
	Julie (5) Anna (2½)
12	Edward and Shirley JACKSON
	Simon (2½) Elaine (10 months)
13	Andrew and Marjorie JEFFREYS
	Brian (6) Michael (3)

14   Ian and Barbara JOHNSON
        Nicola (5)   Thomas (2¾)
15   Ray and Alice MITCHELL
       Rachel (2¾)   Kenneth (13 months)
16   George and Helen MOFFAT
        Pamela (5½)   Ruth (2½)
17   Ben and Sheila PRINGLE
        Monica (5)   Helen (3)
18   Derek and Maureen RANKIN
        Lynne (6¼)   Jonathon (2½)
19   Jim and Anna ROBSON
        Martin (6)   Jacqueline (2¾)
20   David and Marjorie RUSSELL
        Kathleen (5½)   Timothy (3½)
21   Roy and Elizabeth VAUGHAN
        Jenny (3½)   Catherine (1)
22   Nick and Louise WILSON
        Jane (4)   Clare (2½)

Notes and References

CHAPTER 1   THE OBJECTIVES AND APPROACH OF THE STUDY

1   Some recent examples are: A. Oakley, *Becoming a Mother* (London: Martin Robertson Press, 1979). J. Busfield and M. Paddon, *Thinking About Children: Sociology and Fertility in Post-war England* (Cambridge University Press, 1977).

2   See for example: J.M. Pahl and R.E. Pahl, *Managers and their Wives: A Study of Career and Family Relationships in the Middle Class* (London: Allen Lane, The Penguin Press, 1971). S. Edgell, *Middle Class Couples: a study of segregation, domination and inequality in marriage* (London: George Allen & Unwin, 1980). R. Rapoport and R.N. Rapoport, *Dual Career Families* (Harmondsworth: Penguin, 1971).

3   See for example: D. Cooper, *The Death of the Family*, (London: Allen Lane, The Penguin Press, 1971). K. Millet, *Sexual Politics*, (New York: Doubleday, 1970). R.V. Speck, *The New Families*, (London: Tavistock, 1972).

4   C. Saflios-Rothschild, 'Family Sociology or Wives' Family Sociology? A Cross Cultural Examination of Decision Making', *Journal of Marriage and the Family* (1974) pp. 290-301.

5   R. Rapoport, R.N. Rapoport and V. Thiessen, 'Couple Symmetry and Enjoyment', *Journal of Marriage and the Family* (1974) pp. 588-91.

6   R.D. Hess and G. Handel, 'The Family as a Psychosocial Organisation', in G. Handel (ed.), *The Psychosocial Interior of the Family* (London: George Allen & Unwin, 1968).

7   See for example: J. Newson and E. Newson, *Patterns of Infant Care in an Urban Community* (Pelican, 1965), (first published by George Allen & Unwin, 1963). H. Gavron, *The Captive Wife* (Pelican Books, 1968), (first published by Routledge & Kegan Paul, 1966). U. Bronfenbrenner, 'The Roots of Alienation', in N. Talbot (ed.), *Raising Children in Modern America* (Boston: Little, Brown, 1976).

8   R.Q. Bell, 'A Reinterpretation of the Direction of Effects in Studies of Socialisation', in *Psychological Review* (1968) pp. 81-95.

9   The seminal articles about the initial impact of parenthood are: E.E. Le Masters, 'Parenthood as Crisis', *Journal of Marriage and Family Living* (1957) pp. 352-5. A.S. Rossi, 'Transition to Parenthood', *Journal of Marriage and the Family* (1968) pp. 26-39. However, much of the extensive American work on parenthood adopts this unidirectional approach. A significant exception to this is the work on changes in the family life cycle. For a summary see: W.R. Burr, *Theory Construction and Sociology of the Family* (New York: John Wiley, 1973).

10   R. Rapoport, R.N. Rapoport and Z. Strelitz with S. Kew, *Fathers, Mothers*

and Others: Towards New Alliances (London: Routledge & Kegan Paul, 1977).

11   T. Parsons and R.F. Bales, *Family, Socialisation and Interaction Processes* (New York: Free Press, 1955).

12   E. Bott *Family and Social Network* (London: Tavistock 1957) ch.VII.

13   E.M. Lemert, *Human Deviance, Social Problems and Social Control* (Englewood Cliffs, New Jersey: Prentice Hall, 1972).

14   E. Bott (1957, first edition), op.cit. Tavistock. In her second edition, published in 1971, she provides a review and analysis of the studies which were inspired by her original work.

15   See for example: M.P. Fogarty, R. Rapoport and R.N. Rapoport, *Sex, Career and Family* (London: George Allen & Unwin Ltd, 1971).

16   M. Komarovsky, 'Learning Conjugal Roles', reprinted in J. Heiss (ed.), *Family Roles and Interaction* (Chicago: Rand McNally, 1968). Here the author presented a brief section on 'The Marriage Partner as a Socialising Agent'.

17   For a general exposition of this approach see: H.S. Blumer, *Symbolic Interactionism: Perspective and Method* (Englewood Cliffs, New Jersey: Prentice Hall, 1969).

18   E.W. Burgess, 'The Family as a Unity of Interacting Personalities', *The Family* (1926) pp. 3–9.

19   G. Handel (ed.), op.cit. 1968.

20   J. Heiss (ed.), op.cit. 1968.

21   W.D. Winter and A. Ferreira (eds.), *Research in Family Interaction* (Palo Alto, California: Science and Behaviour Books, 1969).

22   Much of the work of Alfred Schutz has been collected in: M. Natanson (ed.), *Alfred Schutz: Collected Papers Vol. I* (2nd ed.), (The Hague: Martinus Nijhoff, 1967). A. Brodersen (ed.), *Alfred Schutz: Collected Papers Vol. II* (The Hague: Martinus Nijhoff, 1964).

23   M. Phillipson, 'Phenomenological Philosophy and Sociology', in P. Filmer *et al. New Directions in Sociological Theory* (London: Collier Macmillan, 1972) p. 143.

24   P.R.L. Berger and H. Kellner, 'Marriage and the Construction of Reality', in H.P. Dreitzel (ed.), *Recent Sociology No. 2* (London: Collier-Macmillan, 1970).

25   R.D. Hess and G. Handel (1968) op.cit. p. 15.

26   Since I devised my own research strategy I have come across two books which seem to offer some extremely useful practical advice concerning methodology. See: L. Schatzman and A.L. Strauss, *Field Research: Strategies for a natural sociology* (Englewood Cliffs, New Jersey: Prentice Hall, 1973). J. Lofland, *Analysing Social Settings* (London: Wadsworth, 1971)

27   H. Garfinkel, *Studies in Ethnomethodology* (Englewood Cliffs, New Jersey: Prentice Hall, 1967).

28   A.V. Cicourel, *Theory and Method in a Study of Argentine Fertility* (New York and London: John Wiley, 1974).

29   B.G. Glaser and A.L. Strauss, *The Discovery of Grounded Theory* (London: Weidenfeld and Nicolson, 1968).

30   An outline of the empirical study is presented in Appendix 1.

CHAPTER 2   UNDERLYING ASSUMPTIONS ABOUT FAMILY LIFE

1   A. Brodersen (ed.), *Alfred Schutz: Collected Papers Vol II* (The Hague: Martinus Nijhoff, 1964) p. 72.
     I present the full definition of 'recipe knowledge' at the beginning of Chapter 4.
2   P.R.L. Berger and H. Kellner, 'Marriage and the Construction of Reality' in H.P. Dreitzel (ed.), *Recent Sociology No. 2* (London: Collier-Macmillan, 1970).
3   D. Silverman, 'Methodology and Meaning', in P. Filmer *et al., New Directions in Sociology Theory* (London: Collier Macmillan, 1972).
4   This is introduced in Section IV of the present chapter.
5   See M. Natanson (ed.), (1967), op.cit., pp. 72-4.
6   I indicate from which interview a quotation is taken by the following abbreviations:
     (I)   — preliminary interviews with each spouse individually
     (Jt)   — joint interview with both spouses, without my being present
     (W/E)   — fourth interview with both spouses together
     (F)   — final interview with both spouses together
     Note also that pseudonyms are used for all respondents. A list of the names given to all of the family members is presented in Appendix 2. I suggest that the reader consults this list whilst reading the book. This will enable him/ her to distinguish between parents and their respective children when only christian names are given in the text.
7   I adopt the following conventions when presenting quotations: words or phrases which were emphasised by respondents are given in CAPITAL LETTERS; words or phrases to which I wish to draw attention are in *italic*.
8   This argument is presented in full in J.E. Mayer, *The Disclosure of Marital Problems* (New York: Institute of Welfare Research, Community Services of New York, 1966) pp. 4-8.
9   See Chapter 5.
10   Abstract and grounded images are described in full in Chapters 5 and 6 respectively.
11   See section III(b) (*iii*) of the present chapter.
12   This point will be dealt with in detail in Chapters 7 and 8.
13   This argument is expanded in D.R. Peterson *et al.* 'Parental Attitudes and Child Adjustment', *Child Development* (1959) pp. 119-30.
14   R.D. Hess and G. Handel, 'The Family as a Psychosocial Organisation', in G. Handel (ed.), *The Psychosocial Interior of the Family* (London: George Allen & Unwin Ltd, 1968).
15   See the section entitled 'Projected Images of Children' in Chapter 5.
16   This point is elaborated upon in Chapter 4.
17   P. McHugh, *Defining the Situation* (Indianapolis: Bobbs Merril, 1968) p. 9.
18   The organisation of surrogate childcare is discussed more fully in Chapters 7 and 8.
19   M. Natanson (ed.), (1967), op.cit., p. 19.
20   P.R.L. Berger and J. Kellner (1970), op.cit.
21   D. Cooper, *The Death of the Family* (London: Allen Lane, The Penguin Press, 1971).

CHAPTER 3   NEGOTIATION: THE DEVELOPMENT OF PARENTAL BEHAVIOUR

1   D. Walsh, in P. Filmer *et al. New Directions in Sociological Theory* (London: Collier-Macmillan, 1972) p. 19.
2   P.R.L. Berger and H. Kellner, 'Marriage and the Construction of Reality' in H.P. Dreitzel (ed.), *Recent Sociology No. 2* (London: Collier-Macmillan, 1970) p. 58.
3   M. Natanson, (ed.), *Alfred Schutz: Collected Papers Vol. I,* second edition (The Hague: Martinus Nijhoff, 1967) p. 72.
4   This point will be expanded in Chapter 8.
5   Underlying assumptions about fairness were discussed in Chapter 2.
6   See Chapters 7 and 8.
7   These basic assumptions were introduced in Chapter 2 and will be dealt with in detail in Chapters 5 and 6.
8   These images are discussed at length in Chapter 5.
9   See Chapter 5.
10   See Chapters 5 and 6.
11   This was perceived as necessary to satisfy certain basic needs of the child. I discuss it further in Chapter 5.
12   M. Natanson (1967), op.cit., p. 14.
13   Contextual images are discussed in detail in Chapter 6.
14   See for example section IIb on parenthood as learning.
15   This point is illustrated in the following section of the present chapter.
16   These are discussed in detail in Chapters 5 and 6.
17   P.R.L. Berger and H. Kellner (1970), op.cit., p. 62.
18   See the section on comparative images in Chapter 6.

CHAPTER 4   COPING MECHANISMS

1   A. Brodersen (ed.), *Alfred Schutz: Collected Papers Vol. II* (The Hague: Martinus Nijhoff, 1964) p. 72.
2   T.J. Scheff, 'Negotiating Reality: Notes on Power in the Assessment of Responsibility', *Social Problems* (1968) pp. 3-17.
3   P.R.L. Berger and H. Kellner, 'Marriage and the Construction of Reality' in H.P. Dreitzel (ed.), *Recent Sociology No. 2* (London: Collier-Macmillan, 1970).
4   A similar point to this will be elaborated upon in section II(c) of the present chapter which deals with the division of labour.
5   The qualifications, in practice, of this 'responsibility' will be outlined in Chapter 8.
6   The issue of responsibility is crucial. In Chapter 8 I shall illustrate some of the ways in which respondents sustained belief that the husband was 'involved' in this responsibility.
7   Here projected images of the child played an important part in the negotiation of parental behaviour. For further discussion of such images see Chapter 5.
8   P.R.L. Berger and T. Luckmann, *The Social Construction of Reality* (Garden City, N.Y.: Doubleday, 1966).

CHAPTER 5   MAKING SENSE OF THE CHILD: ABSTRACT IMAGES OF CHILDREN

1   A. Brodersen (ed.), *Alfred Schutz: Collected Papers Vol. II* (The Hague: Martinus Nijhoff, 1964).
2   These two sets of images are discussed in detail in section III of the present chapter.
3   This point is also relevant to my argument about the different levels of validity attached to various kinds of knowledge. (See Chapter 3 Section III). In family matters, knowledge acquired through direct personal experience was accorded high validity.
4   J.K. Jackson, 'The Adjustment of the Family to Alcoholism', *Journal of Marriage and Family Living* (1956) pp. 361-9.
5   See Chapters 7 and 8.
6   See Introduction of the present chapter.
7   The following discussion relates more to the category of 'grounded images' but will be discussed here because it is in keeping with many of the preceding empirical examples.
8   See Section II(a) of the present chapter.

CHAPTER 6   MAKING SENSE OF MY CHILD: GROUNDED IMAGES OF CHILDREN

1   See Chapter 5, Section III.
2   See discussion of 'misunderstandings' in Chapter 3, Section III.
3   This point was discussed in detail in Chapter 3, Section III.
4   This point was introduced in Chapter 5, Section II. Here I explore further the practical implications of this abstract image.
5   This point was discussed in the section on comparisons in the present chapter.
6   This is a similar kind of legitimating tactic to the use of 'explanatory incidents' discussed in Chapter 3, Section III.
7   This point was introduced in Chapter 2, Section III.
8   See the section on 'first or second born' earlier in the present chapter.
9   See Chapter 5, Section II(b).

CHAPTER 7   BEING A MOTHER

1   This was discussed fully in Chapter 2, Section III.
2   See Chapter 5, Section II.
3   Projected images were discussed in Chapter 5, Section IV.
4   This coping mechanism was described in Chapter 4, Section III.
5   See Chapter 5, Section III.
6   My comments on the *actual* similarity of such 'similar situations' are given in Chapter 8.
7   This point is directly related to the discussion of social contextual images in Chapter 6, Section III.
8   The concept of temporal contextual images was introduced in Chapter 6. The present section can be seen as a further elaboration of the points in

Section III of that chapter.

9 In the next chapter I discuss how fathers were usually expected only to occupy the children (i.e. child *mind*) when they took over responsibility. Any other chores which they carried out during that time were viewed as a bonus.

10 See Chapter 4, Section II for some illustrations of the ways in which beliefs that family life should be 'fairly' shared were sustained in the face of this contradiction.

11 See especially section IV(b).

12 The way in which respondents attached meanings to different kinds of knowledge was discussed in Chapter 3.

13 See Chapter 6, Section II.

14 The notion of an 'explanatory incident' was introduced in Chapter 3, Section III.

15 See Chapter 4, Section III, for further illustrations of this point.

16 This was often subsumed under the category of 'common sense' to which considerable legitimacy was attached. This was discussed in Chapter 3, Section III.

17 See Chapter 4 for the full discussion of these coping mechanisms.

18 Aaron Cicourel made this observation during a seminar at Edinburgh University in 1971.

19 See Chapter 5.

20 R. Rapoport and R.N. Rapoport, *Dual Career Families* (Harmondsworth: Penguin, 1971).

CHAPTER 8 BEING A FATHER

1 I would suggest that for the majority of respondents this again was partly mythical. With few exceptions, having maintained that they 'shared' this early division of labour, most respondents then proceeded to describe the women as having done the greater part of the shopping, general housework, cooking, washing and ironing. There were also specially allocated chores, very much along stereotyped sex role lines of car maintenance/odd-jobs/heavy gardening for the men, and sewing/mending/light gardening for the women. The men, however, seemed to have carried out their 'special' chores *instead* of the everyday chores whereas the women did theirs in addition.

2 It seemed, from these retrospective accounts, that, after the birth of the child, it became more necessary to sustain belief in a 'fairly' shared reality through the husband's involvement with childcare rather than housework. There no longer seemed any need to *claim* that housework was a *mutual* responsibility.

3 See Section III(b) (*ii*) of the present chapter.

4 These images were discussed in Chapter 5, Section II.

5 Patrick was trying to make a name for himself in a professional career. This involved him in hard work and long hours away from home.

6 See Chapter 4, Section II(b).

7 See my discussion of this in Chapter 7.

8 All respondents mentioned such pressures. Their statements were usually

legitimated by a temporal contextual image of the child, i.e. that a child's *constant* presence was often demanding and stressful.

9　This was discussed in Chapter 4, Section II(c).
10　These were discussed in Chapter 7, Section IV(c).
11　These points were elaborated upon in Chapter 7.
12　Patrick was, however, very much involved on the administrative level. The Hislops maintained that their children were a predominant topic of conversation in their lives. In their individual interviews they put forward very similar images of the children. This I take to be evidence that Patrick was kept very much 'in touch' by Kathy.
13　See Chapter 7, Section IV(b).

CHAPTER 9　IMPLICATIONS – A PERSONAL VIEW

1　J. Lofland *Analyzing Social Settings* (London: Wadsworth, 1971).
2　See, for example, R. Rapoport and R.N. Rapoport, *Dual Career Families* (Harmondsworth: Penguin, 1971).
3　J. Huber, 'Introduction to "Changing Women in a Changing Society"', *American Journal of Sociology* (1971) p. 765.
4　See the findings cited in M. Row 'Choosing Child Care: Many Options' in R. and R. Rapoport and Janice Bumstead (eds.), *Working Couples* (London and Henley: Routledge & Kegan Paul, 1978).
5　I borrow this term from the Rapoports, *Working Couples* (1978), op.cit., p. 185.
6　See, for example, J. Newson and E. Newson, *Patterns of Infant Care in an Urban Community* (Pelican, 1965), (first published by George Allen & Unwin, 1963). And, H. Gavron, *The Captive Wife* (London: Routledge & Kegan Paul, 1966).
7　In the above studies Gavron simply asked if the father *would* do various things with or for the children. The Newsons asked only very general questions which were unlikely to obtain an accurate assessment of the actual quantity of childcare by the father.
8　R. Rapoport, R.N. Rapoport and Z. Strelitz with S. Kew, *Fathers, Mothers and Others: Towards New Alliances* (London: Routledge & Kegan Paul, 1977).
9　Ibid. p. 233.
10　Ibid. p. 184.
11　J. Huber, 'Toward a Sociotechnological Theory of the Women's Movement', *Social Problems* (1976) p. 371.
12　R.M. Lerner and G.B. Spanier (eds.), *Child Influences on Marital and Family Interaction (A Life-Span Perspective)* (Academic Press, 1978).
13　See for example, J. Newson and E. Newson, *Four Years Old in an Urban Community* (London: George Allen & Unwin, 1968).
14　Most studies by psychologists have, however, presented evidence bearing principally on physical and emotional communication between *mother* and child. See for example, R.M. Lerner and G.B. Spanier (eds.), op. cit.
15　R. Rapoport, R.N. Rapoport *et al.* (1977), op. cit., Chapter 2.
16　Ibid. p. 33.
17　The Rapoports cited recent work by Urie Bronfenbrenner as evidence of

this trend. U. Bronfenbrenner, 'The roots of alienation' in N. Talbot (ed.), *Raising Children in Modern America* (Boston: Little, Brown, 1976).

18   R. Rapoport, R.N. Rapoport *et al.* (1977), op. cit. p. 7.

19   M.J. Bone, *Here to stay. American Families in the Twentieth Century* (New York: Basic Books, 1977).

APPENDIX 1   OUTLINE OF THE EMPIRICAL STUDY

1   I describe my respondents collectively as a 'group' rather than as a 'sample'. This is because, although I controlled for characteristics such as family size, ages of children and socio-economic status, the group was not, however, randomly selected in the conventional sense of sampling.

Bibliography

R.Q. Bell, 'A Reinterpretation of the Direction of Effects in Studies of Socialisation', *Psychological Review* (1968) pp. 81-95.

P.R.L. Berger and T. Luckmann, *The Social Construction of Reality* (Garden City, New York: Doubleday, 1966).

P.R.L. Berger and H. Kellner, 'Marriage and the Construction of Reality' in H.P. Dreitzel (ed.), *Recent Sociology No. 2* (London: Collier-Macmillan, 1970).

M.J. Bone, *Here to Stay: American Families in the Twentieth Century* (New York: Basic Books, 1977).

H.S. Blumer, *Symbolic Interactionism Perspective and Method* (Englewood Cliffs, New Jersey: Prentice-Hall, 1969).

E. Bott, *Family and Social Network*, second edition (London: Tavistock, 1971).

A. Brodersen, (ed.), *Alfred Schutz: Collected Papers Vol. II* (The Hague: Martinus Nijhoff, 1964).

U. Bronfenbrenner, 'The Roots of Alienation' in N. Talbot, (ed.), *Raising Children in Modern America*, (Boston: Little, Brown, 1976).

E.W. Burgess, 'The Family as a Unity of Interacting Personalities', *The Family* (1926).

W.R. Burr, *Theory Construction and Sociology of the Family* (London and New York: John Wiley, 1973).

J. Busfield and M. Paddon, *Thinking About Children: Sociology and Fertility in Post-war England* (Cambridge University Press, 1977).

A.V. Cicourel, *Theory and Method in a Study of Argentine Fertility* (New York and London: John Wiley, 1974).

D. Cooper, *The Death of the Family* (London: Allen Lane, The Penguin Press, 1971).

H.P. Dreitzel (ed.), *Recent Sociology No. 2* (London: Collier-Macmillan, 1970).

S. Edgell, *Middle Class Couples: a study of segregation, domination and inequality in marriage* (London: George Allen & Unwin, 1980).

P. Filmer *et al.*, *New Directions in Sociological Theory* (London: Collier-Macmillan, 1972).

M.P. Fogarty, R. Rapoport and R.N. Rapoport, *Sex, Career and Family* (London: George Allen & Unwin Ltd, 1971).

H. Garfinkel, *Studies in Ethnomethodology* (Englewood Cliffs, N.J.: Prentice-Hall, 1967).

H. Gavron, *The Captive Wife* (Pelican Books, 1968), (first published by Routledge & Kegan Paul, 1966).

B.G. Glaser and A.L. Strauss, *The Discovery of Grounded Theory* (London: Weidenfeld and Nicolson, 1968).

R.W. Habenstein, (ed.), *Pathway to Data: Field Methods for Studying Ongoing Social Organisations* (Chicago: Aldine, 1970).

G. Handel (ed.), *The Psychosocial Interior of the Family* (London: George Allen & Unwin, 1968).

J. Heiss (ed.), *Family Roles and Interaction* (Chicago: Rand McNally, 1968).

R.D. Hess and G. Handel, 'The Family as a Psychosocial Organisation', in G. Handel (ed.), (1968).

J. Huber, 'Introduction to "Changing Women in a Changing Society"', *American Journal of Sociology* (1973) pp. 763-6.

J.K. Jackson, 'The Adjustment of the Family to Alcoholism', *Journal of Marriage and Family Living* (1956) pp. 361-9.

M. Komarovsky, 'Learning Conjugal Roles' in J. Heiss (ed.), (1968).

E.E. Le Masters, 'Parenthood as Crisis', *Journal of Marriage and Family Living* (1957) pp. 352-5.

E.M. Lemert, *Human Deviance, Social Problems and Social Control* (Englewood Cliffs, New Jersey: Prentice-Hall, 1972).

R.M. Lerner and G.B. Spanier (eds.), *Child Influences on Marital and Family Interaction (a Life Span Perspective)* (Academic Press, 1978).

J. Lofland, *Analysing Social Settings* (London: Wadsworth, 1971).

J. Lorber, 'Beyond Equality of the Sexes. The question of the Children', *The Family Co-ordinator* (1975) pp. 465-72.

B.E. Maccoby, T.N. Newcomb and B.L. Hartley (eds.), *Readings in Social Psychology* (New York: Renny Holt, 1958).

J.E. Mayer, *The Disclosure of Marital Problems* (New York: Institute of Welfare Research, Community Services of New York, 1966).

P. McHugh, *Defining the Situation* (Indianapolis: Bobbs-Merrill, 1968).

K. Millet, *Sexual Politics* (New York: Doubleday, 1970).

M. Natanson (ed.), *Alfred Schutz: Collected Papers Vol I*, second edition (The Hague: Martinus Nijhoff, 1967).

J. Newson and E. Newson, *Patterns of Infant Care in an Urban Community* (Pelican, 1965), (first published by George Allen & Unwin, 1963).

J. Newson and E. Newson, *Four Years Old in an Urban Community* (London: George Allen & Unwin, 1968).

A. Oakley, *Becoming a Mother* (London: Martin Robertson, 1979).

J.M. Pahl and R.E. Pahl, *Managers and Their Wives: A Study of Career and Family Relationships in the Middle Class* (London: Allen Lane, The Penguin Press, 1971).

T. Parsons and R.F. Bales, *Family, Socialisation and Interaction Processes* (New York: Free Press, 1955).

D.R. Peterson *et al.*, 'Parental Attitudes and Child Adjustment', *Child Development* (1959) pp. 119-30.

M. Phillipson, 'Phenomenological Philosophy and Sociology', in P. Filmer *et al.*, (1972).

R. Rapoport and R.N. Rapoport, *Dual Career Families* (Harmondsworth: Penguin, 1971).

R. Rapoport, R.N. Rapoport and V. Thiessen, 'Couple Symmetry and Enjoyment', *Journal of Marriage and the Family* (1974) pp. 588-91.

R. Rapoport, R.N. Rapoport and Z. Strelitz with S. Kew, *Fathers, Mothers and Others: Towards New Alliances* (London: Routledge & Kegan Paul, 1977).

R. Rapoport, R.N. Rapoport and J. Bumstead, *Working Couples* (London and Henley: Routledge & Kegan Paul, 1978).

A.S. Rossi, 'Transition to Parenthood', *Journal of Marriage and the Family* (1968) pp. 26-39.

M. Row, 'Choosing Child Care: Many Options' in R. Rapoport and R.N. Rapoport and Janice Bumstead, *Working Couples* (London and Henley: Routledge & Kegan Paul, 1978).

C. Saflios-Rothschild, 'Family Sociology or Wives' Family Sociology? A Cross Cultural Examination of Decision Making', *Journal of Marriage and the Family* (1969) pp. 290-301.

T.J. Scheff, 'Negotiating Reality: Notes on Power in the Assessment of Responsibility', *Social Problems* (1968) pp. 3-17.

L. Schatzman and A.L. Strauss, *Field Research: Strategies for a natural sociology* (Englewood Cliffs, N.J.: Prentice-Hall, 1973).

D. Silverman, 'Methodology and Meaning', in P. Filmer *et al.* (1972).

R.V. Speck, *The New Families* (London: Tavistock, 1972).

N. Talbot (ed.), *Raising Children in Modern America* (Boston: Little, Brown, 1976).

A.J. Vidich, J. Bensman and M.A. Stein (eds.), *Reflections on Community Studies* (London and New York: John Wiley, 1964).

D. Walsh, 'Sociology and the Social World' in P. Filmer *et al.*, (1972).

W.D. Winter and A. Ferreira (eds.), *Research in Family Interactions* (Palo Alto, California: Science and Behaviour Books, 1969).

Index